DAMNATION AND DEVIANCE

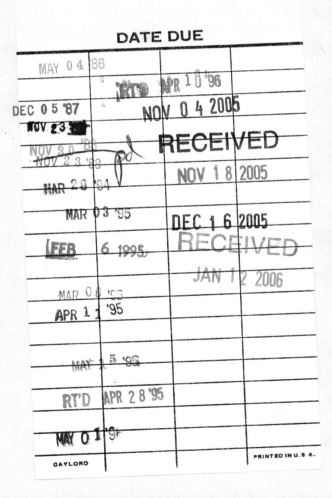

DAMNATION
AND
DEVIANCE

*The Protestant Ethic and
the Spirit of Failure*

Mordechai Rotenberg

THE FREE PRESS
A Division of Macmillan Publishing Co., Inc.
NEW YORK

Collier Macmillan Publishers
LONDON

4057434
DLC

3-9-79
KN

Copyright © 1978 by The Free Press
A Division of Macmillan Publishing Co., Inc.

The Free Press
A Division of Macmillan Publishing Co., Inc.
866 Third Avenue, New York, N.Y. 10022

Collier Macmillan Canada, Ltd.

Library of Congress Catalog Card Number: 77-18432

Printed in the United States of America

printing number

1   2   3   4   5   6   7   8   9   10

Library of Congress Cataloging in Publication Data

Rotenberg, Mordechai.
    Damnation and deviance.

    Bibliography: p.
    Includes index.
    1. Psychiatry—Philosophy. 2. Psychiatry and
religion. 3. Calvinism. 4. Hasidism. 5. Deviant
behavior. 6. Mental illness—Diagnosis. I. Title.
RC437.5.R67   616.8'58   77-18432
ISBN 0-02-927490-7

Copyright Acknowledgments

To the memory of my father,
Rav David Rotenberg

Contents

Foreword

S. N. Eisenstadt

Mordechai Rotenberg's provocative book is, to my mind, a very important contribution to a deeper understanding of contemporary psychiatry—a contribution achieved by focusing on several crucial aspects of psychiatry and of the process of becoming deviant in the broader setting of sociocultural analysis.

Not all the directions to which this book points are, of course, new. It has long been recognized, especially in anthropology, that different cultures have different conceptions of sanity, of mental illness and its treatment. But relatively little systematic, comparative analysis has been attempted in this direction, and so we do not know as much as we should about the basic presuppositions in the different cultures which influence their perception of "normal" as against "abnormal" or deviant or about how different types of mental illness are defined and how these conceptions become related to what in modern parlance is called mental health practice. Beyond this, what comparative knowledge we have has been rarely applied systematically to the study of our own contemporary societies in general or to the analysis of psychiatric and mental health practices and approaches in particular.

There are, of course, exceptions, the most notable probably being the work of M. Foucault in this area. But the more usual approach has been to view the modern conceptions and approaches to psychiatry, the various definitions of mental health or illness, and the disagreements among them as matters of purely scientific controversy or as mere fads or fashions. No doubt this approach has partial validity, but it is certainly not the whole story, and Rotenberg indicates some new and significant ways of looking at these issues. His conclusions will probably become the foci of further controversy, but it will not be possible to ignore them.

The special merit of Rotenberg's study is that he ties in the analysis of the postulates of modern psychiatry as well as of the process of becoming deviant with some of the central theses and approaches in classical sociology as well as with some of the more recent controversies.

One of the central themes of his analysis is the influence of the Protestant Ethic—not only, to follow Weber, on the spirit of capitalism but also on the spirit of psychiatry. Weber's thesis and later interpretations have always stressed the constructive and formative aspects of the Protestant spirit. But creativity has its price; every crystallization of a new human image and of a civilization attuned to it also has its negative features. Rotenberg tries to indicate some of these costs. He proposes, in his own words, that

> ... to the extent that the Protestant Ethic had a general impact on the Western world—in terms of economic and scientific development, as Weber and others proposed—the belief in man's inability to change (from bad to good) has become equally rooted in Western culture, since the development of both is traceable to Calvin's powerful doctrine of predestination.
>
> The dualistic and irreversible nature presumably characterizing contemporary Western mental health diagnostic labels is then traced to Calvin's concept of the "hopeless-damned," to Lombroso's "born criminal" and to Spencer's dichotomous concept of "natural selection" or "dangerous classes," which gained scientific status following the advent of Calvinism during the Renaissance.

On the basis of this analysis he attempts to redefine such phenomena as "psychopathy," deviance, and the like.

Another very important aspect of Rotenberg's thesis relates to the process of labeling involved in becoming deviant. Most of the literature has stressed the labeling done by others. Dr. Rotenberg stresses the crucial importance of *self*-labeling. This is not just a technical quibble; it constitutes a new and crucial analytical dimension to the understanding of the process of labeling, especially its relation to the basic conceptions and self-conceptions that are prevalent in any culture and society.

All these problems are then explored through cross-cultural analysis, based in part on materials collected in Israel from both Israelis and Americans. Of special interest here is the comparison between the Protestant and Hassidic ethics.

Dr. Rotenberg's book bears on some of the central theoretical discussions in the social sciences. Many of these discussions have focused on criticisms of the structural–functional model with its presumed emphasis on society, groups and their needs, and boundary-maintaining mechanisms, or on the stimulus–response model in psychology, with its seemingly fixed view of human nature.

Out of these criticisms two major themes emerged—one stressing that institutions develop through a process of negotiations, the other looking for some "deep" structure which would explain the "real" dynamics of institutional behavior.

Rotenberg's work provides some very interesting illustrations of how it is possible to bridge the gap between these two themes. His analysis of the Protestant—and Hassidic—views of human nature indicates how such conceptions produce some deep, often unconscious (in the sense of being taken for granted) principles which shape activities in many concrete fields of behavior and organization. At the same time, his analysis of the process of labeling and self-labeling indicates at least one classification through which such deeper meanings are institutionally negotiated.

All in all this is an important and provocative book which will certainly give rise to continued discussions and controversies.

Preface

Explicitly or implicitly, theorists of human conduct usually begin their analysis with an axiomatic assumption of one kind or another about human nature. According to Thomas Hobbes (1958), for example, man in the state of nature, like a "brutish wolf," is governed by his egocentric destructive passions. Similarly, psychoanalytic theory assumes that man comes into this world equipped with aggressive-destructive instinctual drives that are classified under the term "id." On the other hand, according to structural-functional sociological belief, not the "war of all against all" but "consensus" prevails in the state of nature, because man is a natural conformist, i.e., a "sheep." As Durkheim (1974: 45) stated: "We feel a *sui generis* pleasure in performing our duty simply because it is our duty."

The thesis of this book is that Western behavioral theories do not *ask* whether man is essentially a "wolf" or a "sheep" but begin by *assuming* that man is *born* either a "wolfman" or an "innocent sheep" and, accordingly, the ultimate goal of social control is not that the "wolf shall dwell with the lamb" (Isaiah 11:6) but the segregation of bad wolves from innocent lambs or, conversely, the separation of successful wolves from black sheep. Hence the study of deviance is bound up with the problems of how men are axiomatically classified and who makes the classification. These categories of man are deeply rooted in religious-ethical definitions of right and wrong, which are transmitted from generation to generation by a socialization process that teaches children (including potential social scientists) at a very early age how to distinguish between the "good guys" and the "bad guys." From this perspective, the study of deviance in terms of the "war of who defines whom" is as important on the micro-level as on the macro-level, since it resembles wars between nations, which likewise often originate in differences in religious-ethical definitions of the "good guys" and the "bad guys."

These firmly inculcated classification-paradigms of man essentially prescribe the scope of human changeability, which is at the heart of the social sciences because, in a Kantian sense, the act of observing and perceiving objects (obviously including human objects) is not a passive but an active process that affects and changes the object itself. The purpose of this book, then, is to provide a new theoretical perspective on the cross-cultural study of deviance by proposing these religious-ethical conceptions of man as explanatory orientations for interpersonal behavior and human change.

Thomas Kuhn (1962), in his provocative essay on the progress of science, maintains that the scientist's unique perception of his environment is based on the particular paradigm that guided his own discipline and training. In order for a transformation to take place in the scientist's perceptual world a "scientific revolution" must occur, for only by changing his existing paradigm can the scientist perceive a new gestalt.

What is the paradigm guiding Western theories and conceptions of man and his normal or deviant behavior? In this book the influential Calvinist doctrine of predestinal-dualism and its subsequent reflection in the generalized secular norms known as the Protestant Ethic will be proposed as a possible model of man underlying the Western social sciences. Moreover, as so much has been written about the positive functional aspect of the Protestant work ethos, an additional purpose of this book is to expose the hitherto unexplored dysfunctional dualistic-discriminating side of the Protestant Ethic. To introduce a new and more optimistic paradigm of man, the book will end with a brief comparative presentation of the Hassidic salvation ethic and its positive conception of man. Thus, selected modern theories of deviance will be critically analyzed, and alternative new models presented, in order to show how at present major Western formulations in the behavioral sciences are imbued with what can be termed the "Protestant bias" and how approaches to deviance can be broadened by drawing on "non-Western" paradigms of man.

To validate statements about reality, either of two methods can be employed: the empirical verification process of repeated observation or the dialectic process of constructive verification. The first method provides the models to predict behavior but not necessarily the insight to explain the underlying nature of reality. The second method is, by definition, an explanatory intellectual system that ties a body of diverse and contradictory facts into an encompassing hypothesis.

To show how the damnation model affects contemporary approaches to deviance in conceptual and behavioral terms, both methods will be used, although major emphasis will be put on the second, since designs for empirical validations are still in their very early illustrative stage. In other words, this is essentially a theoretical work, and the illustrative studies that accompany some of the discussions—which grew out of my interaction with students—are cited only to show how research designs can be formulated to test some of my propositions, and in particular those which demonstrate how the damnation paradigm predicts contemporary attitudes toward deviants.

Since the main endeavor of this work is to reveal the impact of the "Protestant bias" on Western theories of deviance, it is essentially "nondisciplinarian" in its theoretical-empirical orientation, although it is categorically "social-scientific." That is to say, it is not meant as a contribution to sociology or to psychology *per se*; thus some chapters concentrate more on the theoretical and empirical research orientations developed in psychology, while the theoretical perspective used in other chapters may be sociological or historical. This is simply because some theories of deviance have traditionally been treated by psychologists and others by sociologists. Consequently, each chapter also constitutes a separate unit of analysis and can be read independently from different theoretical perspectives. I hope, however, that the book is sufficiently readable and jargon-free to be useful to all students of the social sciences as well as to lay readers interested in the philosophies of man affecting social problems.

In the introductory chapter the general inherent contradiction between the Protestant Ethic and the people-changing sciences is outlined and discussed and the Calvinist-Weberian "success-failure" paradigm is presented. The second chapter provides an illustrative historical case study to demonstrate that the Calvinist conception of the un-changeable-damned man was actually in evidence in daily life among the Puritans of Colonial Massachusetts.

The analysis of contemporary theories of deviance begins in Chapter 3, which demonstrates how and why the "myth of the psychopath" is perpetuated in Western clinical and empirical literature on psychopathology, although it is admittedly an empirically nonexistent entity. The model of "differential insensitivity" is then presented as an alternative approach for studying the phenomenon commonly known as psychopathy. Chapter 4 examines critically the recently popular labeling theory which explains the genesis of deviance as an *irreversible* state resulting from a process of derogatory labeling. To broaden the cross-cultural approach to the problem of derogatory labeling, a four-level theory of self-labeling is then presented. And to expand upon how

Westernization is associated with a deterministic perception of self or others, two illustrative studies are presented in Chapter 5—one of social labeling and one of self-labeling. After showing that in both the new labeling-reaction perspective and the old structural-action theory no explicit assumptions are made about man's ability to change, Chapter 6 presents an action-reaction convergence model that entails more optimistic components for an effective correctional-change model.

In Chapter 7, which analyzes the impact of the Protestant bias on theories of alienation, the positivistic approach to man is further developed by contrasting the Western Calvinist type of "alienating individualism" with the non-Western type of "reciprocal individualism." Finally, in Chapter 8 the heart of the "Protestant bias" in terms of the theory of man and human change is analyzed by means of a comparative study of the socio-historical roots of the pessimistic Protestant salvation ethic. To conclude the book, I present what I regard as a more optimistic paradigm of man, the Hassidic salvation ethic, to counter the Protestant deterministic conception of the inherently damned or elect man.

The reader will notice that the book carries somewhat of a double message. On the one hand, it presents a critique of existing theories; on the other, it attempts to offer new alternative models. Although many writers probably make a good living by criticizing the work of others (and this book will undoubtedly provide material for their livelihood), I could not ignore the point often made by colleagues (to whom I am very grateful) in reminding me that for one who is interested in the cross-cultural study of deviance, the real challenge is not critique but the struggle with alternative and constructive approaches from a non-Western perspective. I can only hope that I have taken at least the first step in the thousand-mile march of developing new approaches to the study of man.

Acknowledgments

I am indebted to many colleagues, students and teachers who helped me along the way, but the fear of omissions forces me to evade the attempt to list them all. I am aware, however, that although the final responsibility for what is printed in this book rests solely with the author, it is the interaction with and the reactions of others that helped to transform my raw musings into communicable ideas. It is in this spirit that I would like to express my gratitude to S. N. Eisenstadt, not only for honoring me by writing the foreword to this book, but for the continuous advice, criticism, encouragement and time he graciously granted me during various stages of my work.

I would like to acknowledge the inspiring and lasting impact on my thinking of my first mentor, Theodore R. Sarbin, who introduced me to the breadth of the dialectic social psychology which exists beyond the experimental "significant test," and Bernard Diamond, who first encouraged me to "shake out the slipcovers of the psychiatrist's couch."

I would like to thank David Bakan to whom I fed *Damnation and Deviance* on an empty stomach early one morning in the Hilton cafeteria during the 1971 APA meetings in Washington, D.C. He was kind enough not only to listen but even to encourage me to organize the first symposium on the main thesis developed in this book (which took place in the APA meetings in Honolulu in September, 1972). It gives me pleasure also to mention my gratitude to Juris Draguns and Benjamin Braginsky, who participated in the APA symposium and have remained supportive friends ever since.

In a similar vein I am grateful to John Dawson for inviting me to present my thesis at the Inaugural Meeting of the

International Association of Cross-Cultural Psychology in Hong Kong in 1972.

I am most grateful to Richard Cloward and Howard Polsky, whose help and encouragement was of a kind which can hardly be expressed in the form of simple acknowledgments.

I would like to extend thanks to my friends Yochanan Wozner, and Delila and Menachem Amir, who never tired of lending me their ears whenever the muse bestowed some of her favors upon me.

I am thankful to David Rothman, who read and criticized the historical chapter, and to Robert Hare, who invited me to Les Arcs in France to participate in the 1975 NATO Conference on Psychopathy, as well as to Israel Nachshon, who read drafts of the chapter on psychopathy. I am also grateful to David Flusser, who helped me to gain some understanding of the complicated theosophy of Protestantism, as well as to Yoav Elstein and Rivka Shatz-Uffenheimer, from whom I learned a great deal about Jewish mysticism and Hasidism during my work on the final chapter.

Ina Friedman was of enormous help during the painful period of editing and rewriting the material into coherent and presentable prose. Likewise, I cannot fail to express my deep debt to Gladys Topkis of the Free Press for developing her kind patience with a novice author into true encouraging enthusiasm for his work.

Last but most, I am grateful to my wife, Naomi, who bore gracefully the long and arduous hours during which I was physically with her *under the same roof* but was actually off somewhere musing *on the roof*, and who was always ready for emergency typing of my illegible handwriting during the oddest hours of day and night.

MORDECHAI ROTENBERG
The Hebrew University of Jerusalem
September 1, 1977

Chapter One

The Protestant Ethic vs. the "People-Changing" Professions

It is a notion commonly entertained that God adopts as His children such as he foreknows will be deserving of His grace, and devotes to the damnation of death others, whose disposition He sees will be inclined to wickedness.
(Calvin, A Compend of the Institutes of the
Christian Religion)

At the turn of the nineteenth century, Max Weber published his influential thesis positing a causal relationship between the Calvinist-Protestant Ethic and success in terms of capitalistic competitive-achievement behavior (Weber, 1930). This book deals with the other side of Weber's thesis: the impact of the Protestant Ethic on failure and deviance.

This introductory chapter begins by presenting a general encounter between the people-changing sciences and the Protestant Ethic. For convenience, I shall use the term "psychotherapy" in its broadest sense, to refer to all professional systems of treatment aimed at changing people. The chapter advances the premise that, whereas the Protestant Ethic appears to have contributed largely to the enhancement of the scientific-rational approach to psychopathology and to the methods used for altering it, the

1

underlying beliefs of Protestantism and of people-changing systems are inherently contradictory.

The following suggestive rather than conclusive propositions will be outlined and discussed:

1. To the extent that the Protestant Ethic had a general impact on the Western world in terms of economic and scientific development, it is equally responsible for the belief in man's inability to change, since both effects are traceable to Calvin's influential doctrine of predestination.

2. The Protestant Ethic, which is characteristically associated with such referents as "striving," "achieving," "individuality," and "rationalism," fitted and facilitated the development of a scientific model that held nature to be changeable by man. The arbitrary extension of this model to a people-changing technology, however, appears to be paradoxical and self-defeating, since it is rooted in the doctrine of predestination, which holds that man himself is unchangeable.

3. According to modern interpretations of the concept of predestination, a person's ultimate success (mainly material) serves as *a priori* proof that he belongs to the "elect," whereas the absence of success indicates that he is numbered among the "damned." It is thus possible that the traditional preference of Western psychotherapists for treating neurotics while shunning psychopaths and psychotics is due not so much to a lack of effective and measurable treatment methods but rather to the therapists' underlying belief that the neurotic is a treatable ("elect") while the others are unchangeable ("damned").

4. In psychopathology it is not so much the medical-scientific labeling system *per se* that causes stigma and its detrimental social consequences but rather the *dualistic nature and origin* of the diagnostic labeling procedures, which produce the dichotomous classification of people as "sick-damned" or "healthy-elect."

5. While the continuity between medieval demonology and the contemporary mental-health movement has often been pointed out, the historical factors accounting for the augmented persecution of deviants during the Renaissance and the following period have been largely ignored. This phenomenon can be explained by the advent of Calvinism at that time.

6. Behavior-disorder models, such as "demon possession" or "pacting with the devil," imply an external cause that could be removed or a voluntary act that could theoretically be avoided. These models, which are perpetually blasted in modern texts, leave more room for change than a predestinal model, which precludes *a priori* any human intervention capable of changing "the damned."

Before elaborating on these propositions, it would be helpful to review the attitudes toward deviance that have held through various periods of history.

Metaphors of Deviance in Historical Perspective

From a historical perspective, it is abundantly clear that rational-prescientific and demonological-mystical explanations of deviant behavior coexisted in ancient times. Methods of remediation and attitudes toward deviance naturally varied in accordance with the specific metaphor used to describe disordered conduct.

Very early in human history, the so-called insane were venerated because they were "in some way too sacred and good or too powerful for anyone to venture to reduce them to the unblessed state of normalcy" (Zilboorg, 1941:23). Similarly, in ancient Egypt, Greece, Rome, and Israel, it was popularly held that either an evil or a good spirit (e.g., the prophet) could take possession of a person and cause him to behave in some bizarre or unusual way.

Treatment procedures varied from the purely physical to the social-mystical. The Greeks and Romans, for instance, used physical-medical practices emanating from the Hippo-cratic-Galenic theory of humors, as well as prayers, bathing, athletics, music, dietetics, and occupational therapy—closely akin to some of the contemporary psychotherapeutic meth-ods. In general, it seems that in ancient times not only was deviance considered an integral part of social life, but de-viants at times contributed to the enrichment of their cul-tural milieu.[1] Consequently, treatment, whether explained in mystical or in rational terms, was rather humane.

During the Dark Ages, however—and, surprisingly, even more so during the Renaissance—Europe slipped into a witch-hunting period that haunted the Western world for hundreds of years.[2] During this time deviants were consid-ered senseless, hopeless, or even dangerous witches or "wild beasts," [3] and as such were treated by methods whose cruelty is unparalleled in history. The question that arises is, What historical factors can be associated with the advent of this inhumane attitude toward deviance during this period?

Conventional textbooks on psychopathology that devote a chapter to a historical review of abnormal behavior usually describe European brutality toward the deviant during the Middle Ages as a matter of fact and dismiss it as part of an era that vanished with the humanistic reform initiated by Pinel and Tuke in the eighteenth century. Paradoxically, the more puzzling phenomenon of "violent regression toward

[1] An excellent exposition on the gradual segregation of the "insane," "mad," and other practitioners of unreason (e.g., poets, painters, and philosophers) out of the mainstream of life since the fifteenth cen-tury is given in Foucault, 1965.

[2] It is interesting that during the Middle Ages the more scientific and progressive approach to mental disorder introduced by the ancient Greeks and Romans was preserved only in the Arab world, where deviants "received much more humane treatment than in Christian lands" (Coleman, 1964, p. 28; Campbell, 1926; Page, 1971).

[3] On the history and origin of the "wild beast" concept, see Platt and Diamond, 1965.

supernaturalism . . . and witch-hunting" during a "period of renewed enlightenment" (Alexander and Selesnick, 1966: 70)—namely, the Renaissance—usually remains unexplained.

Very little attention has been paid to the implications of the changes in conceptions, beliefs, and the use of metaphors (Sarbin, 1969) to describe deviant behavior throughout the ages. It is nevertheless important to note that primitive theories of "demon-possession," "object intrusion," or "loss of soul" all implied an etiology of specific intervention caused by an external power. Since this influence could be removed, no label was necessarily attached to the person. On the other hand, assigning the label "witch" to the deviant shifted the focus from external causes to the person himself, who was then depicted as the source and carrier of the evil seeds. The difference, therefore, between the concept of *"casting out* the Devil" and that of the *"outcast*-devil" is a very significant one.

Thus, from a historical perspective, even very subtle changes in the use of metaphors to describe deviant conduct might be indicative of both implicit social attitudes and the explicit "treatment model" that the specific metaphor pre-scribes. In this sense, the difference between being possessed by a spirit (a metaphor used in ancient times) and being possessed by a demon (a metaphor used in the Middle Ages) is that the former connotes the presence of a neutral or even a godly entity that may well call for veneration of the pos-sessed person, whereas possession by a demon, devil, or Satan implies intrusion or internalization of a negative, un-godly element and thus provokes negative attitudes and harsh treatment, presumably only to "chase out the devil." Nonetheless, in both cases the deviant himself is not accused of carrying the seeds of wickedness, since possession implies invasion by an external entity, which in principle can be removed.

The attitudinal impact of changes in the use of metaphors appears to be parallel to the case of the father who advises his daughter not to marry a certain man because he has heard that the particular man either stole something or had something stolen from him. Until the thirteenth century, the Church officially held that the insane were innocent victims of the devil (Zilboorg, 1941; Page, 1971). Hence they could find refuge in monasteries, where such mild techniques as prayer or exorcism were practiced. But once the derogatory metaphor, devil or Satan, was adopted in relation to deviant people, the innocence or passivity of the deviant was soon questioned, on the ground that there must be something in the victim himself that attracts the devil. Thus the difference between the offender and his victim is obliterated.

The "switch-to-a-witch" model marking the fourteenth and fifteenth centuries, when it is possible to trace a growing belief that some people were actually witches or in league with Satan (Robbins, 1959; Hughes, 1965), is indeed expressed in the extreme intolerance of deviants, for whom the only effective remedy was extermination. This "treatment" procedure, as is well known, was faithfully implemented by the Church's inquisitors (Robbins, 1959; Sarbin, 1969; Szasz, 1970), who burned thousands of people, as prescribed by the witch-hunter's bible, the *Malleus Maleficarum*. It should also be noted that the earlier concept of "pacting with the devil" implied a voluntary act, which—theoretically, at least—could be avoided, disputed, or disproved. According to the later dualistic-predestinal concept, however, if a man was born *damned* and was assigned to that category prior to his birth, practically nothing on earth could be done to change his unhappy fate.

Thus, although obviously some metaphors of deviance were used simultaneously during various periods, it is useful to assess contemporary approaches to deviance by examining the attitudinal and treatment implications associated with a specific metaphor which predominated during various historical phases (see Table 1–1).

Today the prevalent medical model of deviant behavior

TABLE 1.1. The Metaphoric Scheme of Deviance

PERIOD	METAPHOR	TREATMENT	ATTITUDE	ETIOLOGY	STATE
Ancient	humoral or spiritual possession	physiological or veneration	neutral or positive	external intrusion	reversible
Early Middle Ages	demon possession	exorcism	neutral	external intrusion	reversible
Late Middle Ages	devil's victim	rituals and incarceration	suspicious	passive-receptive	uncertain
Renaissance	pacting with the devil	trial and burning	negative, rejecting	voluntary behavior	disputable
Late Renaissance	personification of Satan	burning	negative, rejecting	innate, internal	irreversible
Post Renaissance	damnation	outcasting or punishment	negative, rejecting	innate, internal	irreversible
Modern	medical	stigmatization, incarceration	negative, rejecting	innate, internal	irreversible

and its elaborate scientific labeling system have been attacked by many writers (Goffman, 1961; Szasz, 1961; Scheff, 1966; Sarbin, 1969; Ullman and Krasner, 1969), mainly on the grounds that by the very process of psycho-medical diagnosis, stigmatic labels are attached to people and cast them into irreversible "sick" roles. The underlying implication of some of these writers, notably Szasz (1970), is that today's mental-health movement is, in fact, an extension of the medieval belief in, and persecution of, witches.

The central point here, however, is that the inhumane treatment of deviants practiced in Europe from the sixteenth through the nineteenth century was imbedded in a much older and more deeply rooted concept than the belief in witches—namely, the belief in predestination and dualism, which was revived and sharpened by John Calvin during the sixteenth century and became a major influence in Europe during the centuries that followed. The predestinal-dualistic doctrine, which divides people into "good-elect" and "wicked-damned," has been part of the Christian faith since its inception. Professor Flusser, the world-renowned expert on Judeo-Christian theology, states that, "since Christianity accepted the doctrine of election, it could not easily do without the concepts on which that doctrine was based, such as predestination and dualism" (1958:130).

It is not only the continuity between witch-hunting and Calvinism [4] that is overlooked by historians of psychopathology but—more important—the concept of "unchangeable man" that follows from Calvinist doctrine. It is against the background of a newly sharpened dualism, therefore, that one should examine Calvin's doctrine of predestination in

[4] Trevor-Roper (1967:13), for example, tells how, "obedient to the voice of Calvin," death was prescribed for all witches in Scotland in the mid-sixteenth century. Similarly, Szasz (1970:296) reports that in 1545 Calvin led a campaign against witches in Geneva during which thirty-one people were executed.

the sixteenth century and its impact on people-changing conceptions in the Western world today.

Predestination and the Success-Failure Paradigm

According to Calvin, people "are not all created with a similar destiny; but eternal life is foreordained for some, and eternal damnation for others" (Calvin, 1939:129). Those who belong to the elect are predestined to have the "symptoms" of righteousness, while the damned are born with the unchangeable "symptoms" of wickedness.

It is a notion commonly entertained, that God, foreseeing what would be the respective merits of every individual, makes a correspondent distinction between different persons; that he adopts as his children such as he foreknows will be deserving of his grace, and devotes to the damnation of death others, whose dispositions he sees will be inclined to wickedness and impiety [*ibid.*].

This basic tenet of Calvinist predestination is found in all major writings on Calvinism, including the famous Westminster confessions of 1647 and the Lambeth Articles of 1595, which were officially adopted by the Anglican Church (Campbell, 1892, Vol. II).

Thus, according to strict Calvinism, if a person is born "damned," there is virtually nothing he or anyone else can do to change his fate. Similarly, no act of human intervention can help a man to join the elect if he has not been assigned to it already:

Predestination to life is not foreseen faith or good work or any other commendable quality in the person predestined, but the good will and pleasure of God . . . it is not everyone's will or power to be saved [Lambeth Articles, quoted in Campbell, 1892, Vol. II, p. 150].

Although in ancient times dualist and unitarian conceptions of man or of good and evil overlapped to some extent, and, although predestination and dualism were already proclaimed by Paul and John in the first century (Flusser, 1958), the full-scale translation of predestinal dualism into action strategies did not occur until Calvin's time. Thus its social consequences were never more apparent and lasting than in the European Renaissance and the period that followed.[5]

Calvinist predestination "was the faith over which the great political and cultural struggles of the 16th and 17th centuries were fought in the most highly developed countries" in Europe (Weber, 1930:98). It became the spiritual-historical ancestor of Puritanism in America and England (Campbell, 1892). It caused schism in the Church during the eighteenth and nineteenth centuries, and it served as the major impetus to and forerunner of modern capitalism and the rational, scientific approach to human life and nature in general.

To illustrate the persuasive methods used to inculcate the doctrine of predestination among Protestants, one should take note of how the Calvinist catechism was circulated among the public. According to Campbell, beginning in 1574 and for many generations thereafter, all English Bibles (which were printed only with government permission) "contained this Calvinistic catechism, bound in between the Old and New Testament" (1892:148). Thus, concludes Campbell, since "it was given officially to the Protestants ... almost as a part of the inspired word of God, one need scarcely ask whence the Puritans derived their so-called peculiar ideas of predestination" (ibid., p. 149).

At this point, the critical question is, How, in everyday

[5] In discussing attitudes toward deviants during the Middle Ages, a typical textbook such as Ullman and Krasner (1969, p. 133) contrasts the tolerant, favorable attitude of the Talmud and the Koran with Luther's definition of idiots as a "corrupted mass of flesh with no soul." But the possible relation between predestination and psychopathology is entirely ignored.

reality, did the ordinary man prove to himself that he was of the elect—or, rather, how did he rid himself of the fear of damnation? According to Calvin himself, two factors are important: (1) "calling" (translated from the German *beruf*, meaning both calling and profession)—"In the elect, we consider calling as evidence for election" (Calvin, 1939:129); and (2) "constant striving" for perfection in one's work— "Therefore, let us not cease to strive that we may be incessantly advancing in the way of the Lord" (cited in McClelland, 1961:49).

It was on the basis of these two factors that Weber (1930) developed his thesis regarding the relationship between the Protestant Ethic and the rise of modern capitalism. Moreover, after Weber it was possible for McClelland (1970) to show empirically that Protestant countries in the 1950s were "economically more advanced... than... Catholic countries" and that, in socializing their children, "Protestants stress earlier [than Catholics] independence and mastery training" (McClelland, 1970:63).[6]

According to Weber, "success" (mainly professional and economic) served as technical proof that one belonged *a priori* to the elect rather than to the damned. By implication, then, if a person did not succeed economically, or if he or others were not convinced that his efforts were fruitful, such "failure" would supply living proof that he was damned. This is to say that, on an operational level, Weber's predestinal-success paradigm (see Figure 1-1) does not rule out the effect of behavioral efforts on man's categoric destiny if he strives and indeed succeeds (e.g., the typical American rags-to-riches legend). But it ignores the constant underlying predestinal threat operating on self- and interpersonal

[6] Heckhausen (1967) reports that, according to studies in America and Germany, Protestant males did not "show more pronounced achievement motive" than Catholics and Jews. In my opinion, all this finding suggests is that gradually and progressively the Protestant Ethic had a generalized impact on the Western world.

Figure 1-1. The Calvinist Success-Failure Scheme

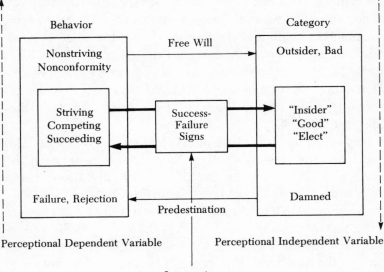

perception: If one ceases to provide success signs (see the heavy arrows), one automatically falls back into the basic damned-outsider category. In the predestinal success-failure scheme, one is categorically damned unless proved otherwise (see Figure 1–1).

Hence the Calvin-Weber predestinal paradigm appears to treat the old free will–deterministic dilemma in a very tricky way. Behavioristically (free will), the provision of success signs leads to one's becoming an "elect-insider," and refraining from striving and succeeding leaves one a "damned-outsider." The operational dependent variable ("insider," "outsider"), however, turns into the perceptual (deterministic) independent variable (see broken arrow): One is damned, therefore he is a lazy failure.

Recent research (Gray-Little, 1973) has shown that, when both positive and negative information were presented to

Danish and American subjects, the negative information was prepotent in impression formation. Since both of these countries are predominantly Protestant, these findings appear to be compatible with the Protestant moral ethic, which teaches that man is essentially damned. Reviewing the wealth of literature that has accumulated since Weber's publication, one finds that much has been written about the "striving" and achievement orientation, as well as about the scientific and economic "success" aspect of predestination (Eisenstadt, 1968) and its resultant effects on economic growth. But very little has been said about the impact predestination may have had on our conceptions of, and attitudes toward, the "unsuccessful" ones.

To demonstrate how individuals were affected by the doctrine of predestination remains an empirical problem with which this book will deal in subsequent chapters.

The remainder of this chapter will deal with the propositions that (1) dualistic-predestinal residuals are clearly reflected in contemporary attitudes toward deviants and (2) rather than minimize the dualistic element in the treatment of deviants, the Western world's rational, scientific approach to psychopathology has reinforced it.

Rationalism and Dualism in Criminology

Matza (1964:1) has suggested that "assumptions (beliefs) implicit in conceptions are rarely inconsequential. Left unattended, they return to haunt us by shaping or bending theories." It should not be too surprising, therefore, that, as the influence of Calvinism spread throughout Europe during the seventeenth and eighteenth centuries, new social theories compatible with predestination enjoyed increasing popularity.

A compelling argument can be made for the compatibility and continuity of Calvinistic predestination in the sixteenth and seventeenth centuries, on the one hand, with such nine-teenth-century conceptions as "natural selection," "dangerous classes," "survival of the fittest" (ascribable to Darwin and Spencer), and the Lombrosean positivistic school in crimin-ology, on the other.

Mayhew has pointed out the link between the Protestant work ethos and the notion of "dangerous classes":

> The concept of the *dangerous classes* as the main source of crime and disorder was very much to the fore at the be-ginning of the 19th century. . . . They were portrayed as a race apart, morally depraved and vicious, living by violating the fundamental law of orderly society, which was that man should maintain himself by honest, steady work (naturally paupers were conveniently included among the dangerous classes). . . . The key factor was the refusal of the pauper or the criminal to work, a refusal arising from some innate moral defect, [quoted in Radzinowicz, 1966: 40].

Popular beliefs about the nature and existence of a crimi-nal class were confirmed by the "scientific findings" of Cesare Lombroso (1876), who believed in a "born criminal type" recognizable by certain definite physical characteristics. Darwin's statement that "born criminals were to be under-stood as atavistic reversions to a lower or more primitive evolutionary form of development" (Lombroso, 1912:137) was extrapolated by Lombroso, who advocated that "born murderers should be put to death . . . as a measure of ex-treme selection . . . supplementing the process of natural selection" (Radzinowicz, 1966:55). If "rational success" proves one's predetermined selection for eternal grace, why not use the same Protestant rationalism to determine "sci-entifically" who belongs to the hopeless damned or to the "dangerous" or "dependent" classes and, consequently, who should be put away and "relieved from competing for survival"?

It seems that condemnation of the damned in the name of a dualistic-scientific approach was long-lasting. Hofstadter (1968) points out that the idea of removing the unfit was echoed in the school of thought that came to be known as "social Darwinism." Braginsky *et al.* maintain that during the late eighteenth century "doctors saw mental illness as one of nature's ways of eliminating the unfit of the species" (1969: 179). Platt (1969) likewise contends that contemporary delinquency-control programs can be traced back to the nineteenth-century social reformers known as the "child-savers," who, in the name of "humanitarianism," invented new categories of delinquency and established institutions to isolate delinquents "for their own good."

Similarly, Kai Erikson, in describing the very cruel penal system prevailing in New England during the seventeenth century, directly attributes the harshness of the Puritan attitude toward deviants to the Protestant doctrine of predestination:

> In order to understand this feature of Puritan justice, one should begin with the doctrine of predestination as it appeared in New England thinking. . . . Given these premises, the Puritan attitude toward punishment had a fairly simple logic. If a culprit standing before the bench is scheduled to spend eternity in hell, it does not matter very much how severely the judges treat him [K. T. Erikson, 1966:190].

Erikson makes a strong case that these harsh Puritan ideologies vis-à-vis deviants remain an important part of the context in which deviants are dealt with today.

Having reviewed the possible continuity between medieval witch-hunting, predestination, and the social-scientific school of positivism, as well as the impact of all three on criminological-penal theories and practices, one should note that the distance from penology to psychotherapy is very short.

Predestinal Dualism and Psychotherapy

The contribution of Protestant rationalism to the development of the scientific method has been discussed by Merton (1936) and others. On the other hand, Hofstadter showed how Calvinist-Darwinian conceptions dominated the outlook of social scientists like Sumner, who "came to preach... predestination ... and the salvation of the economically elect through the survival of the fittest" (1968:66). Nevertheless, while some writers have alluded to the paradoxical implications inherent in a "people-changing science" traceable to a Calvinist conception of man as unchangeable, the applicability of the scientific model to modern psychotherapy is taken for granted by most professional "people-changers" (e.g. Ford and Urban, 1964:14). Mowrer (1964:6), for example, accused Freud of having nicely timed and tailored his paradigm to fit Calvin's doctrine of predestination by adopting a new doctrine of double irresponsibility,[7] according to which "one should not feel guilty about anything." And both Fromm (1960) and Mowrer (1964) have discussed at length how Calvin's doctrine on man supposedly produces a person imbued with feelings of powerlessness and guilt. Nevertheless, they fail to tackle the central question of how this person, who has internalized the Protestant Ethic, can

[7] In discussing moral responsibility for the content of dreams, Freud made his position clear: "Obviously one must hold oneself responsible for the evil impulses of one's dreams." In general it is unclear what Freud's own views about human nature were. It is plausible that he was sentimentally attached to the old hierarchical assumptions, as Rieff (1966:56) suggests, and that his works were later given a predeterministic interpretation by his followers. This view is implied in Freud's own writings. For example, in discussing neurosis, Freud once equated this phenomenon to the "demon-possession" model, not to the witch paradigm. In addition, the similarity between the Jewish concept of *Yetzer* (evil inclination, evil impulse, or passionate desire) and Freud's libido theory further suggests that Freud's ideas were rooted more in a unitarian conception of man (Porter, 1902) than in a Protestant dualistic conception.

be helped and changed by a therapist who is affected by the same doctrine.

Even more paradoxical is the thesis put forward by Davis, who, in a lengthy discussion, simultaneously accuses the mental-hygiene movement of hiding behind the "scientific" guise of Protestant psychologistic individualism, which conceives of human conduct in terms of innate biological traits, and claims that this same Protestant Ethic bequeathed to the mental-hygiene movement an "open-class system" that favors "equal opportunities to rise socially by merit rather than by birth" (Davis, 1938:56)—a typical illusion of the 1930s.

While Davis attributes the mental hygienists' ineffectiveness in treating the "unsuccessful class" to their inability to utilize their own unconscious, "Protestant," open-class conceptions, he fails to realize that while "to rise socially by merit and good works" is inherently at odds with the doctrine of predestination (in which the Protestant mental hygienists' beliefs are admittedly rooted), it *is* compatible with their biological deterministic view of man. In the Protestant system, "the equality of mankind is denied in principle," as Fromm (1960:76) has suggested. To put it differently, the theological-formal causality paradigm (good-elect or evil-damned) is misrepresented by the mental hygienist as a mechanistic-efficient causality paradigm (Sarbin, 1971).

If, as we have seen, the modern "people-changing sciences" are essentially rooted in Calvinist predestinal dualism, it should not be surprising to note that treatment of deviants is likewise dominated by the Protestant Ethic. More specifically, definitions of normalcy and psychological treatment appear to be rooted in Protestant conceptions, and modern psychiatric nosology implies a division into "treatable-elect" and "unchangeable-damned."

In a most detailed attempt to delineate positive mental health, Jahoda (1958) maintained that "the healthy person

displays active adjustment rather than passive acceptance."
This definition, Ullman and Krasner (1969) suggest, is
taken directly from the Protestant lexicon. According to
Davis, whose conclusions are based upon a survey of the
major works through the late 1930s, "lack of ambition is felt
to represent a definite symptom of maladjustment . . . the
normal person is considered to be one who chooses a calling
and tries to distinguish himself in it, while the mentally sick
person is one who needs occupational therapy" (1938:57).

The concept of "will" (motivation) or striving seems to
be central to these definitions and fits neatly into the famous
Protestant ethos of "God helps those who help themselves"
(Weber, 1930:115). At first glance, one might be misled to
conclude that since "will is the object of treatment" (Davis,
1938:58), therapists hold that man is master of his destiny.
But will is precisely the device used to divide people into
treatable-successful-elect and untreatable-failures-damned.
Motivation (will) not accompanied by concrete materialistic
success is unacceptable as a criterion for mental health.

This point has been eloquently illuminated by Fromm,
who points out that "the significance of an unceasing effort
gains in importance, particularly the idea that success in
worldly life, as a result of such efforts, is a sign of salvation"
(1960:77). In other words, not only the will, motivation, or
efforts, but also the resulting success [8] is requisite for membership in the treatable-elect.

If one uses striving, motivation, and the resulting success—
or rather exaggerated compulsive striving as well as willing-
ness and collaboration (with therapists)—as criteria for
treatability, the only psychological type who falls directly
and neatly into this category is the so-called classic neurotic
type. Only the neurotic can be considered "successful," and
he usually has a constant compulsive need to strive for perfection (Fromm, 1960).

[8] Cohen (1955) explains the emergence of delinquent gangs in the
United States as a reaction formation against this dominant Protestant Ethic.

Thus the therapist's traditional preference for treating neurotics (Goldman and Mendelsohn, 1969) and his reluctance to treat psychopaths ("the clinical wastebasket," in professional slang) and psychotics (who are usually segregated but not cured) might reflect a deep-seated belief that the former belong to the "successful-elect" and the latter to the "hopeless-damned." In this sense, neurotics are usually fairly "successful" people who do not require radical hierarchical changes (e.g., from evil to good). Rather, they require the resolution of inner conflicts and need to be taught "how to live with contradictions in life" (Rieff, 1966:55). This distinguishes them from psychopaths and psychotics, who are regarded as a special class of incorrigible nonpersons (Sarbin, 1969) and therefore untreatable.

The proposition that psychodiagnostic labels imply a revived dualistic conception requires brief exposition here. Scientific nomenclature is vital for the organization of accumulated knowledge in any descipline. There is a crucial difference, however, between labeling certain behavior sequences "melancholic," for instance, and reversing the dialectics by saying, "You behave in this melancholic manner *because you are* schizophrenic." The extent of absoluteness and innateness implied in the attached label determines the degree to which treatment can erase the mark of Cain, so to speak.

The deviant behaviors we included under the rubric "mental disorder" are not peculiar to Western societies. Bizarre behavior and the labels applied to it are as old as history. But the irreversible nature ascribed to these diagnostic categories (Goffman, 1961; Szasz, 1961; Scheff, 1966; Sarbin, 1969) and "the gradual segregation of the insane" (Foucault, 1965) seem to be more characteristic of Western societies.

Empirical evidence suggests that in East Africa, for example (Edgerton, 1969), the processes and labels applied to "mental illness" are all negotiable and reversible. Similarly, Kitano (1969) noted that in Japan—a technically advanced but non-Protestant country—the social role and the label "mentally ill" and the resulting rejecting attitudes are practically nonexistent. Draguns (1972) observed that in countries less fueled by the Protestant Ethic, *rejection* of the mentally disordered was much lower than in countries permeated by that ethic.

Specific studies concerning the nature and incidence of perceived predestinal damnation are unavailable at present. But one might entertain the proposition that the irreversibility implied in Western labeling might be rooted in the predestinal-dualistic doctrine of Protestantism. Furthermore, the relative ineffectiveness of psychotherapy (Eysenck, 1966b) and therapists' traditional insistence on the "passive receptive role" (Sarbin and Adler, 1970–71:608) can be attributed to the generalized Protestant disbelief in man's ability to change.

This is not to say that effective, measurable people-changing methods do not exist. There is a wealth of world literature on the alteration of conduct and personality—using procedures ranging from conversion, rituals, and ecstasy to military indoctrination and sensory deprivation—which is rejected as "unscientific and unworthy of serious study" (*ibid.*, p. 600). A prostitute can be converted effectively and predictably to a nun, but the process is not as scientific or as "acceptable" as the individualistic Protestant "soft" methods of treating the neurotic and avoiding the hard-core "damned."

Predestinal dualism, which leads to a fundamental division of people into two camps—the righteous and the wicked—has been part of the Christian faith since the first century A.D. The metaphors employed to describe those predestined to wickedness changed over the years—from "sons of darkness" [9] to devils, witches, damned, and finally psychotics and

---

[9] This term, referring to the wicked, was used by the Dead Sea sect (approximately 100 B.C.) and by Paul and John (approximately A.D. 100). According to Flusser (1958), the Qumran doctrine was not generally accepted by Judaism but directly influenced early (pre-Pauline) Christianity.

psychopaths—but the continuity of these labels can hardly be ignored. Predestinal dualism and its reflections in the Protestant Ethic are at odds with the people-changing conceptions professed by modern psychotherapy. This is the very essence of the tragic circle of self-fulfilling prophecy in Western society, which can be broken, as Merton suggested, "only with the rejection of social fatalism implied in the notion of unchangeable human nature" (1957:436).

This chapter has postulated specific impacts of the Protestant Ethic on Western attitudes toward and conceptions of failure and deviance. Since this book is essentially grounded in the orientation of the social sciences, the following chapters will concentrate on critically examining selective theories of deviance that emanate from the Protestant paradigm of man and on deriving alternative theoretical propositions. One question that remains, however, is whether the Calvinist damnation metaphor was ever used in daily life to describe and treat deviance. To provide an illustrative historical case in point, the next chapter will describe and discuss how the unchangeable conception of the damned man was used among the Puritans of Colonial Massachusetts.

Chapter Two

Puritan Damnation and Deviance: A Socio-Historical Case Study

Cast out all the people among us, as drunkards, swearers, whores, liers, which the Scripture brands for black sheep and condemns them in an hundred places. Set by all Civill men, that are wolves, chained up, tame devils, swine in faire medow.

(Thomas Shepard, The Sincere Convert)

Chapter 1 advanced the thesis that the recently popular "antilabeling" approach to deviance attributes the genesis of deviance to the process of irreversible derogatory labeling. This perspective raises serious questions from a cross-cultural and historical point of view. The most pressing of these is: What are the historical-ideological roots of the presumed absolute irreversible rejection of deviants that characterizes most Western societies?

Historians of psychopathology and deviance usually dismiss the demonological explanation of mental disorder prevalent in medieval Europe and the resulting brutality toward deviants as an attribute of the Dark Ages. However, as alluded to earlier, the more puzzling phenomenon of increased cruelty to and rejection of deviants during the Renaissance usually remains unexplained. In searching for the missing historical link that would explain the presumed irreversible rejection of deviants during both the Renaissance and the modern era, I have argued that it is essentially the Calvinist conception of predestinal damnation and not medieval demonology that underlies the contemporary medical approach to deviance.

More specifically, I have proposed that just as the Protestant Ethic had a general impact on the Western world in terms of economic development and increased achievement behavior—as Weber (1930) and others have posited—the covert belief that deviance and failure are symptoms of an innate and irreversible state of damnation is equally pervasive in Western culture, since both tenets are traceable to Calvin's influential doctrine of predestination.

Following the same line, I have maintained that very little attention has been paid to the relationship between periodic changes in conceptions of man and concomitant changes in the metaphors used to describe deviance. Thus Szasz (1970), for example, who maintains that today's mental-health movement is an extension of medieval witch-hunting, fails to explain the implications for differential treatment methods inherent in specific demonological metaphors and their relationship to contemporary mental-health systems. Similarly, while Kai Erikson has explained the harsh attitudes toward deviants in Colonial Massachusetts as a corollary of the early Puritans' belief in predestinal damnation, the cases he cites to document this attitude describe people who were severely punished either for having made a convenant with the devil or for having been "possessed with Satan" (1966:193–94).

Differences between these metaphors may appear to be very subtle. However, they may nonetheless be revealing of an implicit social attitude and an explicit "treatment model." "Demon possession" implies voluntary intrusion by an external entity, which is in principle removable. "Pacting with the devil" stands for a voluntary act that could, at least theoretically, be disputed and disproved. But "predestinal damnation" connotes an innate, irreversible state of deviance. Accordingly, if Puritan Calvinists in Colonial Massachusetts, for example, indeed believed in predeterminstic damnation (see Miller, 1956; Erikson, 1966) but simultaneously blamed deviants for having freely and willingly made a covenant with the devil, the application of these "mixed" and seemingly paradoxical metaphors requires deeper explanation.

Since much has been written about the Puritan "witch-hunting" period (e.g. the famous witches of Salem), this chapter attempts first to demonstrate how the "predestinal damnation" metaphor was actually used in everyday life by people to label either themselves or others as inherently damned and unchangeable, and then explores the Puritan paradox of punishing people who were presumably "born damned."

To assess the relative impact of a particular metaphor on a group's attitudes toward deviance would require a comprehensive historical study, which is beyond the scope and orientation of this book. It should therefore be stressed at the outset that the goal of this chapter is to establish that the "predestinal damnation" metaphor, among other approaches to deviants, was indeed used by Puritans in Colonial Massachusetts. Thus the selected case material will be presented mainly as illustrative and not as representative historical evidence.

Two aspects of what can be termed "applied damnation" can be identified: (1) the division of people into "hopeless damned" and "righteous elect" on the basis of conformity to or deviation from an ideal religious norm; and (2) the treatment of self and others as "hopeless damned" on the basis of specific failure symptoms in "secular" behavior.

Predestinal Dualism and Religious Deviation

It is reasonable to assume that, in a religious community such as Colonial Massachusetts, the most powerful disseminators and activators of a divine doctrine would be the preachers. Let us therefore begin by taking a glimpse at what preachers said to their people. The following is a typical quotation from the sermons delivered by the preacher Thomas Shepard:

> God has elected but a few. . . . How many do you think shall be saved in this citie? . . . [T]hough there be so many thousands of you, yet there cannot be found an hundred that shall be saved, and I doubt of them, too [1646:124, 132].

In another sermon, Shepard stressed God's absolute and arbitrary freedom to damn any person He wished:

> When God hath an intent to harden an man's heart and to damn him, either he shall have a prejudice against the man or else . . . and the Lord he hardens and blinds and prepares for eternal ruin all the man [1853: 3:381].

The famous eighteenth-century Puritan leader Jonathan Edwards stressed God's arbitrariness in granting grace:

> However you may have reformed your life in many things, and in the house of God, it is nothing but his mere pleasure that keeps you from being this moment swallowed up in everlasting destruction [quoted in Miller, 1962:210].

Similarly, the early eighteenth century's influential Increase Mather preached in a famous sermon:

> I say, God is not bound to give Sinners Grace. He is an absolute soverign, and may give Grace or deny Grace to whom He pleaseth [quoted in Miller and Johnson, 1963:335].

While preachers like Shepard, Edwards, and Mather stressed the arbitrariness of God's will and the slight chance people had to be among the saved, other preachers dramatized and justified the terrifying sufferings associated with the state of being damned. Consider the following:

> They are now hanging over the pit of destruction and just ready this moment to fall into it, that hell-fire now flasters

in their faces . . . and they will oftentimes repeat the awful
words Damned! Damned! Damned! three or four times
[Chauncy, 1743:96].

The point stressed here is that the doctrine of predestination not only was preached as a harsh and terrifying theological concept that would facilitate social control but was
also the source of social discrimination [1] and mutual accusations by dividing the community into "damned" and "elect."
The Puritan divine Davenport, for example, accused the
minister of his town of being an "unconverted man" and a
"hypocritic wolf in sheep's clothing" and declared publicly
that "thousands are now cursing him in hell for being the
instrument of their damnation" (*ibid.*, p. 157). Similarly,
Morgan (1958) tells us how the thousands of immigrants
who flooded into Massachusetts in the seventeenth century
not only had to be "checked off as being saved or damned"
but were trained to check and search the souls of their
neighbors by "placing the mark of holiness on their own
foreheads and the mark of damnation on most of their
neighbors." These experiences, according to Morgan, were
the "breeders of separatism" (pp. 79–80). Indeed, the dualistic doctrine of predestination was used to "divide men into
believers and nonbelievers: saints and damned" (see Rutman, 1965:119) by separatists such as Roger Williams and
Anne Hutchinson, who declared as damned all those who
adhered to the covenant of works (i.e., who relied on good
works instead of a divine grace alone).

Furthermore, it seems apparent that the inclination toward
separatism, discrimination, and the dualistic division of
people that emanated from the application of the doctrine
of predestination was not reserved for religious extremists
and separatists only. Chauncy reports that the suspicious

[1] Loubser (1968) has explained the inequality and segregation practiced by the Afrikaners in South Africa today as a perpetuation of
their Calvinistic background.

spirit of mutual accusation infiltrated all strata of the people in Massachusetts:

> There was so much bitter and rash judging. Parents condemning their children and children their parents. Husbands their wives, and wives their husbands. Masters their servants, and servants their masters. Ministers their people, and people their ministers [1743:170].

In an epitomizing illustration of this damnifying atmosphere, Chauncy describes the case of a fifteen-year-old girl who accused her father of being damned.[2] "At first she began with her father and told him she could see the image of the devil there in his face and that he was going haste-paste into hell ... as heir of eternal damnation" (*ibid.*, p. 169).

The terminology of damnation, however, was not associated solely with passive expressions of disagreement or interpersonal hostility. Verbalization or publication of what were termed "damnable doctrines" (*Massachusetts Historical Society*, vol. 14, chapter 39, p. 6), "damnable errors" (e.g. Herchman, 1771:143–44), or "wicked opinions" was actually punished by banishment or even death:

> And it is further ordered and enacted, that if the said offender shall the second time publish . . . the said wicked opinion, he shall be banished or put to death as the court shall judge [*Records of the Colony of Massachusetts*, 1652, Vol. 4:1, p. 78].

In summary, although the girl described above referred to her father's physical appearance as the image of the devil, the attitude of the separatists vis-à-vis religious deviation usually was not linked to specific behavioral symptoms. However, deviation from specific secular norms (e.g. stealing, sex violations) were nonetheless labeled and judged in religious terms by self and others.

---

[2] Mutual accusations of the nature described here can be identified many generations later in the behavior of the "Hitler *jugend*," children who accused their parents of being disloyal to Hitler.

Predestinal Dualism and Secular Deviance

The road that leads from accusation and condemnation of people who deviated from a religious norm to accusation and rejection of people who behave in a bizarre manner, fail, or deviate from any secular norm is indeed very short. Let us first reconsider how the process of classification, segregation, and casting out of specific deviant types from the rest of the community was triggered by a preacher like Shepard:

> Cast out all the profane people among us, as drunkards, swearers, whores, liers, which the Scripture brands for black sheep and condemns them in an hundred places. Set by all Civill men, that are but wolves, chained up, tame Devils, swine in faire medow. . . . Cast by all Hypocrites, that like stage players . . . act the parts of Kings and honest men; when look upon them in their trying house, they are but base varlets [1646:132–33].

Commenting on the impact that such harsh, stigmatizing sermons had on the congregants, Middlekauff refers to several sources that describe how "the ministers' insistences on predestination sometimes were enough to drive a man out of his wits" (1971:377). It would seem reasonable, then, that the preachers' insistence that one's slim chance to be saved is unrelated to one's efforts and their persistent call to cast out all profane people should be reflected in (1) feelings of hopeless damnation and desperate attitudes expressed toward oneself and (2) punishment and rejection or casting out of others as deviants and social failures.

SELF-DAMNATION

It is well known that many of the Puritan religious leaders expressed feelings of desperation and damnation in the course of their efforts to experience conversion. The famous minister John Bunyan (1628–1688) was described as follows:

> Calvinism led him by means of the given doctrine of election and reprobation to question his own chances of salvation. . . . The "storms" of temptation . . . buffeted him with almost physical violence; voices urged him to blasphemy. . . . Finally, one morning, he believed that he had surrendered to those voices of Satan . . . "down I fell as a bird that is shot from the tree" [*Encyclopaedia Britannica*, 4:413].

Similarly, a certain minister named Gratry (1880) was quoted as having said, "I suffered an incurable and intolerable desolation, verging on despair. I thought myself, in fact, rejected by God, lost, damned! I felt something like the suffering of hell" (quoted by James, 1960:154).

The ministers (who undoubtedly reinforced feelings of desperation and melancholy among the public by their modeling behavior) should not be cited exclusively, however, to demonstrate how damnation affected everyday life. It is the common man who is our main focus of interest here. Bercovitch suggests, for example, that "in New England . . . where anxiety about election was not only normal but mandatory—hysteria, breakdowns, and suicides were not uncommon" (1975:23). The following case, recorded in 1642, ended in a tragic suicide:

> About this time, one Turner of Charlestown, a man of about 50 years of age, having led a loose and disorderly life, and being wounded in conscience at a sermon of Mr. Shepard's, he kept it in and did not discover his distress . . . and after a good space he went out from his wife on the Lord's day at night having kept at home all that day, and drowned himself in a little pit where was not above two feet water [*Winthrop's Journal*, 1642, vol. II, p. 55].

In another case, recorded at approximately the same time, the influence of the doctrine of predestination is again clearly evident in a young man's explanation of his attempted suicide. The man who interviewed him reported: "He said, 'twas in vain for him; his day was out.' I asked, what day; he answered, of grace" (*Massachusetts Historical Society*, Vol. 44, p. 16).

From the present point of view, it is unimportant whether a causal relationship can be established between predestination and such suicidal tendencies. What is important is that those who reported these cases in the seventeenth century interpreted such behavior as resulting from sermons or general feelings of damnation.

Moreover, it was not only laymen who observed the impact of the predestination doctrine on melancholy and mental disorder. The European physician-psychiatrist Weyer (1515–1588), for example, described some of the mentally disturbed people he knew:

> I have seen a man who stubbornly refused to eat and drink, thinking that he was condemned. These are people who are so miserably tormented by little scruples of conscience that they look for five legs in a ram when a ram has but four. . . . They weep day and night, thinking themselves damned [quoted in Zilboorg, 1941:225].

The examples cited here should be sufficient to document how self-damnation was expressed in mental disorders such as depression and suicidal tendencies. A few examples describing how predestinal damnation was used to interpret, punish, or cast out others who performed specific deviant acts are now in order.

SOCIAL DAMNATION

I have argued above that the terminology of damnation was used in various social contexts to refer to an innate, irreversible state of deviance. I have also shown that the notion of predestination precipitated a constant process of differentiation between "good guys" and "bad guys," as was demonstrated by the descriptions of the separatists' mutual accusations and mutual banishments. It should therefore not be surprising that, while various forms of deviant conduct were interpreted as innate, hopeless states, there was also a prominent tendency to punish and segregate deviants as dangerous outcasts or *contagious* lepers.

Jonathan Edwards, for example, drew a dramatic scene to show how a man could ascertain his condition as elect and justify his privileged position by comparing himself to the suffering damned:

> These scenes of awful and everlasting torture would only serve to give the saints a greater sense of their happiness, and of God's grace to them . . . seeing how vastly different their case is from their own. The view of the doleful condition of the damned will make them the more prized for their blessedness [quoted in Adams, 1893:74].

Thus the atmosphere of constant differentiation between the elect and the damned seemed to have paved the way for the growing belief that the state of damnation was somehow contagious and that all unruly or disturbed people should therefore be controlled or put away so that they could not damnify[3] others. A law passed in Massachusetts in 1676 states:

> Whereas there are distracted persons in some townes that are unruly, whereby, not only the familyes wherein they are, but others suffer much damage by them, it is ordered by this Court and the authority thereof, that the selectmen in all townes where such persons are are hereby impowered and enjoined to take care of all such persons that they doe not damnify others [*Records of the Colony of Massachusetts Bay*, Vol. 5, 1676, p. 80].

---

[3] Deutsch has suggested that it was "the fear of damnification" (1949: 43) that attracted public attention to mentally disturbed people. While Deutsch based his observation only on this law, other writers, such as Grob (1966), relied only on Deutsch in their explanations of the aversive attitudes toward mental illness prevailing in America.

The material presented above indicates that the damnation metaphor was extended from the religious arena to refer to mental disorder and its hazards for the public.[4] It appears that sometimes this process was reversed, and the stigma of mental disorder was used to reject people on a religious basis.

> In the year 1628, a young man named Rogers was sent to their minister, without any invitation from the Church . . . or sufficient recommendation. They, however, made some trial of him; and soon perceiving him disordered in brain they were at considerable charge to send him back next year [*Massachusetts Historical Society*, Boston Collec-tion, Vol. 4, p. 109].

It is obviously possible that the young man in question was indeed mentally disturbed, but the carryover from one sphere to the other—the tendency to associate religious devia-tion with mental disturbance—comes through clearly.

Let us consider now how a typical case of mental disorder was described and interpreted in religious terms:

> The wife of one Onions of Roxbury died in great despair: she had been a servant there and was very stubborn and self-willed. . . . She fell withall into great horror and trem-bling so as it shook the room, etc. . . . and crying out of her torment and her stubbornness and unprofitableness under the means and her lying to her dame . . . she ne-glected her spiritual good for a wordly trash and . . . she must go to everlasting torments [*Winthrop's Journal*, Vol. II, 1630–1649, p. 93].

---

[4] In more contemporary settings, Caplan has suggested that nine-teenth century laws inspired by Social Darwinism arranged for the segregation and sterilization of criminals, paupers, and the mentally ill so that they would not "pollute the blood of the community" (1969:301). Similarly, Szasz maintains that in Nazi Germany mental patients were exterminated "in the name of protecting the health of the sane" (1970:214). One therefore wonders what beliefs stand behind the adoption of the popular term "mental hygiene," since "hygiene" is defined in Webster's dictionary as the science of sani-tation, meaning the practice of cleanliness and the prevention of infectious diseases.

In another case, the records describe a woman

> . . . who was fallen into a sad infirmity the loss of her un-
> derstanding and reason which had been growing upon her
> . . . giving herself wholly to reading and writing and had
> written many books. . . . For if she had attended her house-
> hold affairs and such things as belong to women and not
> gone out of her way and calling to meddle in such things as
> are proper for men whose minds are stronger, etc. . . . She
> had kept her wits and might have improved them usefully
> and honorably in the place God had set for her! [*Winthrop's
> Journal,* Vol. II, 1645, p. 225].

The common denominator of these two cases, which describe the etiology of mental disorder, is the straightforward
Calvinist language used to interpret the behavior and to
justify the consequences. In the first case, it is mainly the
term "everlasting torment," used repeatedly by Puritans, that
the woman in question was said to deserve and suffer. In
the second case, it is mainly the futile attempt made by the
woman to step out of her preordained "calling," "in the place
God has set her," that is used to interpret and justify her
suffering.

In the cases of these women, nature took its course, and it
remained only for the Puritan writer to justify their tragic
end. In other cases, where more malice and stubborness were
involved, the tendency of the authorities to cast out and
punish the deviant as a hopeless, *impenitent,* damned person was consistently evident. In one case, for example, a
person brought before the church authorities for stealing
confessed his sins but was nevertheless declared impenitent
and excommunicated:

> Isaak . . . stood impudently and said indeed he owned his
> sin of stealing, was heartily sorry for it, begged pardon of
> God and men, and hoped he would do so no more. . . . The
> Church at length gave their judgement against him, that he
> was a notorious, scandalous sinner and obstinately impenitent
> [quoted in Adams, 1890, Vol. VI, p. 483].

In another case, a man who had married his brother's widow was also declared to be an "impenitent, scandalous, wicked, incestuous sinner . . . and the sentence of excommunication was solemnly performed by the pastor of the Church" (*ibid.,* p. 484).

It is difficult to assess the relative prevalence of a specific metaphor relating to deviance and its impact on everyday life, because one can never be certain whether the prevalence of reported cases of a given sort represents the relative dominance of such cases or the historian's area of concentration. Nevertheless, the few cases described here (which obviously concentrate mainly on one metaphor) should be sufficient to demonstrate that belief in the hopeless, irreversible state of the damned, whether judged in terms of their deviation from a religious norm or secular norms, was actually reflected in the behavior of people toward themselves and others and that the damnation terminology was not merely a figure of speech. While it is obvious from the data that certain forms of deviance were often perceived as reversible by the more enlightened, "soft" Puritan Calvinists, the concept of the predestined-damned state of irreversible deviance was nevertheless also an active metaphor used to interpret and treat deviant people.

It is the possible continuity between the underlying conception of the irreversible state of deviance implied by the early American damnation metaphor and today's medical metaphor that concerns us most here. Indeed, notions similar to those of the seventeenth- and eighteenth-century Puritan beliefs in the impenitent, hopeless, and irreversible state of various forms of deviance may be recognized in the nineteenth-century "Social Darwinist" trend in psychiatry. In 1885, for example, a psychiatrist noted that among the

. . . mass of chronic insane . . . comparatively few . . . recover for the reason, chiefly, that they did not possess in the first place the conditions of recovery. . . . How can reason and volition return to those from whom it never departed? [quoted in Caplan, 1969:293].

Thus, although it is very difficult to establish the historical link between the damnation metaphor and the contemporary medical model of deviance and even Social Darwinist psychiatry (which was obviously influenced by divergent social and scientific developments), it seems more than plausible that the basic belief that some people are hopeless cases and that certain forms of deviance are innate or irreversible has consistently underlain Western conceptions of deviance from the time of the Reformation to the present.

Since examination of the limited available data reveals that even in a relatively pure Calvinist state, such as Colonial Massachusetts, demonological and damnation metaphors were used simultaneously to describe and to treat deviants, a few words should be devoted to explaining the paradoxical paradigm of man that emanates from the doctrine of predestination.

Predestinal Free Will and Deviance

The philosophical paradox inherent in the tendency to blame and punish a person who is by definition not responsible for his condition—whether because he was involuntarily possessed by a demon or because he was "predestined" to fail—was alluded to earlier. To disentangle this paradoxical attitude toward deviance, which is entailed in the Calvinist-Puritan paradigm, one must understand how predestination was translated into action strategies.

It is well known that active Calvinism entailed two contradictory elements, as outlined in Chapter 1 (see specially Figure 1–1). On the one hand, it professed a deterministic concept of man which emphasized that man's destiny to be a successful elect or a damned failure was predetermined and unrelated to his actions, efforts, or choices. On the other hand, by dispensing with the church as a mediator between man and his God, Calvinism gave rise to a new spirit of individualism and autonomy that urged man to concentrate on his independent achievements—the ultimate proof of *a priori* election (Weber, 1930; Lukes, 1973).

Thus, in relation to the old "free will–determinism" dilemma, Calvinist individualism (see Chapter 7) predicated that man has personal freedom of choice and responsibility to purchase his own salvation, although the threat of predestination always hovers over him. The *Kulturkampf* between the New England separatists, who adhered to the Covenant of Grace, and the "soft Calvinists," who advocated the Covenant of Works, evolved precisely around this "free will–determinism" dilemma, although "the absolute freedom of God to choose or reject, regardless of man's achievements" (see Miller, 1956:54) underlay both covenants. The Covenant of Grace complied with the deterministic conception of the predestinal damned or elect, and the Covenant of Works corresponded to the new individualistic concept of man's freedom of choice and personal responsibility, which meant that man could be redeemed by his effort and labors. It is through this "free will–determinism" approach to behavior that one should understand the Puritan's paradoxical attitude toward failure and deviance.

Until the begining of the fourteenth century, the predominant approach to deviance in Europe was grounded in the "demon possession" metaphor, according to which the Church officially held that the insane were *innocent victims* of the devil. Accordingly, such people were not stigmatized, because it was believed that, in the same way that the devil invaded man, he could also be driven out. In the fifteenth century, it was believed that some people—i.e. witches—were actually personifications of the devil (Zilboorg, 1941; Page, 1971). The new Calvinistic individualist spirit that spread through sections of Europe in the sixteenth century, however, held that man is endowed with free will and hence should be held responsible for his failures and blamed and punished for his deviant conduct, even though he is essentially a hopeless, unchangeable, damned creature who is unable "to choose correctly" (see Bercovitch, 1975:21). Indeed, one may notice that during that period the innocence and passivity of the devil's victims were questioned on the ground that there must be something in the victim [5] himself that attracts the devil (as noted in Chapter 1) and he should thus be held responsible for his own bewitchment. In this regard, Zilboorg states:

> The belief in the free will of man is here brought to its most terrifying, although most preposterous, conclusion. Man, whatever he does, even if he succumbs to an illness which perverts his perceptions, imagination, and intellectual functions, does it of his own free will; he voluntarily bows to the wishes of the Evil One. The devil does not lure and trap man; man chooses to succumb to the devil and he must be held responsible for this free choice. He must be punished; he must be eliminated from the community [1941:156].

The new metaphor of "pacting voluntarily with the devil" indeed shifted the focus from blaming external elements that had invaded the victim to blaming the victim himself, who was now depicted as a carrier of the seeds of evil will. "Pacting with the devil," which can be viewed as the derogatory counterpart of positive freedom of choice, should in theory have opened up new avenues of hope for deviants, who could be punished and repent, since they possessed free will. Evidently, however, "pacting with the devil" rarely implied freedom to reform. Rather, congruent with the new self-contradictory individualistic spirit disseminated by Calvinism, it assumed man's *responsibility* for his *failure* and the

---

[5] The behavioristic approach to victimology has actually established a tradition of studying victims in stimulus-response terms, which assumes that the victim serves as a triggering stimulus for the reacting attacker.

consequent blame associated with it but simultaneously condemned him as a damned-hopeless person.

The theme of damnation permeated most of the sixteenth-century Elizabethan tragedies (see Gardner, 1948). But I believe it was Marlowe (1564–1593) who best expressed Western man's plight and tragic fate in being caught in this Protestant "determinist–free will" trap. On the one hand, his Dr. Faustus is blamed for pacting with the devil and for having the power and "ill will" to sell his soul to Satan; on the other he is described as a hopeless, damned person. Hence he goes down into Hell. The devil's agent announces that Faustus's pact with the devil was his own free choice (" 'Twas thine own seeking, Faustus; thank theyself"). Indeed, Faustus declares, "This word damnation terrifies not me." But later he says, "My heart is harden'd; I cannot repent." And Mephistopheles tells Faustus: "Thou art damned. Think thou of Hell!" Again Faustus insists that his act was not one of free will: " 'Tis thou has damn'd distressed Faustus's soul" (quotations from Farnham, 1969:79–84).

Conclusion

While some historians of deviance and psychopathology have highlighted the general continuity between medieval demonology and contemporary derogatory attitudes toward deviants, they have largely ignored the impact of the Calvinist predestinal paradigm of man on attitudes toward deviance and failure. Moreover, because of their ahistorical perspective, labeling analysts have failed to explain the simultaneous application of the individualistic approach to deviants (blaming and punishing them for voluntarily pacting with the devil) and the deterministic model of deviance (perceiving deviance as an innate, irreversible state). This chapter has attempted to trace this paradoxical approach to Calvinistic predestinal individualism.

The contemporary Western model of psychotherapy which rests primarily on the assertion that the client's salvation depends on his own *motivation* and free will to change, appears suitable only for the neurotic (elect), who is usually successful in Weberian materialistic terms and who displays a never ceasing, compulsive need to "succeed" in worldly activities. The criminal psychopath or psychotic, who "lacks motivation" and "volition" (which he never possessed), is blamed for his own failures and at the same time perceived as an incorrigible, a hopeless case. The corrective message of positive criminology seems to encompass this very self-defeating paradox by focusing on the criminal's motivation but discounting his free will (see Vold, 1958). Moreover, the operational definition of the psychoanalytic term "unconscious motivation" seems to stand precisely for the self-contradictory attitude that deterministic individualism entails. Consider a statement made by a contemporary psychoanalytically oriented philosopher:

> Countless criminal acts are thought out in great detail; yet, the participants are acting out fantasies, fear, and defenses from early childhood, over whose coming and going they have no conscious control. Now, I am not saying that none of these persons should be in jails or asylums. . . . Nor am I saying that people should cease the practices of blaming and praising, punishing and rewarding . . . although very often they have practically no effect [Hospers, 1966:27].

Because of the contemporary dichotomy between the "successes," referred to as treatable neurotics, and the "failures," termed untreatable psychopaths or psychotics, it is important to establish that the notion of "damnation" was actually applied, even if only to a small number of people. If Puritanism may indeed be conceived as the cradle of American-Western culture, or as "the origins of the American self" as Bercovitch (1975) recently coined it, then it is in the historically and culturally relativistic sense developed in this chapter that one should examine the claim that the Western "medical model" of deviance casts people in irreversible, degrading, deviant roles. Accordingly, interpretations of human conduct should be based not on the social scientist's hard or soft deterministic conception of man (e.g. Matza, 1964) but rather on the unique ethical-cultural belief systems of real people. Indeed Bercovitch maintained that Puritans, as one example, "diagnosed mankind as . . . 'Execrable beyond the relief of all created help whatsoever' " (1975:16).

Using Colonial Massachusetts as a case in point, I have attempted to provide some socio-historical illustrations in order to demonstrate that this conception of the *irreversibly* hopeless damned man was indeed active in everyday intra- and interpersonal relations. In the next chapter, I shall try to demonstrate how the Protestant bias has imbued contemporary conceptions of deviance by analyzing selective theories and providing alternative and broader models for assessing deviance. It appears best to begin by examining traditional conceptualizations of "psychopathy," which stand for psychiatric disorders as well as criminality, wickedness, and innate inferiority. Since the subject of psychopathy has been treated mainly by social scientists with a psychological orientation, the analysis in the next chapter will inevitably be grounded in psychological theory and research.

Chapter Three

"Differential Insensitivity" and the Myth of the "Psychopath"

"Go away, my boy, or else my man will eat you up for breakfast . . . " Thump! thump! thump! they heard the giant's footsteps.

(J. Jacobs, Jack and the Beanstalk, 1949)

In the 1960s, the McCords noted: "For 150 years, science has known of the psychopath's existence; for at least 140 years, scientists have quarreled over the definition of this disorder" (McCord and McCord, 1964:2). A survey of the major literature on the subject of psychopathy today reveals a consensus that psychopathy is an undefinable and untreatable general form of antisocial personality disorder.

The thesis developed in this chapter is that (1) behaviors subsumed under the rubric "psychopathy" are basically forms of insensitivity, which may be socially functional or dysfunctional; (2) both functional and dysfunctional insensitivities usually result from specific formal or informal desensitizing socialization experiences; and, accordingly, (3) insensitivities should be studied and treated as specific differential behaviors, not as global personality disorders.

Diagnostic Labeling for Nontreatment

A good example of what can be termed as metaphorical "myth-to-mischief" transformation is the manner in which the labels "psychopath" or "sociopath" are employed by professional mental hygienists. While attacks against the use of stigmatic medical metaphors to describe misconduct are often rebutted by the claim that it is a nosological necessity required to facilitate treatment, the label "psychopath" is actually assigned in order *not* to treat the person so labeled.

It is pertinent to note that the category "sociopathic personality disturbance" of the 1952 *Diagnostic and Statistical Manual of the American Psychiatric Association* was reformulated in the 1968 revision as "antisocial personality," without the direct use of the terms "psychopathy" as "sociopathy." The careful omission of such labels is apparently due both to their embarrassingly elusive and ambiguous connotation and to a lack of agreement about the nature and very existence of such mental disorders as psychopathy and sociopathy, which had never been clearly defined in legal or medical terms (see Rotenberg and Diamond, 1971).

Nevertheless, empirical studies, especially those using psychophysiological correlates of so-called psychopathy, have proliferated recently; and in standard textbooks of psychopathology published since 1968, loose definitions of psychopathy, as well as illustrative case material, still abound. Moreover, diagnostic transactions between clinicians, through which clinical reports containing the labels psychopath and sociopath are passed under the counter, continue to flourish.

By diagnostic labeling "under the counter," I mean the cautious use of such evasive diagnostic descriptions as "indications of sociopathic disorders," "behavior patterns of psychopathic nature," and so forth, which usually convey the message, "You know what I mean" or "He seems to be 'it.'" And, whether intentionally or not, such descriptions appear to be functional for therapists in rationalizing stalemate, failure, or refusal to treat uncooperative or unpleasant patients [1]—i.e., in using "psychopathy" as a "wastebasket category" (Buss, 1966:430)—or in disguising the Western therapist's basic doubt of man's ability to change. When such clinical dialogues take place, most clinicians "get the picture," as Millon (1969:427) indicates; and except for rare altruistic or "messianic" therapists (e.g. Karpman, as mentioned by Zax and Cowen, 1972), most clinicians comply with the informal code of *not* treating such "incurable" cases. [2]

How are we to understand the recent accumulation of "rigorous psychopathy studies" in the face of the tendency of the clinical authorities to abandon the concept entirely, at least as an official psychiatric category? Are the "official" clinicians evading new "scientific evidence" that attempts to revalidate the diagnostic category "psychopathy" because it is more functional to preserve it as an "unofficial" "wastebasket category"? Or are the researchers to be blamed for reviving a myth through their careless operationalization of this ambiguous clinical category? A brief review of recent empirical literature reveals that, in their zealous search for identifiable correlates of psychopathy, the researchers have lost sight of what they are after; that is, they have evaded

---

[1] The McCords quote the psychiatrist Dr. Leo Kanner's statement, "A psychopath is somebody you don't like" (quoted in McCord and McCord, 1964:2).

[2] In this context, it is of interest to cite Zax and Cowen's comment on Karpman's straightforward distinction between incurable anethopaths and treatable pseudo-psychopaths: "Karpman's designation aroused considerable uneasiness in many students of psychopathy. In essence, his argument was that there existed a group of psychopaths that he had been able to understand and work with psychotherapeutically" (1972:312).

the problems involved in operationalizing the independent variable, psychopathy, which they treat as an established empirical entity.

We ought, then, to examine first how the independent and dependent variables are defined in psychopathy studies. I shall limit myself mainly to psychophysiological investigations, which constitute the most influential and conspicuous trends in recent research.

Who Is the "Empirical Psychopath"?

Let us begin with the independent variable, the selection of psychopathic and nonpsychopathic subjects. There are two major obstacles to operationalization of the independent variable: (1) the nature and quality of the variables under consideration, and (2) the number of subvariables involved.

First, unlike the relatively more "abnormal" symptoms universally associated with schizophrenic behavior, such as specific identifiable patterns of irrational thinking (Schmidt and Fonda, 1963), psychopathy refers, by definition, to many *normal* human traits, such as callousness, guiltlessness, impulsiveness, egocentrism, and immaturity, all of which are presumed to be exaggerated in the so-called psychopath. It is therefore difficult to determine when, where, and why such behavior is desirable and normal and when it is psychopathic.

The irony in circumstantially (but arbitrarily) interpreting behavior either as normal and desirable or as sociopathic is epitomized in attitudes toward behavior featuring "self-control." This term can imply internalization of social norms under certain conditions and apathy and coolness under other conditions. I think this dichotomy is what Albert Camus had in mind in describing how his "outsider" was condemned and executed, not for murder but for behaving in a self-controlled, apathetic—i.e., "sociopathic"—manner at his mother's funeral. " 'In short,' he concluded ... 'I accuse the prisoner of behaving at his mother's funeral in a way that showed he was already a criminal at heart.' " (1968:97).

Moreover, if "psychopathy" indeed refers to a number of exaggerated normal yet innate and "incurable" (Jung, 1954; McCord and McCord, 1964) or "irreversible" (Frankenstein, 1959) behaviors, this leads us, on the one hand, to the paradoxical conclusion that "normal" behavior is unchangeable and, on the other hand, raises the question as to why psychopathy, which is presumed innate and irreversible, is the only clinical category for which no exemptions from criminal responsibility are made by modern law.

Secondly, students of psychopathy have enumerated up to seventy-five (Albert *et al.*, 1959) and more behavior patterns characteristic of this disorder. However, they usually falter when it comes to discussing the status of diagnostic reliability regarding psychopathy (Buss, 1966; Zubin, 1967; Hare, 1970).

Cleckley (1964), the most frequently cited authority on this disorder, lists the main features of psychopathy as including: (1) superficial charm and good intelligence; (2) absence of delusions and other signs of irrational thinking; (3) absence of nervousness or other neurotic manifestations; (4) unreliability; (5) untruthfulness and insincerity; (6) lack of remorse or shame; (7) antisocial behavior without apparent compunction; (8) poor judgment and failure to learn from experience; (9) pathologic egocentricity and incapacity for love; (10) general poverty in major affective reactions; (11) specific loss of insight; (12) unresponsiveness in general interpersonal relations; (13) fantastic and uninviting behavior under the influence of alcohol; (14) impersonal, trivial, and poorly integrated sex life; (15) failure to follow any conscious life plan.

We thus deal with a broad spectrum of behaviors that are almost impossible to pinpoint, given the formidable difficulty of establishing how much impulsiveness, plus how much guiltlessness, plus how much callousness, egocentrism, immaturity, etc., add up to full-fledged psychopathy. Consequently, it is generally accepted that ideal-type "psychopaths as such do not exist" because of difficulty in identifying "individuals who warrant the label psychopathic" (Hare, 1970).

Nonetheless, these normal but exaggerated, multiple but not necessarily related characteristics (impulsiveness and lack of anxiety may actually be contradictory traits attributed to psychopaths) have been taken by researchers to stand for the psychopathic type, and there is high agreement in studies as to which characteristics mark a "true psychopath" (*ibid.*).

Accordingly, in operationalizing the independent variable "psychopathy"—i.e., in subject selection—"rigorous" psychophysiological studies of psychopathy (e.g., Hare, 1973; Schalling and Rosen, 1968) have usually employed such clinical conceptualizations as Cleckley's behavior list (where each of the behaviors can be further subdivided) in a completely undifferentiated manner. Thus, selection is usually accomplished by asking professionals acquainted with potential subjects to rate them on a scale derived from Cleckley's "definition." On the basis of these ratings, subjects are then divided into psychopathic and nonpsychopathic groups.

While Cleckley's conceptualization has enjoyed popularity among researchers, other investigators have used other or additional—but unfortunately no less differentiated—measures for subject selection, such as the Minnesota Multiple Personality Inventory (MMPI) (Dahlstrom and Welch, 1960), Quay's factorial scale (Quay, 1964), and procedures used by Dinitz *et al.* (1973) advocating a multiple-criteria measure, including demographic and sociological variables, which results in a broader and even less differentiated definition of the independent variable, psychopathy.

Unlike the undifferentiated clinical definitions of the independent variable, dependent variables are defined in very specific operational terms, especially in the physiological studies. Thus, since psychopathic characteristics are taken to include (among many other attributes) a relative lack of emotional tension, anxiety, or arousal, or autonomic correlates such as low electrodermal or cardiovascular activity, or cortical correlates such as slow brain-wave activity, if these attributes are found among subjects deemed psychopathic they are presumed to corroborate the low-arousal or low-anxiety hypothesis concerning psychopaths. This, of course, does not imply that low reactivity, low arousal, or even low anxiety in themselves, whether found among students or among offenders, are a pathological indication, even if low reactivity is recorded when the subject anticipates some stressful situation. Below I shall attempt to differentiate between *excitability* and *sensitivity* and shall suggest that, if a subject does not become easily excited under stressful conditions, this does not necessarily presuppose general insensitivity. We now must carefully assess, however, the relationship between low physiological responses and the "vices" attributed to psychopaths, even before we determine whether these various physiological measures intercorrelate (which they do not; see Hare, 1975), and must understand the meaning of reactivity differences obtained under restful and/or boring, stressful and/or exciting, or during recovery conditions.

To put it more bluntly, according to all the physiological measures used in studies hitherto, "psychopaths" have been found to differ consistently from "nonpsychopaths" only in exhibiting less spontaneous fluctuations in skin conductance under restful conditions and in anticipation of receiving shocks (see *ibid.*). Thus it is the presumed basic relationship between specific physiological dependent variables and the undifferentiated clinical independent variable, psychopathy, that comes into question here. Most investigators are (justifiably) very cautious—or, rather, evasive—about explaining the meaning of low autonomic reactivity in anticipation of or during recovery from stress. Even if we accept for the moment the "scientifically reserved" but rather wishful suggestion that low electrodermal reactivity to anticipated stress implies lack of anxiety, this finding is still in no way related to the pathological parameters comprising the independent variables as defined by these investigators. In other words, lack of anxiety in the face of stress, whether among students or among criminals, may, at best, indicate a *low* disposition to avoidance learning or, rather, a high degree of adjustability to uncertainty, danger, or arousing stimuli. However, it certainly does not bear any necessary relation to the unsocialized behavior—the selfishness, callousness, irresponsibility, impulsiveness, and, especially, lack of guilt and conscience—attributed to psychopaths by Cleckley and others. Besides, if low reactivity is related (spuriously?) to one of Cleckley's variables, we certainly cannot gather from these studies to which specific behavior it is related.

Moreover, if one of the traits attributed to the psychopath is egocentrism, wouldn't it be somewhat self-contradictory to suggest that the "egocentric-narcissistic" psychopath does not love his skin enough to show high reactivity in anticipated stress but rather seems willing, almost "altruistically" and calmly, to receive a shock for the "benefit of science" (Milgram, 1963)—unless we interpret his low reactivity in other terms?

It seems, then, that the replicable relationship between low reactivity and psychopathy, which is so often concluded in recent studies, is actually between specific but unidentified insensitivity zones (e.g. lack of anxiety or neurotic manifestations on Cleckley's list) and their physiological correlates. If this is indeed true, then why not design studies accordingly? The insistence upon clinging to an undifferentiated and unverifiable definition of psychopathy seems to do little more than breed a myth about a "wicked-born," unchangeable, generalized type of psychopath who exists somewhere out in the cold. In other words, I would argue now that in Western culture the presumed innate-irreversible deviant label "psychopath" [3] may actually be traced to Calvin's paradigm of the predestinal "damned" man, as I have generally suggested in Chapter 1.

A good example of how wickedness is psychiatrically interpretated as "innate psychopathy" is the famous case of eleven-year-old Mary Bell:

> . . . [T]he evidence of the two psychiatrists called by the defence for Mary, Dr. Orton and shortly afterwards Dr. Westbury, was heard.
>
> "The abnormality of mind to which you have referred," said Mr. Robson to Dr. Orton, "did it arise from a condition of arrested or retarded development of mind, or any inherent cause, or [was it] induced by disease or injury?"
>
> "Well, psychopathic personality," said Dr. Orton, "is thought to arise from a combination probably of genetic factors, which are inherent, and there are also environmental influences" [Sereny, 1972:152].

The danger of perpetuating the myth concerning the existence of a "Big Bad Psychopath" is not only that some people might be so labeled unjustly and not treated but also that it obscures the clinical, theoretical-functional, and empirical implications inherent in differential manifestations associated with such phenomena. The dualistic myth-making about how untreatable "damned/bad seed" psychopaths differ from the treatable, successful "elect" [4] (see Chapter 1)

---

[3] Rotenberg and Diamond (1971) argued that the biblical "stubborn and rebellious son" seemed basically to resemble the contemporary category of psychopathy. Interestingly enough, the Talmud apparently took cognizance of the myth of an ideal type "stubborn-rebellious son." Because of the impossible combination of such multiple behavioral and social variables, the Talmud states that such a case "never happened and never will happen" (*The Babylonian Talmud*, Sanhedrin, Vol. II, 1959, p. 483).

[4] Investigators of psychopathy have often agreed that some men of genius display immature, emotionless behavior similar to that of "psychopaths" (Cleckley, 1964; Frankenstein, 1959). Strangely

is illuminated by Harrington in his book on psychopaths, which begins with Linder's old statement: "There walk among us men and women who are in but not of our world" (1972:11).

If, however, the characteristics constituting "psychopathy" were to be conceived not as generalized personality traits but rather in terms of differential insensitivities, then (1) functional insensitivity would in fact appear to be socially desirable and hence would be fostered through social and psychological systems of desensitization and (2) dysfunctional insensitivities could be studied and treated as specific differential behaviors resulting from specific desensitizing experiences.

So far, I have attempted to show why the concept "psychopathy" is obsolete. Before the functional perspective of desensitization is developed, however, we must determine *conceptually* whether the global label "psychopathy" does indeed stand for what can be termed "differential insensitivity."

Psychopathy, Neurosis, and "Differential Insensitivity"

Let us begin with the assumption that, in spite of the countless behavioral features presumed to represent psychopathy, we are basically dealing with one human quality, namely, the quality of *insensitivity* (chiefly social insensitivity). As indicated above, Cleckley (1964) enumerates fifteen broad characteristics of psychopathy; McCord and McCord (1964) have suggested that the two essential fea-

---

enough, however, although they admit that the "psychopath" and the genius may be comparable in overt behavior and intelligence and that in the final analysis only the eventually recognized success differentiates empirically between them, they take pains to point out the basic difference between the two.

tures of psychopathy are *lovelessness* and *guiltlessness*; and both Foulds and Buss consider *egocentricity* and lack of *empathy*, i.e., social insensitivity (Gough, 1948), to be largely responsible for psychopathic disturbances (see Hare, 1970). One need not be a supersensitive psychopathologist to conclude that these features may be subsumed under the rubric "insensitivity" as implied in Aronfreed's behaviorist definition: "The designation of primary psychopath sometimes has been applied to a person whose behavior seems to be characterized by an absence of the usual sensitivities to the affective values of a social environment" (1968:207).

If this proposition has merit, the next step would be to argue that psychopathy (insensitivity) and neurosis (oversensitivity) may be conceived, in fact, as representing two extremes along a single continuum and hence "psychopathy," like neurosis, could be conceptualized in differential terms, i.e., as differential insensitivities related to specific behavioral areas. To explain the functional-differential perspective of psychopathic insensitivity, let us look at the neurosis-psychopathy continuum.

In one of his attacks on Freud's conceptions of therapy, Mowrer submits that Freudian

. . . psychoanalysis has one of two outcomes: either the analysis is technically unsuccessful, which means that it fails to lessen the presumed over-severity of the superego, with the result that the patient continues to be neurotic; or the analysis is technically successful, i.e., the superego is softened up and inner conflicts are resolved, but the patient then develops a "character disorder" [1961:235].

Mowrer concludes:

If, as Freud insisted, the neurotic is a person with an excessively severe over-developed superego or conscience, the three major character types—criminal psychopaths, normal, and psychoneurotic—could be aligned as . . . a standard bell-shaped distribution curve . . . with the normal

type . . . being average model, and therefore most fre-
quent, and with the two deviant forms of personality—
psychopaths and psychoneurotics—trailing off in opposite
directions [*ibid.*, p. 236].

Apart from the humor one might find in a therapeutic
paradigm that depicts both the neurotic and the psychopath
as having, in the final analysis, a "clean" conscience—the
former due to his compulsive need constantly to "wash" his
conscience and the latter because "he never uses it"—there
are important implications in Mowrer's analysis. For if
Mowrer's contention that, according to Freud, "The therapeutic objective is . . . to help the patient move from his
position of excessive-superego severity, in the direction of
psychopathy" (*ibid.*, p 236) *is* valid, then we have an overt
admission of the generally covert assumption that "part-
time" psychopathy and "psychopathy training" (psychotherapy for neurosis) is indeed functional under various circumstances and in certain areas. The aim of treatment is
naturally to stop somewhere in the middle of the continuum,
but the functionality of "psychopathy training" cannot be
discounted if one recognizes the significance of conscience-
softening or guilt-lessening in Freudian therapy.

This may be the reason that, on a theoretical level, orthodox psychoanalysts have usually referred to so-called psychopathy as a subtype of neurosis and hence have encompassed
the "neurotic character" (Alexander, 1930) or character-
neurosis under one general theory of neurosis (Fenichel,
1963). It is important to note here that Freud's own preoccupation with conscience-ridden neurosis resulting from
overcontrolling, moralizing, and restricting education probably fitted the Victorian era during which he wrote. At that
time, as Price has indicated, "society's attitudes toward im-
moral behavior were considerably more strict than they are
today" (1972:122). In our era of moral permissiveness, however, an interpretation of neurosis in terms of an overwhelm-
ing superego would be misleading and unproductive. If one

interprets neurosis as "excessive emotionality," in Eysenck's (1957) terms, or as "differential oversensitivity," then a less morality-laden and more fruitful model of "differential insensitivity" could likewise substitute for the older model of the superegoless "psychopath."

With such a frame of reference, one could conceive of a person being oversensitive in some areas and insensitive in others. Empirical evidence to support this proposition would naturally be difficult to obtain at this stage, since studies on "psychopathy" are usually carefully designed to detect only selective insensitivities as dependent variables. In behavioristic terms, however, it is possible to demonstrate that one will show less anxiety or sensitivity in areas to which one has previously been desensitized—or in areas to which one was never sensitized in the first place—while being highly sensitive in other areas.

According to Ullman and Krasner (1969), the so-called psychopath is one in whom wrong acts have been reinforced at the wrong time and who, for that reason, has developed a kind of selective inattention to various social stimuli. In this sense, then, "lack of emotion" in McCord and McCord's (1964) archetypal psychopath, Billy the Kid, is not innate but can be traced to an early history of desensitization to anything emotional—in much the same sense as the experienced parachutist's low anxiety level (insensitivity) upon jumping (Epstein, 1967) is also a result of desensitization or fear-reducing habituation (Rachman, 1974).

Desensitization Systems for Functional Insensitivity

A careful examination of insensitivity in a differential framework will reveal that not only is insensitivity found to various extents in the general population but it is functionally necessary for the individual's and the society's existence. Consequently, desensitization is differentially fostered via various formal and informal socializing systems. Consider, for instance, how the quality of being "cool" or "detached" is inculcated in the West, via the mass media, as an ascriptive symbolic feature of masculinity: The modern fictional hero; the cool, clean-cut businessman; and the cool, detached scientist or politician (Lyman and Scott, 1970) are but a few examples of this generalized socially desirable trait.

Moreover, it is generally agreed that psychosomatic disorders refer to severe tissue damage or organic malfunctioning resulting from such oversensitivities as prolonged emotional stress, anger, fear, and disappointment. Thus, studies have shown that socially sensitive people are more prone to develop such psychosomatic ailments as peptic ulcers, heart diseases, asthma, and the like than are less sensitive people. Robbins, Tanck, and Meyersbury (1972) found, for example, that among undergraduate students tension and frustration were significantly related to somatic complaints. Similarly, Eastwood and Trevelyan (1972) found that people with psychiatric disorders such as chronic mild neurosis, anxiety, and depression (i.e., oversensitivities) had a significant excess of major psychosomatic disorders (mainly coronary diseases) over subjects without psychiatric disorders. Subjects in this study were drawn at random from the community, and over 90 percent of the subjects with detected cardiovascular pathology did not know about their condition, which controls for the possibility of psychiatric disorders resulting from knowledge of heart problems. It follows, then, that genuine coolness or insensitivity should by implication be inversely related to psychosomatic disorders.

While research to establish the association between psychosomatic disorders and oversensitivity is at present scant, studies exploring the *inverse* relationship between insensitivity or psychopathy and psychosomatic tendencies are not available. It is worthwhile, therefore, to report the results of a preliminary empirical observation concerning the relationship between psychopathy and psychosomatic tendencies among prisoners.

Eighty-five prisoners were randomly selected from a maximus security prison in Israel. The total sample was subdivided into psychopathic subjects and nonpsychopathic subjects in the following manner: Files of all subjects were carefully studied, and only those who were unequivocally diagnosed by a clinical psychologist or a psychiatrist as psychopathic—i.e., those who were never diagnosed differently (e.g. as neurotic)—were selected as tentative psychopathic subjects. Then Cleckley's criteria of psychopathy (Hare, 1975) were discussed with three staff members in the prison who were presented with names of all eighty-five subjects and asked to divide the total sample into those who they thought fitted Cleckley's descriptions and those who they thought did not. The final subsamples consisted of thirty-one psychopaths and fifty-four nonpsychopaths. Next, the medical files were studied, and again the total sample was subdivided, this time into psychosomatic and nonpsychosomatic subjects. A subject was included in the psychosomatic sample only if a psychosomatic disorder such as peptic ulcers, asthma, or heart disease was established medically, not if the subject had merely complained about it.

The resulting distribution of psychopathic and nonpsychopathic subjects with and without psychosomatic disorders is shown in Table 3–1.

TABLE 3.1. **Psychosomatic Disorders among Psychopathic and Nonpsychopathic Inmates**

Disorder	Psychopaths	Non-psychopaths	Total
Psychosomatic	6	24	30
Nonpsychosomatic	25	30	55
Total	31	54	85

Note: $X^2 = 6.58$, df = 1, p < .02

Of the fifty-four nonpsychopathic inmates, nearly half had diagnosed psychosomatic disorders, while only about 20 percent of the thirty-one psychopathic inmates suffered from psychosomatic diseases. Thus, certain forms of social insensitivities usually associated with so-called psychopathy appear to be situationally functional for individual and social existence. The question is only how "cool" our socializing thermostat should be set. If Camus's (1968) "outsider" had fallen gravely ill or attempted suicide at the sight of his mother's death, society would have considered him a warm (albeit weak) human being. But the display of extreme "self-control" condemns him as a criminal psychopath. This fictional case illustrates the very paradox with which we are dealing, since the kind of "insensitivity" described by Camus may result from that same very ambigious "self-control" so subtly fostered by society.

Returning to our major point, what precisely is meant by "functional insensitivity," and how is desensitization for selective coolness or detachment inculcated through the various channels of socializing systems? It is well known that even the most unusual experiences can eventually become familiar to the human animal, a creature of habit, through desensitization. Funeral directors and medical interns may enjoy their lunch in the presence of corpses. Pilots and sailors may learn to feel less safe on the ground (often for sound reasons) than up in the air or on a stormy ocean. The politician may become insensitive to personal attacks, the hard-nosed scientist may be conditioned to view plagues as interesting structural phenomena and, similarly, a middle-class bourgeois may learn to participate in group orgies as part of a routinized custom. More specifically, follow, for example, a delicate middle-class woman through the training phases in nursing school (see Williams and Williams, 1959). After repeated contact with defecation, urination, sexual organs, death, disfigurement, and pain, she usually becomes insensitive to situations and scenes to which many ordinary people would react by fainting, vomiting, or feelings of revulsion.

Desensitization is not just an incidental by-product of becoming a nurse but a planned process. Olesen and Whittaker (1968) describe how, through institutionalized processes of "testing," the student nurse is thrust into new and gradually more shocking predicaments. Similarly, in their study of student culture in medical schools, Becker *et al.* report that students' traumas, so often described in novels, "were so startlingly rare" that "none mention the cadaver as traumatic" (1961:103, 106). As one student explained: "I went to a post-mortem this morning. It doesn't really bother you too much. I guess you get kind of calloused about it. Especially little infants. When they die there's just no feeling about death anymore." (*ibid.*, p. 326). In fact, Becker *et al.* observed that "in anatomy . . . medical students harass the girls in the class by gags with sex organs of cadavers or profane the lab by throwing around the detritus of dissection" (*ibid.*, p. 103). In 1974, the Israeli community was appalled by the sensational trial of some medical students who were accused of eating human brains during a dissection class (*Jerusalem Post*, Aug. 8, 1974).

Dramatic descriptions of desensitization processes in socializing novice morgue attendants are provided by Sudnow. Learning how to wrap a corpse is one example:

> As the novice fumbled in trying to put the tag on gently without having its wire touch the body itself, the old timer . . . interrupted . . . and quite forcefully, with exaggerated nonchalance, jabbled the wire through the feet section, seemingly trying, on purpose, to catch some flesh on the way (1967:80).

Extremely insensitive behavior is consequently displayed by experienced attendants, as noted by Sudnow, who observed that occasionally portions of the wrapping are done before death, leaving only a few moments of final touch-up work with the dead body (*ibid.*, p. 82).

Another case of social desensitization is police training. In analyzing the psychological consequences of the policeman's role, Toch (1970) describes how (continuous) contacts with antisocial people are likely to give policemen a "veneer of hardness"; thus the police officer gradually "loses his feeling of communality with the public" and "exaggerates the prevalence of apathy." Similarly, Toch found that, as a result of training, advanced police officers perceived more violence in an experiment than did officers in their first year of training, and McNamara was able to show that police officers' legitimization of force "increased during the training and then increased more during the first year of field experiment" (1967:214).

The examples cited above are extreme cases of social desensitization systems, but in essence formal and informal socialization processes for functional insensitivity are present in almost every profession and are usually geared to desensitizing different affective components in prople's behavior. The point to be stressed here is that such desensitization systems are intended to be functionally linked to specific social contexts. It is socially functional that nurses and physicians maintain stable blood pressure and stay generally calm while performing surgery, even in the face of unexpected stress situations. Likewise, it is functional that pilots maintain relatively low and stable heart and respiration rates while flying planes. There is no evidence, however, to indicate to what extent desensitization is generalized or remains linked to specific behavioral constellations or social contexts.

There is also no evidence to suggest how, and to what extent, specific desensitized dispositions can be resensitized, since society does not normally provide institutionalized resensitization systems. Insensitive dispositions of an ex-army major might be quite dysfunctional in civilian life.

In conclusion, the perspective presented above attempts to emphasize that insensitivities viewed in differential terms result from socially planned or unplanned desensitization experiences that may sometimes be functional and at other times dysfunctional. Society's ambivalence about dysfunctional consequences resulting from planned desensitizing socialization were most dramatically demonstrated in the trial of Lieutenant William Calley for the atrocities and cruelties committed by American soldiers at My Lai (see Goldstein, 1975).

Thus far I have elaborated upon the functional aspect of insensitivity in order to rationalize the differential nature of the insensitivity usually associated with psychopathy. However, empirical as well as clinical implications pertaining to dysfunctional insensitivities are, from our perspective, obviously of major concern. I therefore turn now to a discussion of implications for research and then shall present a new clinical treatment approach for differential sensitization.

Research Implications of Dysfunctional Insensitivities

If specific physiological measures can be found to be stable and replicable predictors of specific dysfunctional insensitivities, then assessment of the relationship between specific social and physiological insensitivities could be developed in two directions:

1. *Comparisons between groups of subjects presumed to have had similar desensitizing experiences.* In such a design, athletes or parachutists could be compared with burglars (assuming that these subjects were desenitized to frightening experiences or to personal injury). Accordingly, empathy and sympathy tests (Rotenberg, 1974) could be administered and skin-conductance and/or heart-rate measures recorded in anticipation of noxious simuli to be inflicted on the sub-

ject himself or on another. The following results might then be expected: While no differences might be found between burglars and athletes in their physiological reactivity to receiving shocks, differences might be observed in the empathy or sympathy tests, which assess the subject's understanding of, or emotional involvement in, another's suffering or mental state. (I shall later describe such a pilot study, which attempts to challenge traditional interpretations concerning psychopaths' low electrodermal reactivities to anticipated stress.)

Similar studies could also be constructed to compare various groups of subjects who presumably have had various desensitizing experiences in relation to specific aversive stimuli inflicted upon the self and/or others. It can thus be expected that social and physiological responses to future specific noxious stimuli (to be inflicted on the self or others) by physicians, nurses, policemen, or various criminals might vary according to their specific desensitizing histories. A physician's or a nurse's autonomic response might be quite low while observing a subject receiving a shock (assuming that physicians and nurses are more accustomed than others to witnessing physical injuries), while their reactivity might be quite high upon observing someone suffering from mental cruelty. Conversely, a white-collar criminal might not react significantly to observing mental cruelty, while his autonomic reactivity might be higher upon observing someone receiving an electric shock.

2. *Comparison of specific dysfunctional social insensitivities with specific physiological correlates on the same subjects.* To verify empirically differential parameters of a social insensitivity such as outward toughness, coolness, or apathy, which might often be the referents of clinically operationalized psychopathy, it would be of utmost importance to correlate specific social and physiological insensitivities on the same subjects. Rotenberg (1974) has found, for example, that, while American institutionalized delinquents scored

lower than nondelinquents in affective role-taking (i.e., their disposition to reduce or increase another's suffering), they were in no way deficient in their cognitive role-taking ability or in their intuitive social sensitivity (i.e., their prediction accuracy of another's mental state).

In two other studies (Rotenberg and Nachshon, in press; and Nachshon and Rotenberg, 1977) it was found that, while Israeli institutionalized delinquents were more impulsive than nondelinquents, and while delinquents perceived more violence than nondelinquents, in an ambigous-person perception test they did not inflict more suffering on another person (using a design similar to Milgram's, 1963) than nondelinquents did. In the studies cited above, cognitive and affective sensitivities to others were assessed differentially on the same subjects. Thus, measures were taken to compare delinquents and nondelinquents in their reactions to the suffering and well-being of others, and not in anticipation of an aversive stimulus to be inflicted on the subject himself. Further, in those studies, no physiological correlates of social insensitivities were used.

A good beginning in comparing specific social and physiological correlates is the work done by Schalling *et al.* (1973), who found that criminals who were high on Gough's delinquency (*De*) scale (Gough and Peterson, 1952) also had lower spontaneous skin-conductance reactivity than those who scored lower on Gough's *De* scale. As in many previous studies (see Hare, 1970), galvanic skin response (GSR) was, however, the only differentiating measure; no differences were obtained, for example, in finger-pulse volume.

Although Schalling *et al.* used the *De* scale as a measure of psychopathy, Gough's scale may in fact be one of the best standardized nonbehavioristic measures of social sensitivity, since it actually detects the subject's empathic or role-taking ability. Behavioristic measures of social sensitivity that differentiate between affective and cognitive role-taking are obviously preferable (Rotenberg, 1974). But, more important, in Schalling's study measures of skin conductance were not taken when the subject anticipated a noxious stimulus that was to be inflicted on himself or on others in an interpersonal situation. As pointed out earlier, low physiological reactivity, even with anticipation by the subject of receiving a shock, is probably related only to the low-arousal hypothesis (the shock could possibly come as a welcome exciting stimulus in a boring test) but not to social insensitivity (i.e., concern for others). It should therefore be the task of future research to concentrate first on assessing differentially the relationship between various parameters of social and physiological insensitivities.

Assessing Sociophysiological Insensitivities

I shall mention briefly two possible designs of such studies, the one to assess subjects' responses to the *suffering of others*, and the second to assess subjects' responses to *suffering from others*. But first we should determine how and why specific social and physiological insensitivies can be logically interrelated so that future "replicable findings" (Hare, 1973) will somewhat comply with the criterion of face validity.

Although dysfunctional insensitivities might include audiovisual and other sensory spheres, what should concern us most here are certain socially dysfunctional insensitivities. More specifically, we would like to identify more accurately, for example, the variables associated with the social insensitivities of people who tend to get into trouble with others or who trouble others because their ability to "give a damn" or to care is somewhat impaired, or because they are detached, aloof, or affectively unable to be involved with others to a degree that makes this trait dysfunctional, at least from society's perspective. Our search for physiological correlates of such social insensitivities would thus be productive to the extent that specific physiological variables could be found to be stable and measurable predictors of specific socially dysfunctional insensitivities, and not in their general verification of a global personality category such as "psychopathy." It would seem useful, therefore, to spell out the presumed relationship between certain physiological and social insensitivities in very specific and logical terms.

I have stressed earlier that if our main concern is with social insensitivities, which involve the inability to feel the sufferings of others or the self in an *interactive* situation, then measurements of autonomic responses to future stress not related to social involvements are ambiguous and even paradoxical. The ability to receive electric shocks, for example, might often be socially prestigious. Accordingly, it would be sensible to compare, for example, various paper-and-pencil and behavioristic measures of role-taking ability or concern for others with the subject's physiological reactivity to the suffering of others. Such comparisons are important not only in order to facilitate cross-validation of certain research instruments but mostly in that they may produce reliable indices for determining whether or not outward verbal or behavioristic toughness or apathy to the suffering of others or social indifference to suffering from others (which so often impresses, and possibly misguides, diagnosis of typical delinquents) is actually accompanied by a parallel inner physiological process. In other words, it would be important to know whether the paraded coolness or indifference of certain delinquents is genuine or, conversely, is a possible indication of defensiveness negated by inner sensitivity.

This point, alluded to by Hare (1970), is clearly illuminated in Milgram's (1963) studies, which report that his subjects continued to administer increasingly severe shocks to a victim supposedly involved in a learning experiment, although they expressed stress orally. Milgram did not record physiological processes during his experiments, but it would be instructive to know whether and in which subjects the oral expression or, conversely, the nonexpression of stress was accompanied by autonomic activity.

Using traditional procedures for subject selection, Mathis (1970) found, for example, that psychopathic inmates gave lower skin-conductance responses than did noncriminal subjects upon observing slides of severe facial injuries. Similarly, Hare and Craigen (1974) found in a modified prison-dilemma game that, compared to normal subjects, psychopathic subjects gave lower unconditioned skin-conductance responses to shocks received or delivered to others, although the groups did not differ in the intensity of shocks chosen to be administered to the self and others or in heart-rate responses under either condition.

In the above studies, physiological measures were recorded while subjects inflicted suffering upon, or observed the sufferings of, others. No parallel measures were taken, however, in regard to social sensitivity. To identify predictors of a subject's responses to the suffering *of* others, it would seem useful, therefore, to design studies in which a subject's social sensitivity, in terms of empathic and sympathic dispositions (Rotenberg, 1974), would be compared to the subject's autonomic reactivity upon observation or infliction of suffering on others in a variety of interactive situations.

To identify predictors of a subject's responses to suffering *from* others, an example of a study design would be a comparison of the social and physiological variables associated with group dependence vs. social detachment. That is, assuming that genuine detachment or social indifference is a major component of dysfunctional insensitivity, it would be important to investigate what happens to a subject's autonomic system, not only to his outward behavior, upon experiencing suffering from others in a group situation. Accordingly, a subject's need for affiliation, attraction to the group, and feeling of loneliness and isolation should be compared to his physiological responses upon being publicly shamed, blamed, or insulted, for example, in a structured social game situation or in another form of group interaction.

I have briefly discussed psycho-physiological research possibilities pertaining to major dysfunctional insensitivities concerning the interpersonal sphere. To provide an illustrative, empirical test of "differential insensitivity," results of a pilot study will now be described to demonstrate how low skin conductance (the only measure that has heretofore been used with considerable success in differentiating between psychopathic and nonpsychopathic subjects) is related more to previous desensitizing life experiences than to delinquency *per se.*

"Differential Insensitivity" and Desensitization: A Pilot Study

In this exploratory study, my aim was to compare skin conductance in anticipation of receiving electric shock among subjects who may be presumed to have had various desensitizing experiences of physical-body pains similar to electric shocks.

I assumed that Israeli high school students might represent a group of subjects who were generally desensitized to frightening-injuring conditions because their socialization in school and in youth movements includes physical (paramilitary training) and mental (idealization) preparation for future service in selective combat units. I further assumed that in addition to the generalized paramilitary anticipatory socialization experiences, students of a vocational high school who are studying to be electricians might have been specifically desensitized to electric shock during their vocational training. Finally, I assumed that, while socialization of institutionalized delinquents (who probably constitute the typical, though younger, group of psychopathic subjects usually used in studies) might have included general desensitizing experiences to body pains, such as physical punishments, street fights, etc., anticipatory socialization for service in combat units seemed atypical of this group.

Thus, the subjects for the study were twenty inmates selected at random from an institution for hard-core delinquents (Ds); twenty randomly selected subjects from a class of future electricians in a vocational high school (Es); and fourteen control subjects selected at random from an academic high school (Rs). The age range (15–18), the socioeconomic background (mainly working class), and the ethnic origin (mainly Afro-Asian) of all subjects were generally comparable.

It was expected that, because their previous direct desensitizing experiences in relation to electric shocks, Es would show lowest GSR activity in anticipation of electric shocks. Next would be the Rs, who, because of their more generalized desensitizing socialization to personal frightening experiences, would show more skin fluctuations than electricians but less than Ds. Ds were expected to show the highest GSR activity, since their previous socialization was presumed to include stealing "behind the back" and perhaps occasional physical punishments, but not future service in combat units. (Formerly institutionalized delinquents usually do not serve in the army.)

PROCEDURE

To be consistent with procedures used in traditional physiological studies of psychopathy (e.g. Hare and Craigen, 1974), skin resistance was recorded by a Stoelting multifunctional portable-type polygraph. Electrodes were attached to the first and third fingers of the left hand. Electric shock was produced by a constant-current generator and was delivered through concentric electrodes placed on the right wrist.

To use the most popular measure of psychopathy, a counselor or teacher in each institution who presumably knew the subjects better than other staff members rated each subject on Cleckley's (1964) psychopathy scale, so that the subjects could be divided into high and low "psychopaths" on Cleckley's scale. (Unfortunately, we could not find more than one rater in each institution who knew all subjects equally well.)

The experiment was always conducted in a quiet room where only the experimenters and one subject were present. To minimize unnecessary suspicion and to maximize a relaxed atmosphere, each subject was first introduced to the instruments and to the staff and then told that we were interested in measuring his sensitivity to electric shocks. He was then seated with his back to the instruments, attached to the electrodes, and given increasing sample shocks, beginning from zero (feeling no shock) until he said, "I feel the shock." Then a five-minute skin-conductance baseline was taken until a stable GSR pattern was obtained. Next, the subject was told that he would receive three kinds of shocks, the first of low intensity, the second of high intensity, and the third of medium intensity. (In reality, the same mild shock was delivered at all times, without the subject's knowledge.) The experimenter then told the subject that each time, before administering the shock, he would first announce its intensity and would deliver the shock only after asking "Ready?" Between the announcement of intensity and the "Ready?" the experimenter always waited eight seconds, during which the subject's skin fluctuations were recorded. The procedure of three shocks was repeated twice, so that each subject was given a shock six times. Mean skin activity of anticipations to all the six shocks constituted a subject's GSR score.

RESULTS

Although Ds were found to have the highest means among all three groups on Cleckley's psychopathy scale, a one-way analysis of variance showed that the differences among the three groups did not reach significance. Moreover, no correlation was found between skin conductance and psychopathy, either when the total population of all three groups was divided into "psychopaths" and "nonpsychopaths" or when each group was divided separately into subjects scoring high and low on Cleckley's psychopathy scale. This may mean that, because we used one rater, our method of selecting psychopathic subjects was inadequate, or it may mean, as I have suggested earlier, that the operationalization of the independent variable, psychopathy, in terms of global personality traits could not predict the specified physiological dependent variable, skin conductance.

Results were as expected, however, when the independent variable was defined by groups according to their presumed desensitizing background. Thus, Ds showed highest skin activity in anticipation of shocks (mean = 18.05), next were Rs (mean = 13.98), and lowest skin conductance was found among Es (mean = 13.27), as expected. A one-way analysis of variance showed that differences were significant ($F = 9.7309$; $df = 19$; $p < .01$).

It should be further noted that the conspicuous difference in skin conductance, found mainly between Ds and the other groups, not only was expressed in terms of Ds' increased skin activity but also was accompanied by their oral expression of fear of being shocked, whereas the other groups usually remained quiet.

DISCUSSION

Because low GSR was hitherto the only physiological variable that discriminated between so-called psychopaths and nonpsychopaths, the goal of this pilot study was only to determine (for the first time) whether anticipation of receiving electrical shocks is indeed lower among delinquents than among groups presumed to have had various desensitizing experiences to physical pain. The most revealing outcome of this study is that delinquents have not lower but rather higher skin fluctuations in the face of a specific adverse stimulus when desensitization history is used as the independent variable. This raises questions concerning previous findings in physiological studies of psychopathy.

Obviously, further systematic and imaginative research is needed before the relationship between specific desensitizing experiences and skin resistance can be determined. The fact that the subjects in the present study were adolescents, while in most psychopathy studies they are adults, might have a slight confounding effect simply due to differences attributable to the age factor.

It is important to stress, however, that in what can be termed the "physiological school of psychopathy," which so far has been able to show only that "psychopaths" differ from others mainly in their low skin conductance (the low-anxiety index), the possible effect of situational variables or specific desensitizing experiences on skin resistance has been largely overlooked. Thus, although Israeli teenagers might be unique in that they are usually desensitized to frightening conditions in the course of their socialization for future service in combat units while delinquents usually do not serve in the army (which might explain why Ds appeared more apprehensive than others and why Rs and Es did not differ significantly), the contribution of the present study is that it subjects previous "myth-scientific" physiological findings, presumably corroborating the existence of "psychopaths," to empirical testing from a new angle.

Moreover, this study, which found delinquents to be quite "anxious" in anticipation of shocks, may suggest that, while it is possible that many hard-core delinquents are indeed *socially* insensitive, they are also *egocentric* (as psychopaths are presumed to be) and consequently are afraid of shocks because they "love their own skin." Hence, social insensitivity to others and egocentricity may in fact entail two contradictory elements attributed to psychopaths. Considering our findings from a different perspective, this study may have some implications for criminal interrogation. Since GSR is used also as a lie-detecting device, it is actually possible that sophisticated criminal groups may "train" their members, through systematic desensitization practice with private polygraphs during simulated interrogation sessions, to display low skin conductance.

In conclusion, if future research addresses itself to assessing a variety of specific dysfunctional socio-physiological insensitivities, the concept of "differential insensitivity" may help to shatter the myth concerning the existence of the global, innate (born-damned) personality type: "psychopath."

I shall now turn to an examination of the potential clinical implications inherent in a concept of differential sensitization (to be distinguished from undifferentiated sensitivity training practiced in some encounter groups) for specific manifestations of dysfunctional insensitivities.

Sensitization of Dysfunctional Insensitivities

Studies of "psychopathy" have repeatedly pointed out two major findings:

1. Avoidance learning in "psychopaths" is usually low owing to lack of anxiety, as indicated by low physiological and social reactivity to pain and anticipated stress.
2. The "psychopath" lives in constant need of novel excitements because of boredom and a low level of social, cortical, and autonomic arousal.

The low anxiety-sensitivity scores typically found among "psychopaths" are usually taken during periods of rest or stress but not necessarily under *exciting* or novel conditions. Investigators have found, however, that skin conductance of "psychopaths" increased dramatically when GSR was taken under challenging cognitive activity (see Hare, 1973). Schacter and Latane (1964) were surprised to find also that "psychopaths" who did not avoid electric shocks when injected with placebo learned dramatically better by avoiding shocks under the influence of adrenalin. And Schmauk (see Hare, 1970) found that, while "psychopaths" did not avoid shocks or social disapproval, they learned to avoid monetary loss.

These findings suggest, first, that the insensitivity of "psychopathic" subjects is not a generalized or innate phenomenon, but can be affected by exciting stimuli or such excitement substitutes as adrenalin, and, second, that psycho-physiological reactivity and learning ability of "psychopaths" might be in part related to their differential need for stimulation and excitement. Moreover, according to Lykken (1957), "psychopaths" preferred frightening activities over boring experiences; and according to Petrie (1967), for the stimulus-governed psychopathic delinquent, experiencing pain might be one method of overcoming "boredom"—i.e., sensory insufficiency. (It is thus possible that traditional studies using GSR activity as indicators of anxiety in anticipation of electric shocks are partially on the wrong track, since for "psychopaths" the anticipated shock might be a welcome change to overcome the experience of a boring experiment.)

Thus, it would be useful at this point to make a conceptual and operational distinction between *excitability* and *sensitivity*. If a subject does not become easily excited under stressful conditions, this does not necessarily mean that he is generally insensitive and will not become excited under novel challenging situations. Excitability, as used here, refers to one's psycho-physiological spontaneous reactivity to stimuli (see Harter, 1967), and sensitivity refers to one's affective-cognitive differential awareness of various stimuli. These variables are not contingently related; one could get excited without being aware of the specific stimuli that triggered the reaction, and one could be sensitive to specific stimuli without getting excited about them.

Yet sensitivity and excitability can be interrelated sequentially: One can be conditioned to become very excited about something he is sensitive to, if this sensitivity is turned into a drive so that stimulation and deprivation increase excitement. The operational definition of sensitization would then refer to increased differential accuracy in identifying objects (e.g. smells, visual objects, or social situations) plus increased psycho-physiological reactivity (e.g. GSR or heart rate) to various stimuli. This is to be distinguished from covert sensitization, which was used to refer to imaginary aversion therapy (Rachman and Teasdale, 1969). Thus, sensitized behavior refers to increased excitability corresponding to specific increased sensitivities.

If differentially *exciting stimuli* (whether in smell, sound, or touch) can be interpreted as catering to *differential sensitivities,* then basically one should be able to use excitement-arousing stimulations as reinforcers for differential sensitization of so-called psychopaths. This approach would appear essentially to be no different from the traditional operant-conditioning techniques that were reformulated for changing criminal behavior by Burgess and Akers (1969) and were found to be effective in upgrading delinquents' educational level (Cohen, 1968) and in reinforcing certain socially desired behaviors of offenders (Schwitzgebel, 1967). Using exciting-novel activities to reinforce adjustment of psychopathic offenders was also found by Ingram *et al.* (1970) to be a significantly better method than verbal therapy. In these studies, however, reinforcing stimuli were undifferentiated and activated collectively. The present perspective advocates a differential "excitement-boredom" sensitization system by assuming that a distinct positive reinforcer combined with its opponent negative reinforcer is more effective than a distinct positive reinforcer by itself by virtue of the "enslaving process" (Solomon and Corbit, 1973); that is, an attempt will be made to integrate into a differential pleasure-pain sensitization-reinforcement model the premises that "psychopaths" are (1) in constant need of novel, exciting stimuli (sensory input) because (2) they are unable to withstand extended boredom and confinement (sensory deprivation; see Petrie, 1967; Hare, 1970).

The "Excitement-Boredom" (Pleasure-Pain) Principle

Studies have shown that the process of becoming enslaved (addicted) to a rewarding stimulus (A)—i.e., a hedonistic tone—through the process of learning to enjoy it is interconnected to an opponent stress stimulus (B) of craving, withdrawal, etc. Thus the parachutist's stress (stimulus B) before jumping is related to the pleasurable stimulus (A) of descending, and the lovers' stimulus B (withdrawal and separation) is associated with their stimulus A (meeting and enjoying each other). Hence, A (positive reinforcer) increases and conditions B (negative reinforcer), and B amplifies and conditions A (see Solomon and Corbit, 1973).

We know that, in general, boredom and confinement (stimulus B) mean punishment—i.e., negative reinforcement—for "psychopaths," and exciting-novel experiences (stimulus A) mean generally rewarding-positive reinforcement. We need only to identify each subject's unique differential positive-negative reinforcers emanating from his unique history and natural dispositions. Thus music, for example, should be more exciting for a subject with a good and/or trained ear and consequently "musical noise" should be more irritating to him than to others, as would a bad odor (B) for a subject who is differentially sensitive to and used to good smells (A).

Theoretically it should be possible to have institutionalized offenders (the usual subjects in psychopathy studies) go through a routine of multiple (or specific) stressful and enjoyable contrived experiences (perhaps in a special reception center) while they are hooked to GSR electrodes. One could then have a chart for each subject, aligning his physiological reactivities (excitability scores) on a continuum from the lowest reactivity to the highest. In addition, a base rate of accuracy scores in identifying smells, tones, visual objects, and social situations involving enjoyable interactions, suffering, or guilt can be recorded (sensitivity scores). It is to be expected that most subjects will be unaware of many of their sensitivity or excitability responses. Recording multiple reactivities of the same subjects and comparing the scores of so-called psychopaths and nonpsychopaths would in themselves contribute to neutralization of the myth of generalized insensitivity attributed to "psychopaths." But, more important, the identification of a stimulus A—i.e., zones of increased sensitivity and/or increased excitability—can then be amplified by gradually increased training and experiencing (creating dependency), which can then be matched with an opponent negative stimulus B. For example, if subject 1 is found to be sensitive to musical tones (stimulus A) and/or mildly excited while listening to a piece of music (stimulus A'), he can be trained to become increasingly aware of music and learn to enjoy it by listening or learning to play an instrument and so become increasingly "addicted" to it. Stimuli A and A' would then be followed by stimulus B—e.g., frustrating experiences with a "broken" record player or instrument; hearing white noise plus extended periods of boredom and confinement. It is to be expected, then, that after increasing frustration with unpleasant noise, deprivation, and boredom, the yearning for stimulus A and excitation A' will increase just as the heartbeat of lovers increases after extended separation. Skrzynek (1969), for example, found that the need of "psychopaths" for novel-complex stimuli increased after perceptual isolation (forty minutes in the dark). The result is that a sensitivity area A (mere awareness) is complemented by an amplified excitability area A' (e.g. increased GSR). The same procedure can be repeated with regard to other sensitivity-excitability areas, even those that are lower on the subject's baseline and are dysfunctional.

If the major dysfunctional insensitivities of the so-called psychopath are presumed to be in the social realm, this paradigm can now be extended to include social insensitivities as well. The major opponent stimulus to boredom, isolation, and confinement is undoubtedly *sociability*, and the "psychopath's" need to associate and have exciting collective fun can be structured so as to include the experience of guilt, remorse, and suffering of others, first on an awareness level (A), then as a conditioner for the very exciting experience (A') of association and collective fun, involving concern for others. For example, a game could be structured to give points each time a subject expresses remorse or feels guilty, so that the feedback of the other person becomes an exciting reward, A'.

Conclusion

The main endeavor of the model sketched above is to show how the very process of "differential sensitization" is possible. Obviously, the ultimate effectiveness of such a model would depend on careful and repeated experimentation, and even then one could not expect massive success in changing such uncooperative subjects as usually constitute the population labeled "psychopathic." However, as a substitute for the non-treatment tradition emanating from the myth of the generalized hopeless personality type psychopath, as in desensitization systems for functional insensitivity, differential sensitization of dysfunctional insensitivities, even if applied successfully to only a small number of cases, could eventually be linked to realistic social roles and identities (e.g. musicians, comrades, etc.) so that concrete, role-linked pleasure-pain mechanisms will operate as a self-maintaining reinforcement system.

In this chapter I have used Calvin's paradigm of the "damned man" to analyze the broad psychiatric-criminological concept of "psychopathy" in order to show how a myth about the existence of a global, innate, hopeless personality type is perpetuated in the West, although admittedly there is no "true clinical-empirical psychopath." By integrating a sociological functional approach with psychological empirical and clinical perspectives, the chapter went on to develop the empirical and clinical paradigms emanating from the concept "differential insensitivity," which was introduced to substitute for the generalized derogatory label "psychopath."

I shall now examine the more general claim of the recently popular labeling theory, which explains deviance as an irreversible state resulting from a process of derogatory labeling. To broaden the cross-cultural approach to the study of deviance, I shall also offer a new theory of differential "self-labeling" and attempt to show again that the socially deterministic assumption of irreversible derogatory labeling may be valid only in a cultural system where people believe that failure or deviance causes one to be reassigned to a category (e.g., the damned) to which he belonged *a priori*.

Chapter Four

The Antilabeling Crusade
and Self-labeling

I have called thee by thy name, thou art Mine.

(*Isaiah 43:1*)

The theoretical approach to deviance that has come to be known variously as the "labeling theory" (Becker, 1963), the "social-reaction perspective" (Kitsuse, 1962), or simply the "new perspective" (Gibbs, 1972) has in recent years become one of the most popular and influential directions in the study and analysis of deviant conduct. This perspective, which puts great emphasis on processual and phenomenological analysis, shifts our focus from action to reaction.

In spite of critical evaluation of the labeling approach calling for clarification of the kind and degree of reaction required for a type of act and/or actor (Schur, 1971; Gibbs, 1972; Warren and Johnson, 1972), social labeling and/or societal reactions have been taken as the major independent variables explaining how deviance is produced and maintained. However, the differential impact of social labeling on self-labeling has been largely neglected. For example, Schur acknowledges "variations in individuals' susceptibility and resistance to such labeling" while recognizing the difficulty in shaking it off "once it has been successfully imputed"

(1971:15). Similarly, in the introduction to their presentation of the societal reaction-labeling perspective, Cressey and Ward state: "Even a man in prison might admit that he committed the crime for which he was convicted yet feel inside that he is not really a criminal" (1969:581). Two lines later they state: "The adjectives 'hardened,' 'confirmed,' and so on are used as defaming, stigmatizing terms referring to persons who conceive of themselves as criminals."

Schur's evasive treatment of the self-labeling problem and the two previous statements by Cressey and Ward concerning persons who feel and do not feel like criminals clearly reflect the confusion in labeling theory regarding the meaning of labeling from the labelee's perspective.

In this chapter, the generality of the labeling paradigm will be examined by dealing with the question: What makes the label stick from the actor's perspective? It will be maintained that, while the basic tenets of labeling theory seem correct, the theory is still incomplete, since labeling theorists have taken self-labeling largely as a matter of fact and, hence, have not specified the conditions under which social labeling is accompanied by or results in self-labeling. A general scheme for analyzing the sources and properties of self-labeling will be presented and an attempt will be made to identify the specific ideological and theoretical roots of major labeling formulations in the proposed framework.

Labeling Analysis and the Antilabeling Crusade

The most frequently cited labeling theorists with a sociological commitment have generally maintained that "deviance is not a property inherent in certain forms of behavior, it is a property conferred upon these forms by the audiences which directly or indirectly witness them" (Erikson, 1962: 308), or that "it is the responses of the conventional and conforming members of the society who identify and interpret behavior as deviant which sociologically transforms persons into deviants" (Kitsuse, 1962:253). Similarly, it has been suggested that deviance results from society's application of rules and sanctions; hence "the deviant is one to whom that label has successfully been applied" (Becker, 1963:9).

In psychological-psychiatric circles, labeling analysis has taken the form of a crusade against the medical model of mental disorder and its elaborate diagnostic labels. For example, in endorsing the 1963 Action for Mental Health, the Board of Directors of the American Psychological Association strongly criticized blind acceptance of "traditional labels of health and sickness" (Milton and Wahler, 1969); in discussing "Classifications of the Behavior Disorders" in the *Annual Review of Psychology*, Phillips and Draguns (1971) found it necessary to present new objections to the traditional diagnostic system.

Laing (1967) suggests that the act of diagnostic labeling sets in motion the vicious circle of a self-fulfilling prophecy, as a result of which the patient finally internalizes the diagnostic stereotype and behaves accordingly. Sarbin (1967) contends that the use of the reified medical metaphor to refer to mental disorder results in social rejection of persons labeled mentally ill. Likewise, Szasz (1970) maintains that the label "mentally ill" is an extension of the stigmatic medieval label "witch," in that both serve as a legitimate basis for the persecution of people so labeled.

As I implied in Chapter 1, the underlying implication of labeling analysis is that, by the magic process of negative labeling, a person is *transformed* irreversibly into the deviant entity that the label connotes, or, as Schur puts it, "deviance is created through processes of social definitions" (1971:3). But is the labeling process really so magical and so effective as to turn a person into a "frog" just by calling him one? And if labeling is so powerful, cannot the same magic process turn the frog into a prince? In other words, since labeling logically can also be favorable, does labeling theory assume a two-directional process?

One could argue that labeling is nothing more than a classification system and that scientific nomenclature is vital for the systematic organization of accumulated knowledge in any discipline. Furthermore, since it is important for scientists to classify things, it is also natural for laymen to identify people as social types (Strong, 1943).

If the label "schizophrenic" is assigned only for "scientific convenience," why should it be so pernicious and detrimental to the person so labeled, and on what basis do we assume that labelees accept this definition differently from any other descriptive label assigned to their physical behavior—e.g. "diabetes"? While it seems reasonable to accept the premise that human beings may be more vulnerable to derogatory labels than are chromosomes or historical documents, the generality of the irreversible self-fulfilling labeling proposition claimed by psychiatrists and sociologists (e.g. Laing, 1967; Becker, 1963) should be seriously questioned. The question is: Precisely what is the labeling paradigm proposing? How does a given name or tag transform a person?

One approach to that problem might be that implicit in the labeling-transforming hypothesis is the proposition that the act of negative labeling involves a process of social reification; namely, that there is a difference between labeling certain *behaviors* "melancholic" or "schizophrenic" and reversing the dialectic by saying that one behaves in a schizophrenic manner because "one is a schizophrenic." In this process, the dependent variable (schizophrenia) is fallaciously taken as the independent variable (see Table 4–1). This revised proposition would state that a successfully reified derogatory label may have a transmuting effect on the labelee. But when and why are labels reified by labelers and labelees alike?

There is no denying the sociologists' contention that social

TABLE 4.1. **Reified and Nonreified Labeling**

LABELING STATE	INDEPENDENT VARIABLE	DEPENDENT VARIABLE	DESYMPTOM-IZATION
Nonreified labeling	specified behavior	schizo-phrenia	reverses label
Reified labeling	schizo-phrenia	non-specified behavior	label irreversible

labeling and societal reactions may sometimes be very painful to the actor—especially if such reactions include isolation, rejection, deprivation, or physical attack. However, the proposition that "labeling creates deviance" does not explain why some labelees do *not* internalize the label. Nor does it explain how some people can label themselves when no social reaction or external labeling has taken place previously.

The central question in labeling theory, then, involves the conditions under which social labeling results in self-labeling. The question here reflects the famous joke about the mother who tries to convince her frightened child that "a barking dog does not bite." The child answers: "I know that, but does the dog know it?" Labeling may create deviants—but do all labelees know this and accept it?

From a theoretical point of view, the overemphasis on societal reactions and social labeling as the major determinants in the process of creating deviants presents a social-deterministic model in which man is viewed as a pawn of society, with no will of his own. If the orientational ancestors of the labeling approach are Alfred Schutz's phenomenological sociology and Mead's interactionist perspective (Kitsuse, 1962), then the offspring have done an injustice to their forefathers. After all, the phenomenologists profess to deal with "what people know as reality in their everyday life" (Berger and Luckmann, 1966), and they stress that "the world must be recognized as it is directly experienced by human actors" (Schur, 1971:116). Yet labeling theory, which derives from these orientations, largely ignores the actor's perspective.

Furthermore, taking the side of the underdog labelees (Becker, 1967), as some theorists do by leading an "anti-labeling crusade," is by no means synonymous with studying the differential meaning of labeling from the actor's real experiential perspective. The question always remains: Do both the dog and the child know that "barking dogs don't bite"?

Similarly, although Mead assumed that selves arise through the symbolic, reflective process of others' evaluation of and reactions to the actor, it seems that, by overemphasizing societal reactions, one is entirely forgetting Mead's conception of the minded man's ability to *interpret* reactions and control his environment and the special self he wants to build. This self-deterministic perspective was, after all, Mead's great disagreement with Spencer, Sumner, and other Social Darwinists, who understood evolution as a passive process of man's adaptation to his environment (Mead, 1936).

The degree of congruence between group-assigned labels and incumbents' self-concepts might vary greatly (Secord and Backman, 1965; Sarbin and Allen, 1968; Rotenberg and Sarbin, 1971). Goffman (1959), Turner (1956), and others have convincingly analyzed not only the conditions under which role-type behavior is incongruent with self but also how people elicit societal responses to misrepresent and obscure their selves. Likewise, Sykes and Matza (1967) discuss the various techniques used by delinquents to neutralize deviant self-images imputed to them by official social labelers. It is also well known that "ideological-political patients" in Russian mental hospitals rarely internalize their socially assigned labels. Similarly, one may notice that in recent years black ex-convicts in the United States have persistently rejected the labels attached to them by white rule-makers.

The most dramatic demonstrated discrepancy between

social labeling and self-labeling is Rosenhan's (1973) report about the adventure he and his associates experienced after gaining secret admission to mental institutions and being diagnosed, labeled, and related to as mentally ill. One can assume that Rosenhan and his associates not only rejected the derogatory label but even strengthened their own self-label as scientists.

It is my contention, then, that the relations between social labeling and self-labeling are a function of the degree of significance of referent others to the actors in the specific labeling context. In other words, it is insufficient to establish that particular stereotypic responses prevail in society (Schur, 1971) without determining their differential effect on the actors. A social response is not synonymous with its psychological impact.

In summary, labeling analysis has hitherto either minimized or taken for granted the differential aspects of self-labeling involved in the process of becoming deviant. Any theory of social labeling that does not provide the conceptual framework for analyzing the properties of self-labeling accompanying the social process is incomplete.

By pointing to what I have termed the "Protestant bias" in conventional labeling analyses, I shall deal here with the question, *"What makes the label stick?"* from the actor's perspective. In addition, an attempt will be made to expand the labeling approach to deviance by presenting a conceptual scheme for the analysis of conditions and sources of differential self-labeling. It will be proposed that specific beliefs and cultural roots underlie major Western and Eastern labeling systems.

Since labeling theorists have largely failed to deal both with the problem of continuity between social labeling and self-labeling and with compatibility between established labels and subsequent social labeling, it would seem useful first to explain briefly (1) the difference between primary and secondary others and (2) the difference between pri-

mary (categoric) and secondary (descriptive) labeling. (In
Chapter 6 the differences between these two dimensions will
be further explained.)

PRIMARY AND SECONDARY OTHERS

Rotenberg and Sarbin (1971) demonstrated empirically
that self-identity (self-labeling) is directly related to the
degree of significance of those who make valuations of a
person's involvement in specific roles. Those whose valuative
reactions are incorporated into the actor's self-identity are
termed *primary others.* Audiences who have power or prestige for the actor and whose valuative reactions are situationally significant but are not incorporated into the actor's
self-identity (e.g. prison guards' valuations of prisoners' behavior) are referred to as *secondary others.*

Both positive and negative self-labeling will occur only if
the labeler is a primary other to the labelee. This would rule
out most labeling applied by official social-control agents,
who, owing to inevitable "social distance," are in most cases
only secondary others to the labelee. It follows logically that
any positive role valuations by a primary other may be incorporated into the actor's self-identity if the actor's self-
concept is essentially positive (e.g. "I am a competent
person"), as a result of the valuator's primary significance to
the actor. Similarly, it seems reasonable that a primary other's
negative reactions to the actor's role behavior will be incorporated into the self-identity if the actor's self-concept regarding his primary roles (e.g. his sex roles) is negative
(e.g. "I am a nonperson.")

But if an actor has a positive self-identity initially and a
primary other changes his valuative reactions in regard to
the actor—as often happens when concerned relatives react
negatively to the actor's suddenly disordered conduct? In

this case it would seem necessary for a complex transformation to occur in order for self-labeling to result.

CATEGORIC AND DESCRIPTIVE LABELING

A *categoric label* refers to one's basic social identity and self-identity and is related to his position, rank, sex, class, etc. It categorically classifies him in his own eyes and in the eyes of others as a "success" or "failure," as "in" or "out," "good" or "bad."

A *descriptive label* refers to concrete behavior that is usually related to one's secondary roles (e.g. occupational roles). It might be positive or negative and will be incorporated into one's self-identity if the labeler is primary and if the descriptive label is compatible with one's categoric label. Descriptive labels, usually resulting from ongoing processes of social typing in small groups (Strong, 1943), can stick only within the category. If a man's categoric label is "successful businessman," the label "schlemiel" will not stick unless he is first delabeled. But the label "alcoholic" might stick, since it is not incompatible. This might explain the relative success observed in delabeling and relabeling "alcoholics" (Trice and Roman, 1970).

Labeling theorists have not yet explained how negative labels stick to previously established labels. There is a difference between the labeling process through which a wayward youth or a pauper is labeled a "thief" and the process through which a rich professional is so labeled. Only in the first case the descriptive label "thief" is categorically compatible with waywardness or poverty, in the sense that the actor is an outsider or a failure to begin with. It seems that many labeling theorists, particularly Matza (1964), have limited their analysis to the former case. In the latter case, however, a labeling-transformation process is required to make the label stick from the actor's perspective.

The Roots of Self-labeling

The model that will be presented briefly here draws on four sources:

1. psychological literature on pathological distortions in self-perception and processes of self-misrepresentation
2. socio-psychological interaction theory of social typing and transformation processes
3. anthropological sources related to the cultural meanings attributed to various naming procedures
4. theological belief systems concerning human nature underlying social and self-labeling contexts

These four perspectives commonly view self-labeling as an outcome of the specific interaction between man and his environment. They are, therefore, naturally interrelated. But the relative dominance of any one will depend on the specific context in which the labeling occurs.

AUTOSUGGESTIVE SELF-LABELING (THE PSYCHOLOGICAL PERSPECTIVE)

In autosuggestive or introjective self-labeling, transformation results from an intrapsychic process. Self-labeling is not triggered by social labeling or societal reactions, although it might be followed by them. The key explanatory concept here is modeling; that is, labeling oneself according to the character features or total personality of an imagined or known figure.

Although modeling usually refers to cases in which others' behavior influences the self, the point here is that there is no directed evaluative reaction or social labeling involved in this case of self-labeling. Societal reactions and/or social labeling *following* self-labeling may be compatible or incompatible with the self-labeling.

In most cases, self-labeling is an attempt to reduce strain. One might label himself "thief," "swindler," or "failure" in reaction to imagined or actual (but undetected by others) norm violations or self-disappointment. The strain produced by feelings of guilt or incompetence is reduced through self-blame and self-labeling. A good case in point might be a typical upper-middle-class "nice Jewish boy" who labels himself a radical "hippie" in order to reduce the strain produced by his "Jewish mother's" pressure to become a materialistic, successful scientist, doctor, or businessman. In this case social labeling usually will not occur until this "nice Jewish boy" has successfully changed his life-style and outward appearance (as if crying out, "I am a hippie, believe me!") in order to validate his self-labeling.

An extreme example: The strain of just being oneself is so unbearable that the actor diverts attention from himself and labels himself somebody else—say, Jesus Christ or Napoleon. Interestingly, although societal reactions of primary others are usually forthcoming in this kind of self-labeling, these reactions may not be compatible with self-labeling—e.g. when family members or professional helpers try to convince the labelee that he is David, not Napoleon. And if a professional diagnostician labels him "schizophrenic," the actor will probably reject this label, at least temporarily, and insist that he is Napoleon. It is important to note here, of course, that the labelee might react to some transcendental primary others—say, God or a dead relative—who he believes conferred the label on him. But this is not the same social labeling referred to in traditional labeling theory.

In other, less extreme or more adaptive cases of self-labeling, the actor may misrepresent himself under a false label by emulating a selected model. In such cases of calculated self-labeling, people use all the gadgets of "impression management" described by Goffman (1959) to elicit appropriate and desired societal responses in order to reinforce the self-assigned label. These cases range all the way from the full-fledged impostor to the office clerk who plays the role of junior executive.

Again, although in the final analysis autosuggestive self-labeling usually involves some societal reactions, the labeling transformation process is reversed because self-labeling arises within oneself. Thus, self-labeling is the independent variable, and the resultant social labeling and societal reactions are dependent variables.

TRANSFORMATIVE SELF-LABELING (THE SOCIAL-PSYCHOLOGICAL PERSPECTIVE)

If no intrapsychic labeling process occurred and an assigned label is incompatible with an established categoric self-identity label, then categoric delabeling must occur before the new label will stick. The process is well known from the social-psychological literature of transformation processes and will thus be presented very briefly.

In reviewing literature describing the self-reconstitution processes, such as conversion, shamanism, thought reform, Synanon, and military indoctrination, Sarbin and Adler (1970–1971) identified specific operational phases common to all change systems. These include destruction of the old identity; the influence of significant others; and ritual involvement in the new self.

DESTRUCTION OF OLD IDENTITY (CATEGORIC DELABELING)

Symbolic death or destruction of the old identity label as a prerequisite for acquiring a new categoric label was found to be a recurrent theme in all self-reconstitution systems, whether it took the form of a public degradation ceremony (Garfinkel, 1956)), the stripping or mortification of the self in Goffman's (1961) terms, or the ritual dying ceremony of the volunteer convert or the prisoner who is "brainwashed." The assault on the labelee's old categoric identity can be brought about by the "hot seat" therapy used in some groups, by Synanon's "haircut" sessions, or by accusations and torture. But these procedures must break old loyalties and lead the old self-identity into total crisis and bankruptcy, as described by Schein (1958), Lifton (1961), and others. The symbolic death and rebirth process might involve an abrupt future-oriented act of repentence, which allows one to accept his new self-label instantaneously, such as may happen in "Hassidic" groups, or it may require a prolonged past-oriented guilt-solving process, such as characterizes most Western therapy systems.

THE INFLUENCE OF SIGNIFICANT OTHERS

It is apparently easier to bring about the degradation and mortification of one's old categoric label than to make the new categoric label stick, especially from the actor's perspective. Garfinkel (1956) tells us about "successful public degradations." Becker (1963) contends that "a deviant is one to whom that label has *successfully* been applied." But conditions for successful deviant self-relabeling are generally unknown. In line with interaction theory, valuators of the new categoric label must become primary to the actor in order for self-labeling to occur. Significant others functioning as role models have also been found in all self-reconstitution systems.

The representative other—whether priest, guru, therapist, sergeant, coach, professor, or guard—usually functions as a teacher who reinterprets reality and valuates the actor's new behavior. The significance of these powerful others to the actor may be no more than secondary at first. But to the extent that the previous categoric label and old loyalties were successfully destroyed, the significance of the new helpful other may become primary. This has proved to be the case in voluntary conversion; but in coercive negative labeling, it seems to be the major stumbling block in the process of self-relabeling, as described in Schein's (1958) account of attempted brainwashing.

RITUAL INVOLVEMENT IN NEW BEHAVIOR

It seems unlikely that one would label himself a "soldier" or "Hassid" just by reading about army life or Hassidism— or even by being officially drafted or socially labeled a "Hassid." In order for self-relabeling to occur, one has to be organismically involved in the new role carrying that label.

After disinvolvement in the old categoric identity is successfully accomplished via ritualized or symbolic death procedures, the actor's involvement in his new categoric label must be functional. Organismic involvement in most self-reconstitution systems was found to be functionally geared to reorganize the boundaries of the new self. Kneeling, ecstatic dancing and singing, "speaking in tongues," hunger, prayer, regulating breathing, and other methods were used to focus the actor's concentration on the new identity and to induce quietude in it.

From a social-psychological perspective, then, categoric self-labeling transformations occur if, after delabeling, one becomes organismically involved in the new label and if the labeler becomes a primary other to the actor. But there are two other processes of self-labeling in which these variables are not necessary conditions.

TRANSMUTIVE SELF-LABELING
(THE ANTHROPOLOGICAL PERSPECTIVE)

Nomen est omen, says the Latin phrase. Self-labeling refers in essence to the process of acquiring a belief about oneself. Thus, if I behave as the label says (under coercion or voluntarily) and my primary others react to me as such, then "I must be it"—"I am what the name says." Naming systems and the concomitant acquisition of beliefs about self are culturally bound. In ancient and primitive societies, the process of naming implied creation, authority, and control over the named person (Fortune, 1932; Sarna, 1966). Adam's assignment by God to give names to the animals symbolized his control over them as well as their destined characteristics (Genesis, 2:19).

The custom of giving a child the name of some outstanding personality in the belief that the essence of the namesake will thus be transmitted to the child is well known in both primitive and modern societies (Honigman, 1954). Moreover, in some societies the fear that the soul of the namesake will be transported into the body of the infant stands in the way of naming children after living parents (Trachtenberg, 1974). Some Africans have been known to take on the names of European ship captains in order to acquire the supernatural power that they thought the white man had (Ruel, 1971). A person without a name is often not considered a real person. Goffman (1961), for example, considered the loss of one's name in asylums a major parameter in the process of self-mortificiation by inmates. In some tribes the child is thought of as a nonentity until it is named; if it dies before the naming ceremony, it is not even buried (Stenning, 1965:390).

The magic power attributed to naming is often extended to various kinds of name manipulations and renaming processes. The renaming of the patriarchs and prophets during biblical times, for example, was said to have transformed their character and destiny (Sarna, 1966). Three forms of name manipulation can be mentioned:

1. *Name pronunciation:* In some societies pronunciation of specific names is believed to inflict disease on people, cure them (Fortune, 1932), or provide the demons with power to command evil against them (Brendt and Brendt, 1964). Hence a night name (referring to any false name used purposely instead of the official name) (Abbie, 1969) or a de-

rogatory name (e.g. "filth"; *Encyclopedia Britannica*, 1970) might be used to mislead the devil.

2. *Name inscription:* The execration technique practiced in ancient Egypt involved smashing a piece of pottery inscribed with the name of the enemy to destroy his power (Pritchard, 1955), and the Hebrew expression "erased be his name" (*"yimach shmo"*) is known to be a most powerfully devastating curse. Conversely, various customs involving manipulations of name inscriptions to cure people (e.g. eating cake with the patient's name on it) are widely practiced among Arabs and Oriental Jews in the Middle East.[1]

3. *Name changing:* In many societies an ill person's name is changed in order "to strengthen his soul" or to change his fortune (Burrows and Spiro, 1957). Likewise, the Jewish custom of adding the word "Haim" (life) to the name of one who is gravely ill is believed to help save his life (Babylonian Talmud, 1938). Moreover, according to Maimonides, the great twelfth-century Jewish jurist and philosopher, one effective repentance method involves name changing (see Ben Maimon, 1955).

In general, the magic process of naming, in which the labeler and labelee believe that transmuting power is inherent in the act of naming itself, can be equated with the self-fulfilling-prophecy process. Transmutive labeling is not necessarily derogatory. Since labeling is externally induced, the process might operate effectively in both directions: The prince can be turned into a frog, and the ugly frog into a prince.

The transmutive labeling process appears to be more characteristic of Eastern and primitive societies. Here the labeler, who is usually believed to possess alchemic power by virtue of his status (fairy, holy man, medicine man), might be a

---

[1] Two of my students have observed that, among Jews from Kurdistan, name-manipulation procedures closely akin to execration techniques are very popular. For example, the eating of a cake with the troubled person's name engraved on it has been observed.

secondary other to the labelee, yet social labeling will result in self-labeling because of the magic power attributed to the naming *per se*. A process of social reification occurs in which social naming is the independent variable and behavior accompanying self-labeling is the dependent variable, as often happens in the extreme case of voodoo death.[2]

This magic process is to be distinguished from cases in which the label merely describes some aspect of the labelee but in itself has no transforming power and from cases in which the name is used among other labels to signify the ascriptive category into which the labelee should be placed.

INDICATIVE SELF-LABELING
(THE THEOLOGICAL PERSPECTIVE)

How can social labeling trigger a self-fulfilling labeling process, as many labeling analysts presume, if no magic power is attributed to the labeling *per se* or to the labeler and if one has not gone through the full process of transformative labeling?

The proposition advanced here is that a self-fulfilling labeling process is possible if labeler and labelee believe in man's *a priori* categoric ascription, which the labeling process signifies. A derogatory label would be used to indicate that the labelee is originally and categorically "bad," regardless of what he appears or claims to be—"He was always a no-good," as people say. Here negative labeling is not the efficient *cause* of deviance, it is only an aid to the independent

[2] A counter-example in Western society of magic belief attributed to a diagnostic label has been documented by Gordon Allport (1964). Allport describes a "dying" patient who was led by his physicians to believe that his disease was incurable because the diagnosis was unknown. When he finally overheard a famous specialist diagnose it as *"moribundus,"* the patient was cured. After many years, he thanked the diagnostician for saving his life—although *moribundus* means incurable. For him, the assignment of any diagnostic label meant he would live.

variable: *a priori* categorization. Signifying labels have no magic transforming power, and many names may serve the indicative purpose of exclusion or inclusion in the original category.

A good example is the Protestant belief in the doctrine of predestination. According to that doctrine, man's life is characterized by constant doubt as to whether he was assigned, prior to his birth, to the category of the hopeless "damned" or to the "elect." He thus forever searches for reassuring signs of election and grace. According to Weber (1930) and McClelland (1961), striving and its consequent material "success" serve as technical proof that one was assigned to the elect—or, rather, they help him to rid himself of the fear of damnation. Thus, behavioral features such as striving and competing, which are commonly referred to as the Protestant Ethic, have now become generalized Western norms. Since we know virtue through vice, beauty through ugliness, and normality through abnormality, by the same token one would seek signs to identify the "damned" in order to ascertain his self-definition as "elect." Resharpening the lines between the deviant-damned and the conforming-elect is one of the functions of deviance in Western society (Erikson, 1959), where lack of success is self-perpetuating in many facets of life. Consider the high probability that lower-class deviants will be labeled schizophrenic rather than neurotic, and that they will be institutionalized rather than receive psychotherapy (Hollingshead and Redlich, 1958).

Indicative labeling [3] is not an independent variable explaining the genesis of deviance, as Lemert (1967) suggested; labeling, as such, is merely a *signifying* act of

[3] An example of a physiological indicative method for recategorization might be *phrenology,* the "scientific" method for analyzing the mind-phrenia by examining the shape of the skull. During the nineteenth century, Combe and Gall used phrenology to determine whether insanity or criminality was innate—i.e. whether people were born with these features.

identification and recategorization. In indicative labeling, it is sufficient for the labeler to be a secondary other (e.g. social-control agent) for self-labeling to occur if the labelee believes in the categoric signs he or others produce. Hence, if one ceases to produce success signs [4] and reaches the point of self-doubt, a vicious circle of self-victimization [5] is set into action and results in social labeling and self-labeling, effectively placing the person into the basic irreversible damned category. Delinquents' infractions, I would argue, are therefore often committed not to restore their sense of control, as Matza (1964) suggests, but to reinforce self-victimization. Similarly, it is not reaction formation against the values of goodness but against the material success goals dominating the West (Cohen, 1955) that accounts for the subculture of the unsuccessful-damned-retreaters and that explains the nonutilitarian process of self-victimizing vandalism, on the one hand, and the Western subterranean tradition of succeeding via any means (Matza, 1964), on the other.

The predestinal-indicative paradigm presented above might now reconcile social-deterministic labeling with Meadian self-deterministic labeling. One may reject a social label or control a self-label operationally; but once negative

---

[4] It should be emphasized that, whether or not reaction theorists take a firm stand in relation to the free will–determinism issue, they seem unable to explain why physical deviants (the blind, the epileptic, the dwarf) are often stigmatized (Goffman, 1965) and negatively reacted to (Scott, 1969)—although the labelee is obviously not responsible for his condition (Freidson, 1965). In predestinal terms, such deviants are assigned *a priori* to the category of the "damned" and are "foreordained to everlasting death" (Weber, 1930:100) and rejection. On the other hand, the signs of material and social "success" provided by the physician-addict, for example, prevent him from being negatively labeled despite his use of drugs.

[5] Here abused or misperceived "insight therapy" may reinforce the self-victimization circle rather than achieve the more difficult task of breaking it. Similarly, voluntary hospitalization of "mental patients" may serve only to enhance the process of self-victimization by arranging for the person himself to conclude that, as a hopeless "damned," he belongs in the other world.

signs outweigh positive signs, social labeling may become perceptually deterministic in relation to self-labeling.

I shall conclude by indicating briefly how major formulations in labeling theory addressed their analysis to typical Western social contexts in which a self-labeling process (possibly rooted in predestinal-dualistic theology) may automatically follow the process I have termed indicative social labeling.

Social Darwinism and Labeling Theory

New approaches to deviance and what I have termed the recent "antilabeling crusade" are implicitly directed at the innate and irreversible conception of deviance and the dualistic, discriminating rejection of deviants that presumably dominates the West. It is not surprising, therefore, that the hard-bitten dualistic approach to life advocated in Darwin's "natural selection" and Spencer's "survival of the fittest" is viewed as a continuation of Calvin's dualistic predestination.

Hofstadter, in his excellent study of the perpetuation of Social Darwinism in modern social thinking, summarizes Sumner's extremely pessimistic sociology as follows:

> Like some latter-day Calvin, he came to preach the predestination of the social order and the salvation of the economically elect through the survival of the fittest [Hofstadter, 1968:66].

While interactionist and phenomenological labeling analysts definitely do not preach dualistic survival of the fittest but rather take a nonevaluative and noncorrectional (Gibbs, 1972) stand in their observations (Warren and Johnson, 1972), the explicit and implicit continuity between Social Darwinism and the analytical content of the "new perspective" of deviance is striking.

A few examples from the literature will suffice to demonstrate how recent approaches to deviance address themselves to neo–Social Darwinism and how major labeling formulations deal mainly with indicative labeling. In his orientational introduction to a collection including the most recent critical evaluation of labeling theory, Scott proposes Berger and Luckmann's phenomenological approach to reality and Erikson's functional perspective as a general framework for analyzing the social properties of deviance. Based on Berger and Luckmann's conception of deviance as chaos threatening the stability of the symbolic universe, Scott's language is astonishing in its resemblance to that used by Calvinists and Social Darwinists. One need only cite Scott's discussion of "nihilation," which is one of Berger and Luckmann's "universe-maintaining mechanisms":

> One such set of mechanisms consists of techniques of social control that are used against deviants who cannot be changed. . . . By putting the madman or the criminal away, a social order removes the symbolically noxious elements from its midst. . . . I believe it is a highly significant fact that few social orders use killing as a mechanism for dealing with recalcitrant forms of deviance . . . certain deviants are regarded as subhuman animals or savages who are unfit for living in civilized society [Scott, 1972:27].

The belief in subhuman deviants "who cannot be changed" conforms to Calvin's predestinal conception of man, and the removal of the unfit was advocated by Darwin, Lombroso, and Spencer. As Hofstadter notes: "They were unfit, he [Spencer] said, and should be eliminated" (1968:41).

Deviant labeling is similarly explained by Scott in Erikson's functional terms as helping to classify people in order to demarcate the symbolic boundaries between the society of "insiders" and the deviant "outsiders." In an apparent attempt to condemn prevailing attitudes toward deviants in the West, Scott concludes that "in our society, more effort is expended in detecting deviance" than in changing it. Judging from other cultures, Scott notes that this is by no means a universal quality but is perhaps "related to a deep-seated intolerance [in Western society] of anything that deviates" (1972:31).

If society's treatment of deviance can be explained as the need to label and remove the unfit, "who cannot be changed," then it should not be surprising that major labeling analysts concentrate on what I call indicative labeling, which Schur (1971) referred to as retrospective interpretation.

A few examples of indicative labeling or retrospective interpretation taken from major writings in the societal-reaction and labeling traditions are in order. Goffman (1961) notes, for example, how case records are used by diagnosticians as retrospective substantiations of patients' present diagnosis and their essential character. Lofland observed a similar process in what he terms biographical reconstructions: "The *present evil* of current character must be related to *past evil* that can be discovered in biography" (1969: 150). Rosenhan, in his demonstration of how pseudo-patient researchers were diagnosed and treated as schizophrenics, provides compelling evidence of how biographical facts were simply "distorted by staff to achieve consistency with . . . the dynamics of a schizophrenic reaction" (1973: 253). In his study of reactions to sexual deviates, Kitsuse likewise notes that in light of new information, subjects were "searching for subtle cues and nuances . . . to support the conclusion that this is what was going on all the time" (1962: 248).

Indicative labeling, in the sense of retrospective classification to an inferior, outcast category, is most succinctly described in Garfinkel's account of degradation ceremonies:

> He is not changed, he is reconstituted . . . the former identity stands as accidental; the new identity is the basic reality. What he is now is what, after all, he was all along . . . the denounced person must be ritually separated from a place in the legitimate order . . . he must be placed outside [1956:24].

Conclusion

It is only when the labelee believes in his own *a priori* categoric ascription (based on failure signs) that self-labeling will automatically follow indicative social labeling. Thus indicative labeling may explain the substance of the self-fulfilling prophecy hypothesis.

As I believe that major labeling formulations concentrate mainly on what I have termed "indicative labeling," in which the implicit assumption is that deviance is innate and irreversible, the next chapter will present two preliminary studies of indicative labeling. The first study analyzes cross-culturally people's tendency to recategorize others as born "successes" or "failures"; the second shows how indicative self-labeling among mental patients is related to their degree of Westernization, in terms of ethnic origins and hospital socialization. These studies do not by any means represent comprehensive empirical tests of the theory of man developed in this book. They are intended only to demonstrate for the emipirically oriented reader how selective research designs could be deduced to test some of the conceptualizations developed here.

Chapter Five

Empirical Explorations of Indicative Labeling

"I accuse the prisoner of behaving at his mother's funeral in a way that showed he was already a criminal at heart."
                                                    (Camus, The Stranger)

Indicative Social Labeling: Americans and Israelis [1]

I have suggested earlier that, following Weber (1930), it has been widely accepted that the typical Western need to compete, strive, and achieve and consequently to perceive oneself or the other as a success can be traced, at least in part, to the influence of the Calvinist doctrine of predestination, in which success signs serve as technical proof that one belongs *a priori* to the "elect" and not to the "damned." Behavioristically, this attribution of present success or failure to a predetermined fate to be "successful" or "to fail" would involve a process of retrospective reinterpretation of a person's past in such a way as to be consistent with his present state. Thus, in retrospective labeling, or what I have termed "indicative labeling," positive success labels or de-

[1] The senior author of this study was Bernard Goitein (see Acknowledgments), who designed and directed this research project.

rogatory diagnostic labels such as "schizophrenic" or "psychopath" are secular reifications of the Calvinist predestined "damned" category. Such reifications indicate how to reclassify people retrospectively into either the "damned" or "elect" category to which they "originally" belonged.

Indeed, a process of retrospective interpretation and reclassification in relation to people labeled homosexuals, mentally ill, or criminals has been observed by some investigators mentioned in Chapter 4 (e.g., Garfinkel, 1956; Goffman, 1961; Kitsuse, 1962; Lofland, 1969; and Rosenhan, 1973). These authors point out that, once a derogatory label has been assigned, the labelee's nature is "rediscovered" in his biographical case history, so that the present label will signify what he "always was," regardless of what he claimed or appeared to be before.

Fischoff (1974; 1975) has experimentally studied a similar process in event perception. Once the outcome of a situation is known, this is seen as having been more likely to occur than it appeared to the same subjects before they knew the outcome. Moreover, the subjects seem quite unaware of this change in their perceptions. Thus, it can generally be hypothesized that if A is provided with some information about a person's past and is asked to rate the probabilities of this outcome (present state), and B is given the same past information plus the outcome and is asked to rate the probability of said outcome, then B should find the outcome more probable than does A. This difference could be a result of the process of retrospective labeling discussed above. Furthermore, even if B is asked to ignore the information about the present state and to predict the outcome on the basis of the past information alone, he will still find the outcome more probable than will A, who was never given the outcome (Fischoff, 1974), because for B restrospective labeling has already occurred. Thus in person perception for Protestants (or Westerners in general), the increase in probability ratings from the predictive condition (giving only past information) to the "postdictive" condition (giving present state *and* past information) should be greater than for non-Protestants (Westerners). Again, this would be a result of the process of retrospective labeling hypothesized here to be characteristic of Protestants. Similar differences should be expected within cultures more or less imbued with the values of the Protestant Ethic.

Fischoff has also found that in event perception (e.g. historical events), if people are asked to ignore the present-state information (e.g. that event C occurred) and to rate the probability of an *alternative* (mutually exclusive) outcome (e.g. event D), their probabilities drop from the predictive condition to the postdictive condition. Accordingly, it can be expected that in person perception, if Westerners are asked to ignore that a certain outcome (e.g. mental patient) has taken place and to rate the probability of an alternative outcome, (e.g. businessman), the decrease from pre- to post-condition will be greater for them than for non-Westerners. Again, this expectation could be attributed to the hypothesized process of retrospective labeling that has already occurred; i.e., the person was already categorized cognitively as a mental patient and not as a businessman (*ibid.*).

A slight distinction must be drawn, however, between the Calvinist-type perception of people and event perception as studied by Fischoff. For Calvinist perception of people, the present is not *caused* by the past; rather, the present *is* the past. That is, past events or behaviors do not *contribute* to present states, for the present only *indicates* what always existed in the past. Accordingly, Calvinism would not influence people's perception of *causal* relationships between specific past and present events in a person's life.

Westerners (who are presumably most imbued with the Protestant Ethic) should, however, find that past information is generally more *indicative* and diagnostic of people's nature than non-Westerners, since the key factor determining pre-destinal perception of people as "successes" or "failures" is the provision of suitable signs. Furthermore, as has been repeatedly demonstrated among Westerners, *negative* past information has greater indicative value of a person's nature (being damned) than positive information (e.g. Pastore, 1960; Gray-Little, 1973). Thus, since for Calvinists the "damned" classification is the basic category into which one falls back once one ceases to provide success signs—even without having to provide overt signs of failure—it is possible that Westerners would find negative outcomes in particular more probable than non-Westerners on the basis of the same information. Again, similar differences should be observed within cultures whose values are more or less Protestant.

The purpose of this study, then, is to determine whether Americans (mostly Protestants) differ from Israelis (non-Protestants) in their perception of others, both in predicting and in "postdicting" others' present states of failure or success.

METHOD

SUBJECTS

The subjects were 330 Israeli students and 100 American students (including Canadians). The American subjects were about two-thirds Protestant and about one-third non-Protestant (mostly Catholics); the Israeli sample was overwhelmingly Jewish with about 10 percent Moslems. The experiments were administered in groups during class time.

DESIGN

Subjects in both American and Israeli samples were randomly assigned to one of three experimental groups: (1) the PR—"prediction" group (present state unknown); (2) the PB—"post-business" group (currently "elect" successful businessman); or (3) the PM—"post-mental" group (currently "damned" mental patient).

PROCEDURE

Subjects were given an "interpersonal perception questionnaire," including fictitious information supposedly taken from the *Brazilian Statistical Yearbook*, with the percentages of people who are unemployed, hospitalized in mental institutions, successful businessmen, and the like. Then fictitious information about a thirty-one-year-old Brazilian bachelor's past was given: The bachelor ("Carl") had studied law at one time, and when he was eight years old he went through a battery of psychological tests as part of a research study conducted at his school. The battery included three tests (each of which supposedly concentrated on a different set of traits) that gave the following profile of Carl: In the first test Carl was described as emotional, diligent, and angry; in the second test he was described as friendly, irresponsible, restless, and active; and in the third, as unintelligent, independent, aggressive, and wasteful. These eleven adjectives were selected from Anderson's (1968) norms. The specific traits were selected so as to be (1) not conspicuously contradictory, (2) translatable to Hebrew, and (3) as a group, roughly one-third negative, one-third neutral, and one-third positive traits for both Americans and Israelis.

While this was all the information given to the subjects in the PR (prediction) group, in the PB and the PM groups a single phrase was added giving Carl's current state (businessman or mental patient, respectively). Subjects in the PR group who did not know Carl's present state were asked to rate, on a six-point scale, the possible contribution of each trait to Carl's being today (1) a successful businessman and (2) a hospitalized mental patient. Then, to assess their indicative perception under neutral conditions (present state unknown), they were asked to rate on a nine-point scale Carl's general chances (based on all the information available to them) of his being today (1) a successful businessman and (2) a hospitalized mental patient. Similarly, in the PB and

PM groups, after each subject had filled out the six-point contributory questionnaire which aimed at eliciting their spontaneous tendency to attribute retrospectively past success or failure signs to present state (which was different for both groups), they filled out the nine-point general indicative questionnaire. Indicative perception was thus obtained by the subjects' ratings—on the basis of all the information available to them (including the subjects' own biased ratings on the six-point contributory questionnaire)—of Carl's chances of being a successful businessman or a hospitalized mental patient as they would have listed them had they not known his present state.

In order to ascertain that Americans in our study were indeed more Protestant in their value orientation than Israelis, after giving their probability ratings, subjects filled out a shortened version of the Protestant Ethic questionnaire of Mirels and Garrett (1971), translated into Hebrew for Israeli subjects, which included only those items with a part-whole correlation of .40 and above. This procedure eliminated items with a heavy cultural bias and/or those not translatable into Hebrew. Thus, eight items were used in the present study:

Items Selected for the Shortened Protestant Ethic Scale
1. Our society would have fewer problems if people had less leisure time.
2. Most people who don't succeed in life are just plain lazy.
3. People should have more leisure time to spend in relaxation.
4. Any man who is able and willing to work hard has a good chance of succeeding.
5. People who fail at a job have usually not tried enough.
6. Life would be more meaningful if we had more leisure time.
7. If one works hard enough, he is likely to make a good life for himself.

8. A distaste for hard work usually reflects a weakness of character.

On a split-half reliability test performed on a sample of 102, internal reliability of the shortened scale was .52; applying the Spearman-Brown formula (Guilford, 1954), reliability was .69, which is significant at the .001 level. In subsequent studies the shortened scale was also found to be useful in discriminating successfully between various ethnic groups, such as Moslem and Christian Arabs.

RESULTS

From the total sample of 330 Israelis and 100 Americans, missing data eliminated 15 Israeli and 12 American subjects, resulting in a final usable sample of 315 Israelis and 88 Americans. A mean score on the Protestant Ethic scale was computed for each subject for those items answered by the subject. To minimize differences resulting from unequal numbers of subjects for this test, subjects in the American sample were split around the median (computed for a larger sample available during pretesting) to form high-PE (Protestant Ethic) and low-PE groups. However, since the Israeli sample was larger, only top and bottom quartiles of the PE distribution were selected in this sample.

In regard to Protestant Ethic endorsement, Americans scored significantly higher than Israelis on the Protestant Ethic scale ($t = 1.6862$, df $= 99$, $p < .05$, one-tailed).

RETROSPECTIVE LABELING

As it was assumed that in the Calvinist perception differences between Protestants or Westerners and others would be observed mainly when "indicative labeling" was assessed, comparative results of indicative perception will be presented here briefly. Let us first compare prediction and "post-

TABLE 5.1. **Mean Probability Ratings of Americans and Israelis in Prediction and Post-Mental-Illness Conditions for the "Failure" Outcome**

	PRE	POST
Israelis	4.129	3.776
Americans	4.517	4.724

diction" of Americans and Israelis in the PR (prediction) and PM (presently mental patient) condition regarding the mental-illness outcome (see Table 5–1).

An analysis of variance shows that a main effect for the pre-post factor was not found: $F(1,270) = 2.17$, not significant ("ns").[2] Overall differences between Americans and Israelis are significant, as predicted for this (mental illness) outcome: $F(1,269) = 12.82$, $p < .001$. While among Israelis there is a drop in probability ratings from the pre- to the post-condition, and among Americans there is a rise from the pre- to the post-condition (see Table 5–1), this interaction, though in the expected direction, is not significant: $F (1,268) = 1.37$, ns.

Since, in indicative perception, subjects were also asked to rate the probability of the alternative event (which did not occur), let us now consider the probability of Carl's now being a businessman for the PM (present-mental-illness) group. We predicted that probability would go down from the pre- to the post-condition, particularly among Americans (see Table 5–2).

An analysis of variance indicates that Americans record significantly higher probabilities than Israelis: $F (1,269) = 5.75$, $p < .25$, for the businessman outcome. As expected, there is a significant drop from the pre- to post-condition in

[2] Because of the unequal Ns a regression solution was used. The changing degrees of freedom are due to the stepwise testing of effects, which were tested in the order reported. There were 259 subjects involved in the prediction and PB comparison, and 270 subjects in the prediction and PM comparison, as unfortunately slightly more PM questionnaires were administered than PR or PB questionnaires.

Table 5.2. **Mean Probability Ratings of Americans and Israelis in Prediction and Post-Mental-Illness Conditions for the "Success" Outcome**

	Pre	Post
Israelis	4.713	4.290
Americans	5.103	4.812

estimates of the probability of the event that did not occur: $F(1,270) = 5.23$, $p < .025$. The expected interaction is not found, however: $F(1,268)$, ns.

Let us now consider the pre and post effects for the PR and PB group (presently successful businessman) regarding the businessman outcome (see Table 5–3).

Results of the analysis of variance again reveal that Americans record significantly higher probabilities than Israelis: $F(1,275) = 7.26$, $p < .01$. The main effect for the pre-post factor was not significant: $F(1,258)$, ns. Examining Table 5–3, we may note also that while for Israelis there is a drop from the pre- to post-condition and for Americans there is an increase from the pre- to post-condition, this interaction, while in the expected direction, is not significant: $F(1,256)$, ns.

Finally, we shall examine whether there is the predicted drop from the pre- to post-condition in regard to the event that did not happen (here, being mentally ill) and whether this effect is greater for the American sample (see Table 5–4).

Analysis of variance again shows that, for the PB group, the probabilities of the event that did not occur—i.e., mental

Table 5.3. **Mean Probability Ratings of Americans and Israelis in Prediction and Post-Business Conditions for the "Success" Outcome**

	Pre	Post
Israelis	4.713	4.653
Americans	5.103	5.310

TABLE 5.4. **Mean Probability Ratings of Americans and Israelis in Prediction and Post-Business Conditions for the "Failure" Outcome**

	PRE	POST
Israelis	4.129	3.337
Americans	4.517	3.862

illness—dropped significantly, as predicted, from the pre- to post-condition: $F (1,258) = 17.31$, $p < .001$. Again, differences between Americans and Israelis are significant: $F (1,257) = 5.20$, $p < .025$, but the expected interaction is not found, $F (1,256)$, ns.

DISCUSSION

Using the Protestant Ethic scale, this study found that Americans endorse the values of the Protestant Ethic to a greater extent than Israelis, which provides more specific support to the hypothesized greater impact of Calvinism on Americans than on Israelis. Differences between Israelis and Americans on the Protestant Ethic scale, however, were not very great, which may mean that the Protestant Ethic has become a more generalized secular Western norm (Israel seems highly affected by Western and American norms) or, alternatively, that the scale is not sufficiently refined to catch the existing differences.

Comparing American subjects with Israeli subjects, we find, as predicted, that Westerners are consistently more deterministic than non-Westerners in perceiving present success or failure from general indications in one's past history, insofar as they assigned higher probabilities to all outcomes in all information sets. Differences of this type between English and Hebrew speakers have also been noted in event perception (Fischoff, 1974). It was also suggested that Westerners may be particularly more deterministic in regard to the failure category than non-Westerners, since, according to the doctrine of predestination, most people are presumably damned. Americans, however, were found to exceed Israelis in their determinism to the same extent for the success category as for the failure category. Although a variety of cross-cultural variables might plausibly be useful to explain such differences between Americans and Israelis, those findings may suggest that interpretations of Calvinism in contemporary America, while predestinal in nature, assign equal opportunity for success ("grace") and failure ("damnation"), at least when the suitable concrete signs are provided, as I have suggested. Thus, both election and damnation are seen as predetermined and probable.

The study also showed that Fischoff's findings concerning the retrospective reduction in probability for the event that did not occur (in event perception) can be successfully replicated in the case of person perception, since probabilities for the outcomes that did not happen dropped significantly from pre- to post-conditions in both the PM and PB groups. On the other hand, although results in relation to the event that did take place were in the expected direction, there was no overall rise in retrospective probabilities, as was found by Fischoff in event perception. It is possible that instructing subjects to rate indicative probabilities after asking them to *ignore* the given information about the present state (mental illness or businessman) created some cognitive confusions, which were reflected in the result. In a subsequent study in which interpersonal perception was assessed without requesting subjects to ignore the present state, differences in retrospective probabilities were also found as expected in relation to the event that did take place. Thus the attempt to apply the probability model used successfully by Fischoff to study event perception may require some simplified modifications in the case of person perception.

In conclusion, the study showed that Americans (i.e., Protestants or Westerners) score higher than Israelis (i.e., non-Protestants or non-Westerners) in Protestant Ethic endorsement and are consistently more deterministic in their perception of people's future. As this was the first time Protestantism was involved as a predictor for retrospective-indicative person perceptions, this study may provide important guidelines for future research. Since the Protestant Ethic may have become a more generalized Western normative value orientation, more conclusive results might be obtained regarding the effects of Calvinism when Western societies are compared to technically advanced countries that are relatively uninfluenced by Western mores and lacking an indigenous predestinal orientation, such as Japan. Most important, while the Protestant Ethic scale has been used successfully to discriminate between various ethnic groups and in predicting, for example, attitudes toward salvation and poverty (MacDonald, 1972), attempts should also be made to develop a more adequate "Calvinism" scale that will not account merely for the Protestant work ethos (which seemed to be the main focus of Mirels and Garrett's scale) but also for other norms and behavioral referents attributable to the Protestant Ethic. Moreover, since in the present study the Israeli sample was not subdivided according to Eastern and Western ethnic origin (simply because the attempt to divide Israeli students into ethnic subgroups failed), the impact of the Protestant secularized value orientation as a relative generalized Western norm seemed to be strongly manifested in this study, as differences between American and Israeli (nondifferentiated) samples were after all as expected.

In summary, the study presented above showed how a probability model designed to study event perceptions was modified and applied to investigate indicative social labeling in terms of retrospective interpersonal perception among American and Israeli students. I shall now turn to describe a simpler research design that was specially constructed to assess self-labeling among mental patients.

Indicative Self-labeling: Mental Patients [3]

To explore how self-labeling originates and operates differentially, we began by operationalizing and comparing two major self-labeling systems: "transmutive labeling," presumably characterizing mostly Eastern societies, and "indicative labeling," presumably characterizing Western society. Thus, we generally hypothesized that while the label "schizophrenic," for example, might be perceived by mental patients of European descent as an "indication" of an innate irreversible state, this same label might be perceived by mental patients of Eastern descent as an externally induced "scientific demon" that could be cured by renaming magic-alchemic processes (e.g. rediagnosing the patients as "uniphrenic"). Consonant with Goffman (1961), it was also generally hypothesized that differences in self-labeling between Eastern and European mental patients would be more pronounced during the early stages of hospitalization and that extended hospitalization can be seen as a Westernization process, as a result of which "indicative labeling" would be the predominant pattern of self-labeling.

SUBJECTS AND SAMPLING

Subjects for our illustrative-exploratory study were forty adult mental patients, all diagnosed as schizophrenics, who were selected according to simple stratified random-sampling procedures from three mental hospitals in Israel. Out of the total sample, twenty subjects were males and twenty were females; twenty-four were old-time patients (over four years in hospital) and sixteen were new patients (three weeks to one year in hospital); twenty were of European descent and

---

[3] I am very grateful to my student Gera Shechter for collecting the empirical data reported here.

twenty of Eastern (Middle Eastern and North African) descent. All twenty Eastern subjects had no more than eight years of schooling, and all of the European subjects had at least nine years of schooling. (Since education in Israel is a major component of Westernization, we controlled for educational level to avoid the possible effect of an intervening variable.) The age of the subjects ranged from 17.5 to 58. The mean age of the new patients was 24.5 and the mean age of the old patients was 33.5. While old-time patients were allowed short furloughs (if they had somewhere to go), new patients were restricted to hospital quarters. European and Eastern samples were subdivided so that approximately half of each group were old patients and half were new.

METHODS AND PROCEDURE

To explore general differences in self-labeling among mental patients, "indicative self-labeling" was operationally defined on the basis of five variables: (1) whether the patient perceived himself as sick; (2) whether he perceived his disease to be innate and having originated within himself; (3) whether he perceived his state to be incurable; (4) whether he did not believe in magic-alchemic recovery procedures; and (5) whether he felt rejected by his social environment. Conversely, "transmutive self-labeling" was operationally defined on the basis of the same five criteria: (1) when the patient described himself as healthy; (2) when he perceived his state as being externally induced; (3) when he felt that his condition was reversible; (4) when he believed in magic-alchemic recovery procedures; and (5) when he felt accepted by his significant others and his social environment.

After extensive pretesting, a structured interview for eliciting open responses along the lines of the above five criteria was constructed. Based on the information obtained from the interview, these five criteria were used as dependent variables, while ethnic origin and time spent in hospital were used as independent variables.

Because of the exploratory nature of the open-ended answers, responses were divided into only two categories.

TABLE 5.5. **Mental Patients' Self-labeling**

		INDICATIVE	TRANSMUTIVE
A.	Perception of situation:	Sick	Not sick
	Examples of answers:	I have a nerve disease; I am depressed and sick.	I was brought here for no good reason; I am okay.
B.	Perception of problem origin:	Innate	External
	Examples of answers:	My disease grew inside me; I was born so.	Snakes picked on me; supernatural powers punished me.
C.	Perception of curability:	Hopeless	Hopeful
	Examples of answers:	I cannot be cured; no chance after twenty years.	I can get better. Of course, I can change.
D.	Belief in alchemic recovery:	Disbelief	Belief
	Examples of answers:	I don't believe in this nonsense; I believe in scientific medicine.	I was given an amulet and it helped. Smelling a black dog helps.
E.	Perception of societal reactions:	Rejection	Acceptance
	Examples of answers:	I was degraded, friends consider me crazy; no visits.	My family treats me nicely; my friends are nice to me.

Thus, answers corresponding to the five dependent variables were dichotomized as shown in Table 5–5.

The independent variables were also dichotomized:

A. ethnic origin
   1. Western—subject or both parents born in Europe or United States
   2. Eastern—subject or both parents born in Asia or Africa
B. time in hospital
   1. long—four years or more
   2. short—three weeks to one year

To control for the possibility that answers might be affected by drug consumption (given at different hours of the day) or the presence of other people, all interviews were conducted during the morning hours in an isolated room with no one present but the interviewer and the subject.

Subjects were told that the interviewer was engaged in a research project and was interested in their opinions and beliefs concerning various subjects related to human nature, the hospital, and mental illness, and that, naturally, participation in the interview was voluntary.

RESULTS

To determine differences between the two independent samples with respect to the five dependent variables, an X^2 analysis was employed when $N \geqslant 20$, and the Fisher exact-probability test was used when $N \leqslant 20$—i.e., when subgroups were compared.

Since our general hypothesis was that the differences between the Eastern and Western samples in relation to the dependent variables will be significant only during the early stage of hospitalization, the following testing procedure was employed. In relation to each dependent variable, a Fisher test was first used to compare new Eastern patients with old

Eastern patients and new Western patients with old Western patients. Then an X^2 test was made to compare all "new patients" with all "old patients," regardless of ethnic origin.

PERCEPTION OF SITUATION

In response to questions asking patients to describe themselves as sick or healthy, only two out of eight Eastern new patients perceived themselves as sick, whereas ten out of twelve Eastern old patients described themselves as sick (according to the Fisher test, $p \leqslant .025$, one-tailed). Among Westerners, five out of eight new patients and eleven out of twelve old patients described themselves as sick (according to the Fisher test, $p > .05$, one-tailed). Thus, while among Easterners significantly more new patients described themselves as healthy as compared to old Eastern patients, among Westerners most described themselves as sick, and no significant difference was found between old and new patients.

Upon performing an X^2 test on all patients ($N = 40$), significantly more old patients (21 out of 24) than new patients (7 out of 16) were found to perceive themselves as sick ($X^2 = 6.9$, df $= 1$, $p \leqslant .005$, one-tailed.)

PERCEPTION OF PROBLEM ORIGIN

While seven out of eight new Eastern patients felt that their problems were externally induced, only three out of eleven Eastern old patients felt so. (According to the Fisher test, $p \leqslant .025$, one-tailed; $N = 19$. Note that whenever $N < 20$ in the subgroups, answers were either not received or disqualified.) Among Westerners ($N = 17$), however, eight out of twelve old patients and three out of four new patients felt that their problem was innate (Fisher test $p > .05$, one-tailed.) Thus, while among Easterners significantly more new patients than old patients attributed their problem to an external cause, among Westerners most felt the problem to be innate, and no significant differences between old and new patients were found. Upon performing an X^2 test on all patients ($N = 36$), significantly more old patients (16 out of 21) than new patients (4 out of 15) perceived their problem as innate ($X^2 = 7$, df $= 1$, $p \leqslant .005$, one-tailed.)

PERCEPTION OF CURABILITY

Among Eastern patients ($N = 19$), eight out of eleven old patients did not believe in their chances to be cured, but all eight Eastern new patients believed that they could be cured (according to the Fisher test, $p \leqslant .005$, one-tailed.) Similarly, among Westerners ($N = 18$), six out of eleven old patients did not believe in curability, while all seven new patients believed in their chances of being cured (Fisher test, $p \leqslant .025$, one-tailed.) Thus, all new patients, regardless of ethnic origin, believed significantly more than old patients in their chances to be cured. The X^2 test on all patients ($N = 37$) confirmed the above ($X^2 = 12.7$, df $= 1$, $p \leqslant .005$, one-tailed.)

BELIEF IN ALCHEMIC RECOVERY PROCEDURES

Interestingly, while among Easterners ($N = 17$), eight out of nine old patients believed in alchemic recovery procedures, only one out of eight new patients believed in magic curative methods. (According to the Fisher test, $p \leqslant .005$, one-tailed.) Nevertheless, among Westerners ($N = 20$), only one out of eight new patients believed in magic treatment, and none of the twelve old patients believed in the effectiveness of such methods (Fisher test, $p > .05$, one-tailed). Thus, old Eastern patients believed significantly more than new Eastern patients and all Western patients in magic recovery procedures. An X^2 test on all patients ($N = 37$) indicated that there were no significant differences between old and new patients in their belief in alchemic treatment ($X^2 = 1.7$, df $= 1$, p $> .05$).

PERCEPTION OF SOCIETAL REACTION

Five out of nine Eastern old patients ($N = 20$) felt accepted by their social environment, as did nine out of eleven new Eastern patients (according to the Fisher test, p $> .05$, one-tailed). Among Western patients ($N = 20$), only one out of seven new patients felt rejected, but ten out of thirteen old patients felt rejected by their significant others (Fisher test p $\leqslant .025$, one-tailed). An X^2 test on all patients ($N = 40$) indicated that all old patients (14 out of 22) felt significantly more rejected than did new patients (3 out of 18) ($X^2 = 7.12$, df $= 1$, p $\leqslant .005$, one-tailed).

DISCUSSION

Although no conclusive evidence can be drawn from our small-scale exploratory study, which was intended to illustrate the theory presented, interesting results in the expected direction were obtained. The general hypothesis of the present study was that Western mental patients will perceive their situation in terms of "indicative labeling" and that Eastern mental patients will perceive their condition in terms of "transmutive labeling." It was also hypothesized that extended hospitalization will enhance Westernization and hence will result in increased indicative labeling (referring mainly to Eastern patients). Thus, operational referents of Westernization in terms of "indicative labeling" were: perception of self as sick, perception of sickness as innate, feeling of rejection, disbelief in chances for recovery, and disbelief in magical curative methods.

It was found that the new Western patient perceived himself as sick and his sickness as innate. He did not believe in magical recovery methods, but he did believe in his chances to be cured, and he still felt accepted by his significant others. While the first three variables can be interpreted in Western indicative terms, there seems to be a slight contradiction between perception of the schizophrenic state as innate and belief in curability. One possible speculative explanation for this reality might be that, in contrast to straightforward medieval witch-hunting of the mentally disturbed (Szasz, 1970), the contemporary medical model has a built-in "scientific disguise" that fosters the "release binge fantasy" (Goffman, 1961), which misleads the patient and his accepting significant others, at least during the early phase of hospitalization, into believing that he is curable and that he was "temporarily" hospitalized "only for his own good." On the other hand, the belief in curability might simply reflect the typical reluctance of any new patient to accept his irreversible condition. Similarly, the expression of acceptance by concerned others might reflect merely their need to relieve guilt feelings.

Nonetheless, the old Western patient was found to perceive himself as sick, incurable, and rejected (all old Western patients were unmarried while all married old Eastern patients remained married). He did not believe in alchemic recovery procedures, and he believed his disease to be innate, i.e., the longer he stayed in the hospital, the more he conformed to Western "indicative self-labeling."

The new Eastern patient described himself as healthy and accepted, believed in his chances to be cured, attributed his "temporary" problem to external causes, but did not believe in, nor was he familiar with, alchemic curative methods.

The old Eastern patient labeled himself as sick, believed that his disease originated within himself and that he could not be cured, but felt accepted and, surprisingly, also believed in the effectiveness of alchemic curative methods that were performed on him or others. Thus, while for three variables one can notice the Westernizing impact on old Eastern patients toward increased indicative self-labeling, the belief of the old Eastern patient in magical recovery methods—in contrast to the disbelief of the Eastern new patient in such procedures—is puzzlingly unexpected.

This contradiction can be reconciled as follows: Since Israel is predominantly a Western country and alchemic curative methods are illegal, the new and usually young patient might not have had a chance to become familiar with such practices. He learned, however, during early socialization, to perceive problems as being externally induced. As time of hospitalization was extended, he became increasingly exposed to two conflicting socialization systems: the Western system dominating the hospital and the Eastern system activated by his accepting ethnic group during furloughs. There is ample evidence showing how Eastern ethnic groups not only accept their mentally disturbed members but also use various magic faith-healing procedures, which are geared to reintegrate the deviant into his social group. For example, during our field work in Yemenite villages, we met an ex-mental patient who became a professional "book-opener" in his village—i.e., a holy man who is familiar with various magic curative methods such as name-manipulation techniques through "opening holy books" [4] to read selected, individually suited verses in the scriptures. This man was highly respected among the villagers, who utilized his services quite frequently. In another case (recorded by Dr. A. Menkes), the reaction of neighbors and the husband of a mother of six children who, during periodic "psychotic" outbursts, would attack people and steal was one of pity and tolerance (e.g. recovering stolen goods in the evening). In general, the scene of family and friends gathering in groups to listen and sympathize with "deviant" people who dramatically describe their fears or hallucinations seemed quite usual.

[4] According to an experienced Israeli anthropologist, such "curative" name-manipulation techniques are as common among Eastern Jews and Arabs as drinking tea upon catching a cold among Westerners.

While this is common practice during furloughs, the conflicting socialization pressures on the old Eastern patient seem to cause great confusion within him, which is apparently reflected in his feeling that his sickness is innate and irreversible, on the one hand, but that he is accepted by his group and that their magic methods can cure him, on the other.

When samples were combined, our findings indicated that all old patients, regardless of ethnic origin, differed significantly from new patients in that they described themselves as sick, they felt rejected, they believed their sickness was innate and irreversible, and they did not believe in magic recovery chances. Thus, indicative labeling appears to be the predominant self-labeling pattern after extended hospitalization. This suggests that a process of "transformative labeling" operates in the hospital, which delabels people who consider themselves "healthy" and relabels them as born "sick."

Considering our small sample and the fact that subjects were Eastern and Western Jews living in Israel, not Protestants living in the West, compared with subjects living in Eastern countries, these preliminary findings seem to provide some illustrative evidence concerning the nature and operation of differential self-labeling and raise serious questions about hospitalization effects when labeling is studied from the actor's perspective, especially in relation to patients of Eastern descent.

Conclusion

Preliminary evidence of differential self-labeling among new and older Eastern and Western mental patients in Israel was presented. Results indicated generally that while "transmutive self-labeling" was characteristic of Eastern patients and "indicative self-labeling" was generally characteristic of

Western patients, as time of hospitalization increased, "indicative labeling" became the predominant pattern of most patients, regardless of ethnic origin.

Having presented two illustrative research designs of indicative labeling, which I propose as the most typical labeling context characterizing Western societies, in the next chapter I shall attempt to develop an integrative "action-reaction" model of deviance that entails more optimistic components for an effective change model than are present in either the old structural-action perspective or the new labeling-reaction approach to deviance.

Chapter Six

"Contingent Being" and the "Action-Reaction" Convergence Model

Our existential problem is not: "to be or not to be?" but being appreciated by others and appreciating our own being!

(M. R.)

Theorists attempting to explain deviance have been fluctuating between two polar positions and confining their analysis to social actions or social reactions. So far, I have concentrated on the more recent social-reaction perspective, which, I have argued, explains the genesis of deviance in social-deterministic terms because labeling theorists have generally ignored the self-deterministic aspects involved in self-labeling. One could now go into a lengthy discussion to show how the "Protestant bias" likewise limited the explanatory scope of Merton's (1957) older structural-functional (action) theory of deviance and anomie and of Cohen's (1955) theory of deviant subcultures. Merton, who attributes deviance to gaps between means and Protestant success goals, cannot actually explain whether the "successful innovator" is deviant or not, since in the Protestant Western scheme the end justifies the means, and successful crime is "an American way of life" (see Bell, 1962); and Cohen cannot explain whether the nonutilitarian, vandalistic deviant subculture is a *reaction formation* of the outcasts against unachievable Protestant success goals or a *formation* of successful actors who excommunicate those who prove themselves to be damned-failures by their nonutilitarian, unsuccessful behavior.

However, instead of going into an elaborate critical discussion to show how these theories are of limited use from a non-Western perspective, I shall attempt to present a constructive model that integrates labeling-reaction theory with structural-action or role-opportunity perspectives. The rationale for presenting the integrated model begins with the following analysis of existing theories of deviance.

Unlike Merton, whose anomie theory attributes deviance only to one's differential access to legitimate success-goals, Sutherland and Cressey (1955) and, particularly, Cloward and Ohlin (1960), explain delinquency as a function of the relative availability of legitimate and *illegitimate* opportunities or associations. It follows that availability of differential opportunities begins from a neutral baseline. However, this position fails to explain, for example, what happens to a person whose legitimate opportunities are replaced by illegitimate opportunities or vice versa. We do not know what happens to the person at the "crossroad." Does deviance depend simply on the opening or closing of opportunities; or does the degradation, mortification, or negative labeling that are often involved in closing off one's opportunities imply a more complex process—one that cannot be reversed merely by reopening opportunities? It seems that these theoretical perspectives on deviance fail to account for basic psychological aspects involved in the process of negative labeling and identity stripping that follow from the closing off of opportunities and upon which the nature of new, secondary opportunities is contingent.

The model presented here attempts to account for the contingent relationship between basic identity problems and secondary opportunities. It begins with the concept of "contingent beings."

The term "being" is a verb and a noun. The verb "to be" means to exist, and the noun "being" refers to the sum total of components constituting a person. In a sense, the verb "being" connotes existence from the actor's perspective, and the noun "being" connotes existence from the other's (or others') perspective. "Being" thus includes the subjective and objective aspects of identity: the way one is "being" identified by others and the way he identifies his own "being." It means one's total existential experiences, which constitute an individual's social identity and self-identity. These experiences include needs, role opportunities, and interactions with others in terms of valuations, labeling, and other relationships as he and others see them. The model of "contingent beings" assumes that (1) there are two basic levels of existential or experiential beings—a primary and secondary level—and (2) the secondary state of "being" is contingent on the primary one.

The concept of "contingent being" can be operationally subdivided into several primary-secondary dimensions, which are expanded derivations of existing theories. These derivations include two major dimensions, one pertaining to actions and the other to reactions:

1. primary and secondary roles (actions)
2. primary and secondary labels (reactions)

They also contain two subdimensions—again, one of actions and the other of reactions:

3. primary and secondary others (reactions)
4. primary and secondary involvements (actions)

Primary and Secondary Roles

Let us begin with Linton's (1945) much-cited simplistic distinction between ascribed roles (e.g. age, sex, kinship) and achieved roles (e.g. social position acquired by skill and merit). Since ascribed roles, which relate to the undifferentiated role "person," form man's basic personality structure, Linton's simple dichotomy makes it difficult to classify some achieved roles that carry a heavy freight of personality features. For example, the achieved role of educator is more imbued with undifferentiated, ascribed-personality components than the achieved role of mathematician. Conversely, the role "Casanova" carries achieved components, although it is an ascribed sex-role.

Moreover, since role is a relational concept, any role definition must encompass both the role and its reciprocal. Characteristic of the ascribed roles of person, age, and kinship are primary face-to-face relations in which other's valuations are declared undifferentially to the total personality, while valuations of achieved roles are presumably more differentiated and related to specific skill behavior. But here again, other's valuations of an eductor are applied more on the basis of his general personality and his empathic primary interpersonal abilities than valuations of the "crazy mathematician" are, although both are achieved roles. Since "ascribed" roles are basic, it would seem that all other roles should be seen as being *contingent* on the basic role person, whether these are characterized by achieved or ascribed features. In this sense, it is "basic" that one be a person (i.e., a "mensch" or a "human being") first and only thereafter a carpenter or a doctor. The terms *primary roles* and *secondary roles* are therefore introduced to substitute for Linton's ascribed and achieved role conceptions (Rotenberg and Sarbin, 1971).

Primary and Secondary Labeling

While roles are engendered by actions, social labels arise from reactions. Very closely related to primary and secondary roles is a problem neglected by labeling theorists (see Chapter 4). It pertains to the compatibility between established identity labels and subsequent social labeling. The difference is between adjectives and nouns. The descriptive label "schlemiel," denoting the perennial "loser" or "fall guy," may be assigned to anybody as an adjective if his established identity label is not that of a successful "striver" or "winner." It would be useful, therefore, to expand our conceptual scheme and distinguish between *primary labels* and *secondary labels.*

As briefly mentioned in Chapter 4, a primary (categoric) label refers to one's established social self-identity and is related to position, rank, and class. It categorically classifies the individual, in his own eyes and in the eyes of others, as a "success" or a "failure," as "in" or "out," "good" or "bad." A primary label is not synonymous with a primary role, since it is not related to any specific role but rather to the dominant features attributed to a person in the ongoing process of stereotyping or social typing. A secondary label refers simply to a new or additional label to be assigned to a person. It may be descriptive or categoric, positive or negative. Secondary labels can "stick" from the actors' perspective only within the category. If one's primary label is that of an "intellectual," the added secondary label "intellectual bum" is still compatible with this primary label, although it is negative. But the secondary label "dumb" cannot stick unless the person is first delabeled as an intellectual. Here it might be noted that in some societies the label "unemployed," or even "schizophrenic," is not necessarily incompatible with the role of respected head of household. The rejecting categoric degradation of "laziness" (Davis, 1938) or of schizophrenia (Goffman, 1961) seems to be more characteristic of Western societies. If a secondary label is compatible with one's primary label, it may be incorporated into the self-identity if the labeler is of primary significance to the labelee. Thus, secondary labels are *contingent* on the nature of primary labels.

Primary and Secondary Others

The two observable subdimensions affecting and reflecting levels of being that have been used to assess self-identity are "others" and "involvement" (Rotenberg and Sarbin, 1971). Yet their use gives rise to questions. How significant must a "significant other" be in order to impact on an actor? The terms "significant" or "relevant" other have also been used in the literature without any attempt to differentiate empirically between degrees of significance needed to affect various actors. In contingency terms, the significance of valuations applied by A to B's secondary role performance (plumber) is *contingent* on the kind of valuations applied by A to B's primary role enactment and also on the level of B's acceptance of A's valuations. If B accepts A's definition of himself as a "male" or a "person" he is also likely to accept A's valuations of him as an educator. It is a matter of common observation that others may possess varying degrees of significance for an actor, ranging from zero to situationally significant other (e.g. a prison guard to prisoners) to highly significant others whose valuations are incorporated into self-identity. Those others whose valuative reactions are incorporated into the self-identity are termed *primary others.* Audiences who have power or prestige for the actor and whose reactions are situationally significant (e.g. prison guard) are not necessarily incorporated into the self-identity and are referred to as *secondary others* (*ibid.*).

Primary and Secondary Involvement

It has been demonstrated empirically that the degree of intensity in role-enactment, in terms of time spent or in terms of emotional and visceral participation, reflects as well as affects one's self-identity (Sarbin and Allen, 1968). Thus, even the best process of anticipatory socialization will have little meaning for self-identity if it is not validated by actual organismic role involvement, especially if one has been "stripped" of his established identity components—i.e., the claims concerning "Who I am" will become progressively empty if they are not supported by my enactment of what I claim to be. Involvement in a role may also range from zero, where role and self are presumed to be completely differentiated, to maximal, where role and self are presumably fused. Furthermore, involvement in role behavior or assigned labels may be voluntary or involuntary. In contingency terms, involvement in secondary roles or labels becomes meaningful to self-identity to the extent that it is compatible with primary-role involvement. If I have a chance to be properly involved in my sex and age roles, and I am valuated by my primary others as a "person" and a "male," the secondary role "educator" is meaningful. Similarly, involvement in the masculine role (e.g. Casanova) might be relatively high if masculinity is inadequately valued by others or one has had limited opportunities to enact the role previously, because the masculine role is a primary role. Conversely, if I enact the primary role of a "nonperson," the secondary role of "nosy troublemaker" or "psychotic" is compatible with that role. Moreover, from a cross-cultural perspective it may be assumed that, while in traditional societies one may be valuated mainly on the basis of one's primary involvements, in modern society valuations are based mainly on secondary involvements in achievement-oriented success tasks, since these retrospectively define the primary roles (damned or saved). Thus, for conceptual consistency, the term *primary involvement* will be used to refer to the nature (intensity, degree) of one's actual enactment of his primary roles and labels, and the term *secondary involvement* will be employed to refer to involvement in secondary roles or labels.

Prison Social Types and Contingent Being

To demonstrate how the model of contingent being may explain complex and functional patterns of deviations, we shall use the example of prison social types. Prison social types are labels associated with specific actions and reactions that prisoners assign to each other. Thus, the behavioral referents of each type must first be outlined briefly. The "right guy" refers to the idealized convict (Irwin, 1970) "who pulls his own number," who is loyal, honest, criminally oriented, and tough. The "inmate" is also a criminally oriented type, but one "who cannot be trusted," who is a "nosy troublemaker," and who "would sell his own mother." The "square" type refers to one who "doesn't know anything," who is unfamiliar with both the criminal and the prison system, and who is not criminally oriented. The "politician" is a "big shot," a "con-boss," highest in the prison hierarchy (Mitchell, 1966) and considered to be a smart inmate who can manipulate others and communicate with both administration and prisoners without endangering himself.

Reviewing the repertory of prison-labeled types, two major questions arise:

1. According to the functional perspective, prison social types evolve as a functional response to "pains of imprisonment" (Sykes and Messinger, 1960). This may explain the emergence of certain sexual (e.g. passive or active homosexual) or pedlar (e.g. trafficking illegally in food, cigarettes, etc.) roles, but it does not explain why the "right guy" became the idealized functional type in the first place, since this role undoubtedly inflicts pain on its incumbent and is less functional in many respects than rehabilitation-working roles, which are despised by "right guys" (only "suckers" work).

2. According to the opportunity perspective, to the extent

that illegitimate opportunities are closed off and legitimate opportunities opened up, criminal orientation should be reduced and conformity should prevail. In the prison, illegitimate opportunities are closed off and legitimate (rehabilitation) opportunities are formally opened up. Nonetheless, prisonization theories (Clemmer, 1958) claim that prisons are "crime schools" not only for committed deviants but also for incoming squares and that rehabilitation roles are basically irrelevant and ineffective in reducing criminal orientation (McCorkle and Korn, 1962).

The prison reality can be better explained in contingency terms. Since one's secondary being (e.g. rehabilitation roles) is contingent on the state of one's primary being, the functionality of social typing must be examined in the way it relates to the primary or the secondary levels of being.

By integrating the functional and the cultural-transmission perspectives to explain the prison culture, we may assume that on the outside the illegitimate primary being of "right guy" (Cloward and Ohlin's criminal type) was positive; that is, his primary involvement in age and sex roles (e.g. the pimp-lover, etc.) was positively valuated by criminal primary others. Contingent upon his "positive" primary being, his illegitimate secondary being (underworld professional activities) may also be positive. We may assume also that on the outside the square experienced a normal, legitimate primary and secondary being (e.g. normal sex and professional life). The inmate type (Cloward and Ohlin's retreatist) may have experienced a negative primary and secondary being on the outside; and the politician may have had a chance on the outside for both legitimate and illegitimate options for positive primary and secondary being (see Table 6–1).

Upon entering the prison, processes of identity stripping, degradation, and negative reactions are set in operation, largely mortifying the primary being of all prisoners; i.e., prisoners are denied the opportunity to enact age, sex, and

TABLE 6.1.

PRISONERS' STATES OF BEING ON THE OUTSIDE (BEFORE ENTRY INTO PRISON)	POTENTIAL INSIDE LABELS			
	Square	*Right Guy*	*Inmate*	*Politician*
Legitimate primary being	+	−	−	+
Illegitimate primary being	−	+	−	+
Legitimate secondary being	+	−	−	+
Illegitimate secondary being	−	+	−	+

+ Opportunity to enact the given role.
− No opportunity to enact the given role.

kinship roles. Thus, secondary rehabilitative opportunities become irrelevant and meaningless as long as the problem of primary being is not solved. To solve the problem of primary being, the "incoming" prisoner must choose between two general options:

1. to accept the "nonperson" role and the degraded valuative-reactions assigned by prison guards and other prisoners
2. to enact a quasi-primary role for which he can receive some respect valuations from other prisoners and consequently also from some guards

The psychotic role and the inmate social type (e.g. "homo," "snitch") represent those who have chosen the first alternative. The idealized "right-guy" type represents those who have chosen the second option. Consequently, the "right guy" idealized behavior refers to a set of situationally functional role responses to deprivations on the primary level of being, which everybody strives to enact if he "can make it" (Glaser, 1964); and the "inmate" (distrusted type) behavior is an alternative response to the same problem by those who "cannot make it."

Thus, most criminally oriented prisoners will be preoccupied with trying to enact the quasi-right guy role, while secondary roles will be irrelevant for them. "Inmates" will enact prison-oriented quasi-secondary roles compatible with their negative primary being (e.g. stool pigeon, pedlar); "politicians" will enact quasi-illegitimate roles compatible with their quasi-primary "right guy" behavior (e.g. clerk, con-boss); and the "square" will be severely stressed, being unable to use secondary legitimate opportunities owing to his degraded primary being (see Table 6–2).

It should be noted that, while most prisoners seem to resolve their deprived states of primary being to some extent by enacting quasi-substitute roles ("squares" the least and "politicians" the most), secondary roles compatible with prison primary beings are functional for survival only inside the prison but are dysfunctional for extramural rehabilitative roles on the outside. Moreover, as a rule, not only are criteria for successful post-institutional adjustment defined exclusively in terms of secondary-occupational role behavior, but the *crisis* involved in reenacting normal primary sex roles as male, husband, father, etc., is virtually ignored.

In conclusion, complex levels of conduct can be understood only by assessing actions and reactions in terms of the contingent relationship between primary and secondary opportunities for being. Prison social types are used as a case in point, but the model should be applicable to other deviant or conforming types as well.

TABLE 6.2.

PRISONERS' STATES OF BEING ON THE INSIDE	ROLE OPPORTUNITIES ON INSIDE			
	Square	Right Guy	Inmate	Politician
Legitimate primary being	—	—	—	—
Illegitimate primary being	—	∓	∓	∓
Legitimate secondary being	—	—	—	∓
Illegitimate secondary being	—	—	∓	∓

∓ Pseudo-substitute role.
— No opportunity to enact the given role.

Assessment of Social-Self Type Congruity

Assuming that the mortification or stripping process of the incoming inmate's primary being is gradual and dependent on the degree of involvement and relationship with outside referent others (e.g. wife, gang), we could now assess the degree of social-self-typing congruity at any point in time by observing involvements and others—the two subdimensions presumably affecting and reflecting states of being.

Indeed, Rotenberg and Sarbin (1971) found that, when prisoners were asked to role-play the "right guy" type, their average involvement in that role was highest when the audience present during the enactment comprised other prisoners (mostly "right guys"), as compared to prisoners' involvement in that role in front of other audiences (e.g. students). Similarly, the average involvement of prisoners in a "square" role was comparatively highest when the audience comprised outside square people.

In another study (Rotenberg, 1975), it was found that, when newly admitted patients in a mental institution were motivated to role-play a "normal" role (clerk investigating patients' complaints), their average involvement in that role was higher when the audience comprised staff, as compared to involvement in that role in front of other patients. On the other hand, patients' involvement in the "abnormal" role (a patient disobeying a nagging nurse) was highest when only other patients were present.

Since the subjects in these studies were unaware of the specific effects that changing audiences (others) were expected to have on their spontaneous involvement in social-type behavior, this perspective provides guidelines for assessing states of being. Thus, by observing (1) intensity of role involvement in the presence of various others and (2) the degree of interaction with various inside and outside others (e.g. contacts, letters, visits), social-self type congruity could be assessed. Moreover, assuming that "involvement" and "others" may affect states of being, contingently structured directed involvement in selecting roles with selective others may have important implications for rehabilitation and change. This leads to a discussion of treatment strategies emanating from the model of "contingent beings." First, however, the conceptual relationship between the labeling (reaction) and opportunity (action) perspectives must be viewed in the framework of the contingent-being theory.

Interrelationships Between the Labeling and Opportunity Perspectives

As noted earlier, the differential-opportunity perspective, in Merton's and Cloward's terms, refers to secondary roles. Essentially, no assumptions are made regarding possible differences between people who had no legitimate secondary opportunities and people who were negatively labeled as a result of, or in addition to, lack of access to such opportunities. It follows that future conformity or deviance (i.e., possibilities for rehabilitation) will depend on the availability of legitimate and illegitimate secondary opportunities, regardless of any concomitant variations on one's primary state of being and regardless of whether the actor's conduct was hitherto deviant or conforming.

Moreover, in a contingency framework, if one did enact legitimate or illegitimate secondary roles, this should be *prima facie* proof that these roles are congruent with one's self-identity. If they were incompatible with the subject's primary role opportunities, he should have encountered difficulties in his secondary state of being. This approach presents a simplistic world in which man (i.e., primary being) is not problematic; hence, criminal or noncriminal *normal* socialization establishes one's primary being, on which a legitimate or illegitimate secondary state of being can be structured. Thus, aside from Merton's and Cloward's vague reference to "retreatists," no variations on the primary level are considered.

Nevertheless, assumptions concerning source, level, and intensity of deviance must be implicit in any theory of deviance. That is, implicit in theories of human conduct are usually propositions or axioms regarding human nature that trace the etiology of deviance to man's good or evil nature, to his upbringing, or to the unique social structure of which he is a part. Consequently, questions regarding level and reversibility of deviance can be answered. In other words, the structural-opportunity perspective either assumes that there is no need to change man, since he is essentially good (Durkheim, 1974) and, therefore deviance should be attributed to gaps between means and goals in the social structure; or it assumes that man's primary being cannot be changed and hence the only thing left is to try to change his secondary opportunities. In either case, the question remains whether and how one can change the primary beings of individuals who have been socialized as criminals (Cloward and Ohlin, 1960) cast as sinners (Mowrer, 1964) or otherwise mortified (Goffman, 1961).

From the labeling perspective, it is theoretically possible that a derogatory label may be assigned to one's secondary being (A is a plagiarist), or to one's primary being (B is impotent). As indicated earlier, if a label is descriptive of certain behavior, negative labeling is essentially reversible once behavior changes. Nonetheless, labeling analysts usually insist that derogatory labeling transforms people irreversibly into the entity that the label connotes (see Chapter 4). Thus, the stripping-labeling proposition refers to a mortification process of primary beings but disregards the dynamics of variations on the secondary level.

The irreversible-labeling perspective also assumes that, once degraded and mortified, primary beings cannot usually be reconstructed—otherwise why attribute irrevocable power to the act of negative labeling? This suggests that social labeling and self-labeling can be effective only in social contexts such as certain Western societies, where, because of a belief in the doctrine of predestination, it may be assumed that derogatory labeling retrospectively classifies people into the primary "damned" category, where they belonged *a priori*. It follows that deviance can be controlled not by changing the criminally socialized individual but rather by abolishing some rules and sanctions (Becker, 1963). Therefore, the antilabeling movement actually calls for expansion of the Hobbesian social contract to include some of the Wolves and Sinners in the society of "insiders," because they cannot change. Nevertheless, this social contract can obviously be expanded to include only marginal and basically harmless deviants, not murderers or rapists.

In conclusion, then, there are no implied assumptions in the labeling and opportunity perspectives concerning the repentance of Wolves, Sinners, and criminals or the rehabilitation of degraded primary beings. Hence both perspectives advocate redemption of the "damned" through changes in the social structure, either by minimizing social gaps or by minimizing social sanctions. This is not the case for the model of contingent beings, which assumes that man is neither essentially good nor essentially damned but rather that his primary being can be reconverted via the same variables of involvement (actions) and others (reactions).

Constructive Labeling: A Perspective for Treatment

The studies cited earlier demonstrated how experimentally manipulated audiences increased inmates' role involvement in predicted directions. Other studies have also shown how spontaneous role enactment and intensive involvement changed the subjects' self-conception (Mann, 1956). Thus, by utilizing directed involvements and selective others, a "transformative-labeling" model can be constructed for changing people in total institutions, for example.

By involvement, I am referring to involvement in activities and interactions with other people. Furthermore, involvement implies the notion that, while one is involved in any single activity or with some people, he is relatively uninvolved in other activities or with other people. Thus, meaningful involvements capable of affecting self-identities are necessarily particularistic and differentiated rather than diffuse. However, careful examination of resocialization frameworks in most total institutions reveals that: (1) Very little effort is usually made to separate various social types or to control interactions and undesired mutual involvements of various types (Clemmer, 1958; Goffman, 1961; Sutherland and Cressey, 1955); (2) in most total institutions, opportunities for involvements in rehabilitative legitimate activities are limited to irrelevant, nonconstructive, secondary roles and inmates are otherwise generally "caged" and "available" for nonrehabilitative or illegitimate primary involvements in ritualized activities and ceremonies (Reimer, 1937); and (3) in most total institutions, primary others from the staff are usually *not* available because of the "social distance" (Sykes, 1956) maintained between inmates and staff to prevent affective attachment and staff manipulation by inmates. Unlimited primary others *are* usually available from the inmates' pool, especially from such nonconformist social types as the idealized "right guy" in the prison.

A "transformative relabeling" model, conceptualized in terms of the "contingent being" framework, would therefore require an operational strategy that brings about drastic changes on the primary level of being (i.e., a new sense of being and a new answer to "Who am I?"). That can be attained only through disinvolvement in the old primary label via differentially directed involvement in a new primary label and with new primary others.

As mentioned in Chapter 4, Sarbin and Adler (1970–71) identified specific operational phases common to most change systems, including (1) destruction of old identity; (2) influence of others; and (3) ritual involvement in a new identity. Indeed, socialization in early Christian groups (Mowrer, 1964), in contemporary Hassidic groups (Buber, 1958a), and in Messianic cults (Katcher and Katcher, 1967) are all marked by ritual processes in which the individual is totally and organismically involved to foster specific labeled identities. This involvement is accompanied by a tremendous sense of community or camaraderie ("others").

The point is that, in order to change a person in desirable directions, it is not sufficient to degrade him (Garfinkel, 1956) or destroy his primary being and then "cage or store" him, even if supportive therapy is offered simultaneously. This is so precisely because a passive status quo social structure enhances the inevitable "social distance" between the formal and the informal systems in the institution, which, in turn, prevents staff from becoming primary others for inmates. Moreover, it exposes the uninvolved, "available," and frustrated inmate to other inmates' directed involvement, which creates the idealized primary "right guy" types.

Such a conception of directed involvement to change contingent beings has been inadvertently applied with considerable success by Synanon groups (see Yablonsky, 1965). In these groups, resocialization is accomplished by first drastically forcing the newcomer to switch from the "right guy" primary being to enacting the dependent "child" primary role; only later, in a developmental sequence, is he helped to establish his compatible secondary being.

Thus, delabeling of a negative primary type must be followed by a complete process of desirable primary relabeling in a "Pygmalion" sense. This requires constant involvement in that label (e.g. by dancing, singing, meditation, working) and reinforcement by specially labeled others (e.g. gurus, coaches, "brothers") who become increasingly significant because of their functional-modeling power and support. Only after the new primary being is relatively established by positive relabeling (e.g. I am a monk, "hippie," or Hassid) do compatible secondary-rehabilitation roles become relevant and readily enacted.

The positive effect of "others" was noted in the behavior and attitudes of previously withdrawn and degraded patients following an experimental summer camp (Shaver and Scheibe, 1967) where students and chronic mental patients lived together. Furthermore, differentially directed involvements would mean that one or several *simulated* total-re-socialization-involvement systems operate simultaneously in one institution. It is known, for example, that potential spies are sometimes required to live in simulated enemy towns during their training period. In these micro-cities, the spies become totally involved in their enemy-role behavior by adopting the eating habits, manner of speech, and cultural idiosyncrasies of the enemy, thus assuring their successful disguise subsequently (see Cookridge, 1968; Hutton, 1961). (In this case, special disinvolvement processes will operate to prevent primary internalization of label.)

On the other hand, experience has shown that formerly institutionalized delinquents or ex-mental patients who were highly proficient in a secondary occupational role could not "make it on the outside" because of their incompetence in specific etiquette behavior related to adequate primary-role performance. Thus, in a total institution such as the prison or mental hospital, differential resocialization would require several "Pygmalion" relabeling units in which inmates become totally involved in a new primary being. This transformative relabeling process should include special identity, clothing, etiquette, hair style, and speech style. To compete with or avoid the emergence of a negative idealized primary other, the average "inmate" type will have to be separated from such social types as "right guys," and only specially trained "square" inmates and staff could be promoted as modeling primary others. Furthermore, as in the school for spies, such a unit must be structured so that the total environment provides constant negative and positive reinforcements to foster the new label, including food stores, simulated government facilities, banks, medical facilities, etc., as well as the possibility of living in family units. Another good example of a simulated anticipatory socialization setting is the *"Hachshara,"* used in Europe and the United States, where people learn how to live in a simulated kibbutz before emigrating to Israel.

It is difficult to believe that, while we understand how to involve children spontaneously in a totally simulated environment in summer camps, we seem unable to use this same type of creativity in the resocialization of individuals in institutions. We naively expect ex-convicts or ex-mental patients to be able to handle their affairs on their secondary level of being and to communicate competently with officials and others after years of neglect in such matters, not to mention the crisis involved in trying to reenact primary sex roles sometimes after years of abnormal sex life. Moreover, if the common denominator of people populating total institutions such as prisons and mental institutions is their initial difficulty in living in an open, democratic society, then it is amazing that in a leading democratic society such as the United States people are expected to behave democratically after years of living the parasitic-dependent life-style fostered in the most extremely authoritarian-structured institutions. Thus, prisons in the West symbolize "failures of democracy." Accordingly, it seems that we erect high walls around our total institutions not so much to hide the deviant, who embarrasses us, but rather to hide our own authoritarianism and inability to apply the democratic way of life equally to all members of society. In a simulated resocialization town,[1]

[1] In fact the old exile-banishment penal system was categorically rejected by criminologists such as Barnes and Teeters as "a ghastly failure" and "one of the most repulsive phases of human activity in

democracy and independence would be applied gradually and differentially.

From the "contingent being" perspective, it matters little whether the new label is that of a "gentleman," "pioneer," "Hassid," or "hippie," or whether the method used to establish the primary being is a therapeutic supportive method, as would be appropriate in the case of a depraved "inmate" type, or a transformative method (destruction and reconstruction), as would be suitable for the "right guy" type. If the principles of total involvement (actions) and reinforcing others (reactions) are constantly activated, it is to be expected that primary and secondary beings will be contingently established.

By integrating action and reaction perspectives on deviance, I have attempted to develop a correctional-change model that makes explicit assumptions about man's ability to change. In Chapter 7, which analyzes the impact of the "Protestant bias" on theories of alienation, the positivistic approach to man will be further developed by contrasting the Western Calvinist type of "alienating individualism" with the non-Western type of "reciprocal individualism." Again, some research findings will be presented to show how,

---

dealing with criminals," probably *only* because of "the cruelties connected with such a system" (1965:305). Eliminate the old-style *physical* cruelties and consider the *mental* cruelties and you may notice that, compared to contemporary modern prisons, (1) while in primitive society the deviant is told to leave and try his luck elsewhere if he can't comply with the local norms, in modern society he is "caged in" (and one might wonder which method is more democratic), and (2) in such prisoners' colonies as Australia and Czarist Siberia, prisoners were allowed to live with their families and eventually some warden-governors "transformed the penal settlements into a colony" (*ibid.*, p. 300) by founding banks, industries, and finally a full-fledged independent (though probably quite authoritarian) government system.

by differentiating between the egoistic and the collectivistic types of need achievement, only the former is related to Protestantism and feelings of alienation and loneliness.

Chapter Seven

"Alienating Individualism" and "Reciprocal Individualism"

> *"Reciprocal individualism"* means that while interacting people are different *from each other, they are never* indifferent *to each other.*
>
> *(M. R.)*

Many social scientists believe that after the Industrial Revolution alienation, anomie, and loneliness were the inevitable by-products of the complex modern organizations common to *all* industrial societies. Blauner, for example, states:

> Today, most social scientists would say that alienation is not a consequence of capitalism *per se* but of employment in the large-scale organization and impersonal bureaucracies that pervade all industrial societies [1964:3].

In this chapter I suggest that alienation, in terms of "separateness"[1] between people (Schacht, 1970), is rooted in the pattern of extreme individualism unique to most Western

---

[1] It should be noted here that few concepts have been subjected to as long a history of epistemological and empirical study by so many disciplines as the term "alienation." Beginning with traditional dis-

Protestant societies. I propose that loneliness is, in fact, the other side of "alienating individualism," which is embedded in the social consequences emanating from Calvinistic theology, whereas "reciprocal individualism," which seems to stem from non-Western cultures, might produce less alienating systems even within industrial societies.

To define terms at the outset: "Alienating individualism" refers generally to an individual's self-reliance or independence that is associated with antagonizing others or being separated from them. "Reciprocal individualism" refers generally to an individual's self-reliance or independence that is interrelated or harmonious with others. These two patterns of individualism are obviously ideal types, and it would probably be difficult to find "pure cases" of them in any society owing to the diffusion of Eastern and Western ethics across cultures. My endeavor here, however, is to identify the cultural roots of each pattern and then provide guidelines for assessing their differential social impacts.

The Roots of "Alienating Individualism"

The Calvinistic roots of individualism and loneliness, as reflected in typical Western life-styles, have been identified by many writers (Weber, 1930; Riesman, 1954; May, 1950;

---

cussions by Rousseau, Hegel, Marx (first and second theory), Weber, and Durkheim, students of alienation have used the term to denote man's estrangement from others, from himself, and from objects such as work, products, and nature. Thus, using alienation within different disciplines to refer to a variety of dissimilar relationships between man and his social and physical environment on an objective and subjective level, in collective and individual terms, on conscious and unconscious levels, and in volitional and nonvolitional frameworks, it is not surprising that many have not only questioned the utility of this concept but suggested discarding it (e.g. Israel, 1971). Since this chapter is not intended as a new manifesto on alienation, the concept will be used here more or less in Schacht's terms to refer to *separateness* between man and man.

Fromm, 1960; Mowrer, 1964; Lukes, 1973). Fromm has pointed out two behavioral patterns produced by Protestant individualism in most Anglo-Saxon countries—independence and autonomy—and a negative corollary of isolation and powerlessness.

Similarly, Weber noted, that, owing to the

> . . . complete elimination of salvation through the Church . . . the Calvinist's intercourse with his God was carried out in deep spiritual isolation [creating] a feeling of unprecedented inner loneliness of the single individual [and forming] the roots of that disillusioned and pessimistically inclined individualism which can even today be identified in the national character and the institutions of the people with a Puritan past [1930:104–107].

Very few attempts have been made, however, to explain the special relationships between individualism and loneliness. To understand the hypothesized relationship between these two phenomena, it is useful to establish three premises: (1) that patterns of disordered conduct or emotional disturbances may be understood as exaggerations of culturally *normal* modes of adaptation (see Draguns, 1974); (2) that individualism and loneliness may represent two points on a continuum of *separateness;* and consequently (3) that exaggerated individualism may lead to a more extreme point of the continuum—loneliness.

Employing these premises, it is possible to establish that *exaggerated* individualistic behavior patterns, possibly associated with increased loneliness, may be identified among Protestants and Westerners in general on four interrelated operational dimensions that are highly stressed in Western socialization systems: (1) the inculcation of independence and autonomy as major goals in Western socialization systems; (2) the competitive-egoistic nature of Westerners' need for achievement; (3) the use of independence and autonomy as major criteria of Western maturity and mental health—or, rather, the use of dependency as a criterion of mental disorder; and (4) the egocentric preoccupation with self in most Western psychotherapeutic methods.

McClelland noted that "the Protestant Reformation might have led to earlier independence training" (1961:47). Slater (1970) likewise maintains that, compared to infants in other societies, babies in the United States spend the most time in complete isolation. Indeed, there is ample evidence indicating that training for independence [2] begins significantly earlier in the West (especially in the United States) than in non-Western societies (McClelland, 1961; Rosen, 1962; Whiting, 1963; and Minturn *et al.*, 1964).

The egoistic competitive need for achievement has also been described as one form of Calvinistic individualism. Lukes, for example, notes that "the Calvinists, in their pursuit of the certainty of being among the elect, engaged . . . in concentration in their own independent achievements" (1973:95). Moreover, by idealizing egoistic individualism, such "secular Calvinists" as Hume, Mill, and especially Bentham have in fact developed the famous and influential philosophical tradition of utilitarianism, which taught people to maximize their own selfish happiness even if it "makes others miserable" (see Stephen, 1950:311). Following a somewhat similar line of thought, students of achievement motivation (McClelland, 1961; Heckhausen, 1967) have generally attributed increases in the need to achieve and compete "with a standard of excellence" to the Calvinistic ethic, according to which one purchases one's salvation through individualistic striving to succeed in one's predestinal worldly "calling."

[2] Slater refers to early independence training as "the Spockian challenge," which also reinforces permissiveness. It should be noted that permissiveness also denotes separateness in the sense of "to each his own," so that the child is told "to do whatever he thinks is best for him" while the mother is constantly away philanthropizing; the result is a disturbed, lonely child who did not have even a "stable maid" image.

However, in accepting McClelland's definition of the achievement need as a generalized pattern accompanying universal industrial development, no further consideration is usually given to the possibility that the Darwinistic "dog-eat-dog" competitive struggle for existence may be a unique achievement pattern featured mainly in Western individualistic societies (Johnson, 1973). Indeed, in discussing the individualistic-competitive uses of Social Darwinism in the West, Hofstadter noted that: "The most popular catchwords of Darwinism, 'struggle for existence' and 'survival of the fittest,' suggested that nature should provide that the best competitors in a competitive situation would win" (1968:6).

Independence and autonomy in the West usually represent the ideal or primary ("sacred cow") criteria for maturity and mental health. Jahoda, whose criteria for positive mental health are derived directly from the Protestant Ethic, states that "autonomy singles out the individual's degree of independence from social influences as most revealing of the state of his mental health" (1958:23). In general, Western psychotherapeutic literature is full of statements that residual dependency needs are symptoms of mental disorders and that independence and autonomy are the indisputable primary goals of therapy and criteria for mental health (Ford and Urban, 1964; Cameron, 1963). This, of course, is not to suggest that all Westerners are independent, nor that all dependent Westerners are defined as "deviants," but that independence has become the predominant ideal of Western socialization and psychotherapy.

Moreover, it has been suggested that in typical Western "guilt cultures" psychopathology is self-centered and related to the internalized conviction of sin, whereas in typical Oriental "shame cultures" deviance is socially bound to external sanctions and the consequent feelings of having failed others or to the notion of losing face (Benedict, 1954; Haring, 1956). According to Haley (1967), for example, schizophrenia (in the West?) is the most extreme form of individualism and self-imposed isolation, in that breaking off communication with others is perceived as avoidance of their control. Similarly, Draguns (1974) reports that, in comparing American and Japanese mental patients, such symptoms as volitional withdrawal and expressing feelings of isolation appear significantly more often among Americans.

Accordingly, psychotherapy in a typical shame society, such as Japan, concentrates mostly on correcting interpersonal relations (Doi, 1973; Murase and Johnson, 1974), while typical Western psychotherapeutic methods concentrate on individualized intrapsychic processes of self-searching or on resolving the guilt feelings derived from one's failure to realize one's egoistic potentialities (Friedman, 1972).

Thus, various patterns of extreme individualism traceable to Calvinistic influences seem to permeate Western societies —especially those with a Puritan heritage. Nevertheless, independence, self-determination, personal freedom, or even aloneness are in no way negative qualities *per se,* and if alienation, as I insist, is not the universal result of industrialization, one might wonder about the circumstances that nourished the exaggerated form of antagonistic individualism in the West.

Two socio-historical factors may account for the emergence of the extreme pattern of "alienating individualism" in the West. First, it should be remembered that the conceptions of personal political and economic freedom and the ideology of individualism grew out of the struggle led by European Renaissance liberal philosophers to free people from the enslaving "belonging" to the feudal master or guild during the Middle Ages. Thus, one may notice that collectivizing ideologies or "group-belongingness" slogans were perceived and interpreted by Westerners as neo-enslavement systems and hence were repudiated as oppressive control [3]

---

[3] In analyzing the transition from earlier "mechanical solidarity," referring to simple dependency on the collective, to the modern "or-

methods that threatened to stamp out the individual's newly gained rights and personal freedom. Riesman's (1954) elegy on the disappearance of the "inner-directed" Renaissance individualist illustrates how the West inculcated extreme individualism by denouncing any sign of collectivizing groupism. Another example is Whyte's classic *The Organization Man* (1956).

Bemoaning the decline of the Protestant Ethic, which he perceived as the "pursuit of individual salvation through hard work, thrift, and competitive struggle [that] is the heart of the American achievement" (p. 5), Whyte launches a vigorous attack on the "new social ethic," which "makes morally legitimate the pressures of society against the individual" (p. 7). Whyte then criticizes vehemently Elton Mayo's human-relations school and Lloyd Warner's ideal community, which allegedly attempted to provide a sense of belonging to the alienated industrial worker but admittedly were never successful in that goal.

Whyte seems haunted by the frightening idea that the organizational machinery will robotize man if he shows any sign of loyalty to the work group. Whyte thus quotes Clark Kerr to magnify his warning against the spreading danger of group control: "I would urge each individual to avoid total involvement in any organization . . . to limit each group to the minimum control necessary for performance of essential functions; to struggle against the effort to absorb" (1956:51). The resulting antagonism of individualists to any

---

ganic solidarity," founded upon individual differences, Durkheim (1964) actually attempts to reconcile individualism with society. It is obvious, however, that Durkheim is quite ambivalent about the new cult of "egoistic individualism," and, consistent with his positive-functional conception of man, it may therefore be more justified to refer to him as a "utopian individualist" and yet a "realistic social-control collectivist." One may speculate further and wonder whether their Jewish origin may be associated with Marx's and Durkheim's attack against the nineteenth-century Calvinistic "alienating individualism."

form of collectivism may be associated with the subsequent emergence of the extreme predominant pattern of "alienating individualism."

The second factor which may account for the institutionalization of "alienating individualism" in Western countries is directly attributable to Calvinism. Paradoxically, this suggests that Protestant individualism is rooted in a deterministic doctrine. The paradox exists in that the concept of free will and individualism in terms of *personal choice* imbued with fatalistic feelings of a *predestined choice* [4] do not represent true individualism but a source of anxiety and feelings of powerlessness for the individual facing choices. As Fromm notes: "No doctrine could express more strongly than this the worthlessness of human will and effort" (1960:75).

Moreover, those following this doctrine face the constant hazard that the sudden emergence of failure signs, such as negatively labeled behavior disorders (see Chapter 4), will be perceived as "predetermined" proofs of damnation. To counteract the doubt that threatens "personal freedom," one must constantly reinforce the most extreme form of individualism and complete separateness by glorifying self-imposed loneliness. Hence the possible predominance of "alienating individualism" in the West.

In conclusion, if "alienating individualism" is presumed to result from the overemphasis on independence as a criterion for mental health in the West, and if alienation or loneliness, as I argue, is not an inevitable by-product of *all* industrial societies, then it is of interest to take a look at another

[4] Although Riesman is probably the greatest defender of individualism, he has inadvertently acknowledged the paradox inherent in "predestinal individualism," first by admitting that individualism was adopted primarily by the middle class, which in turn perpetuates the dichotomy between the damned (lower class) and the elect (middle class); and second by conceding that even the "personal choices" of the middle classes are the results of circumstances and parental decisions, which is a "new, more sophisticated doctrine of predestination" (1954:102).

industrial society where dependence, rather than independence, is apparently the goal of socialization and mental health.

"Amae": The Challenge of Desirable Dependency

A most challenging phenomenon related to the central dilemmas discussed in this chapter is the way *amae* (desired dependence) is institutionalized in the Japanese mental-health field and in modern Japanese complex organizations. The concept of *amae*, according to the formulation of the Japanese psychiatrist Doi (1973), is derived from the noun *amaeru*, which means "to depend and presume upon another's love or indulge in another's kindness." According to Doi, *amaeru* conveys "a distinct feeling of sweetness" and usually refers to a child's dependence on his parents—particularly his mother—but it is used also to describe relationships between adults in many social contexts. From extensive clinical observations, Doi concluded that in Japan the wish and need to be taken care of and to depend (as the term *amae* connotes) constitutes basic psychological personality dynamics comparable to Freudian conceptions of the sexuality-aggression drives in the West. Doi indicates that, although the "wish to be loved" and "dependency needs" are popular expressions in Western psychotherapy, no word in English or any other European language is equivalent to *amae*. In his opinion, this reflects a fundamental psychological difference between Japan and the Western world. Doi argues that in Japan parental dependency is generally fostered and institutionalized into the wider social structure. *Amae* exists between husband and wife, between student and teacher, between foreman and subordinate, and between doctor and patient.

From his observations in a Japanese psychiatric hospital,

Caudill (1961) describes how mutual dependency is encouraged on all levels of relationships. He found especially interesting the role of the *tsukitoi*, subprofessional personnel in constant attendance, who nurture the dependency needs of the patients and share their lives with them.

Thus, in complete contrast to the West, "Japanese therapies have the goal of refreshing one's positive reexperiences of the safe dependency relationships established with parents throughout one's life" (Murase and Johnson, 1974:128); hence, to depend on others means *to be normal*. Vogel and Vogel (1968) have found that normal Japanese children showed no personality-disturbance problems although they expressed strong dependency needs.

It should be stressed here that no attempt is being made to present Japanese socialization or therapy methods on other than a culturally relativistic basis, as Murase and Johnson point out. What is important from our viewpoint, is that the system of fostering dependency needs is extended from the family to the large-scale organization without necessarily reducing the efficient operation of the organization. In Japan, mature interdependency is defined in terms of reciprocal responsibilities. Thus, according to some writers, conformity, obedience,[5] and group membership or loyalty to the firm are quite compatible with self-actualization (Murase and Johnson, 1974). "Amaeruing" in the large firm does not merely minimize alienation; a superior might go so far as to offer help with the worker's most intimate problems, as noted by Vogel and Vogel.

Thus, although opinions are deeply divided over the extent to which Japanese socialization facilitates or frustrates a sense

---

[5] The possible difference between authoritarianism in the terms of Fromm (1960) and Adorno *et al.* (1950), among others, and Japanese conformity should be pointed out here. While in the former loyalty and obedience emanated from suppression of independence, which is affectively neutral, the latter encourages dependency and mutual affection.

of individualism or personal identity, the *amae* system presents a challenge to Western individualism not only in that it shows that dependency is quite compatible with advanced industry and mental health, but also in that it challenges the generality of the Darwinist concept of egoistic-competitive need achievement as formulated by McClelland (1961). On the basis of compelling evidence derived from his extensive studies of socialization in Japan, DeVos (1973) challenges McClelland's overgeneralized, individualistic, and ethnocentrically biased theory of achievement. According to DeVos, achievement motivation in Japan refers to self-realization, which is related to strong needs for affiliation, nurturance, role dedication, and familial obligations accomplished through paternalistic reciprocal cooperation within the semi-kinship economic system.

Consequently, Japanese diligence and need achievement are not usually competitive-egoistic in nature (see also Dore, 1965) but are directed toward collective-altruistic ends. As one employee put it: "I don't get much personal inner satisfaction from my work, but I am as diligent as possible . . . because I know it will help my company and improve its reputation" (Halloran, 1969:218). A similar need-achievement pattern of a collective-ascetic nature can be identified in the Israeli *kibbutz* (see Talmon, 1972). In a recent study (Rotenberg *et al.*, 1976), my students and I discovered that *kibbutz* children volunteer for national tasks significantly more often than do city children, especially when they know that the *kibbutz* peer group rather than they themselves as individuals will be credited for it.

Contrasting the Japanese (and the *kibbutz*) need-achievement type with the Western pattern, we may in fact differentiate conceptually between two kinds of need achievement: (1) the egoistic need achievement (E-nAch) and (2) the collectivistic need achievement (C-nAch). The E-nAch would refer to one's need to achieve for himself, even if this involves harm or loss to others, and the C-nAch refs to the fulfillment of one's need achievement through the accomplishments of the collectivity for which he strives.

"Amae" and the Revolt of Existential Groups

I have discussed the Japanese *amae* system not as a representative case of reciprocal individualism but mainly in order to show how industrialization is possible without the presumed inevitable concomitant side effect of separating alienation. At this point, one might rightly ask whether desirable dependence is indeed an ideology monopolized by Japan. Undoubtedly the recent group movements that have emerged in the United States in the form of communes and encounter groups, with their emphasis on the existential "here and now" salvation, represent a genuine revolt against Protestant individualistic materialism. Certain love-oriented behavior systems, such as mutual feeding, bathing, massaging, and general comforting, which are practiced in some existential groups, can actually be compared to *amae* in terms of the desire to be pampered and taken care of.

The differences between a real community (e.g. Synanon and other communes, see Mowrer, 1964) and the encounter-group symbolic community, which lacks any reality function "beyond the group's existence as a place for emotional release and intimacy," were recognized by Fritz Perls's attempt to build a Gestalt community during the last year of his life (Shaffer and Galinsky, 1974).

In an extensive review of the literature on existential humanistic psychology, Greening (1971) uncovers divided opinions among psychologists concerning the new trend of encounter-groupism. He shows how some psychologists refer to encounter groups as collectivizing threats to individual autonomy and to human dignity, while others denounce clinicians' deemphasis of interhuman relatedness in favor of overemphasis on insight and self-centered ego development.

Thus, the question of whether new existential groupism provides lasting desired dependency as a way of life or whether these groups teach people to exploit others (whom, presumably, they may never meet again) for their own egoistic needs [6] is not easily answered. Here, the Protestant heritage might indicate that the "ambivalence about the issue of individualism vs. social-commitment is deep and unresolved" (see Slater, 1970:148). On the one hand, there is increasing experimentation with communes and interdependent togetherness. On the other, the new culture exhorts individuals "to do their own thing." [7] One moment we hear them voicing the unanimous "Portnoyish complaint" against the nurturing-loving "Jewish mother"; the next moment we watch them marching under big banners, yearning, searching for, and preaching "LOVE." And one wonders whether the endless preoccupation with introspective self-searching, finding one's self or identity, and the use of such slogans as "drop out" and "self-actualization" in essence perpetuate the old-style individualism, whether they reflect simple confusion or carry the message of a new kind of harmonious and less alienating individualism.

To facilitate further consideration of differential patterns of individualism from a cross-cultural perspective, it would

---

[6] The general term usually used to refer to most of these "one-time weekend groups" is "human relations laboratories," which in essence connotes technocratic experimentation with others with no lasting commitments, since the underlying assumption is that as a rule members of such groups do not meet again. In a similar vein, one might wonder whether the expression "to make love," which is currently used in place of simply "loving," implies a mechanical rather than a naturalistic approach to sex.

[7] While the old-style utilitarian individualists honestly admitted that the maximization of one's selfish happiness might sometimes involve hurting others, the contemporary hip slogan, "Do your own thing as long as it does not hurt others," would certainly not qualify as a Kantian categorical imperative of social harmlessness. What about the Jewish mother who says to her son: "Do your own thing, but know that it hurts me if you don't become a doctor!"

seem useful to introduce here a new conceptualization of a more socially harmonious form of "reciprocal individualism," primarily predicated on Buber's writings on Hassidism.

The Nature of "Reciprocal Individualism"

To familiarize the reader with the Hassidic communication style, I shall begin with a tale about a Jew who was the sole survivor of a sinking ship and who swam to a barren island, where he built a whole town and lived there alone. Then, long after he was believed dead by his family and community, he was suddenly discovered by a ship that happened to pass this island. Naturally the discovery caused a great sensation, and many expeditions came to see the miraculous survivor and his town. A peculiar thing that struck the visitors' attention was the fact that he had built two synagogues. When asked why he, a man alone, needed two synagogues, he pointed to one of them declaring: "In that synagogue I wouldn't set a foot!"

This little story captures the essence of Hassidic "reciprocal individualism." A Jew lives in a social world of contrasts.[8] Thus, even if he is alone, he is not really alone. He lives in a community that must have a center—the synagogue—and in this center, which gives him the sense of belonging, he can worship, struggle, and express his individuality by disagreeing—even with himself.

This is the crux of reciprocal individualism: constantly living with contradictions, in disagreement, but with "others" in the community. The community is not comprised of an

---

[8] Living in a world of unsettled paradoxes represents in a sense a kind of "Jewish schizophrenia," and it may explain why some studies find less schizophrenia among Jews as compared to Protestants or Catholics (Srole and Langer, 1969), who perceive man in dualistic-absolute good or bad terms.

amorphous "generalized other" [9] (Mead, 1934) but of concrete, interacting people who are never *indifferent* to each other, yet each one is *different* from every other. In his memories of the Hassidic community he knew, Buber writes of "men of many-sided individuality and strong differences, yet each surrounded by a community that lived a brotherly life" (quoted in Pfeutze, 1961:247).

Buber, a most important exponent of Hassidism, rejects both individualism and collectivism. In both conditions, he contends (1967), people try to overcome and escape their loneliness, isolation, and individual responsibility, in the first case by avoiding the group and glorifying solitude, which results in anxiety and egoism, and in the second case by becoming immersed in a massive, deindividualizing mob-group. In other words, both extreme individualism and extreme collectivism mean "running away," in the first case, running away *from* the group, in the second case, running away *into* the group.

The major concept in Buber's "soft individualism," or what can be termed "reciprocal individualism," is the dynamic sphere between person and person in dialogue. Derived from the traditional dialectic method of studying the Talmud, the contrasting debate between the I and the Thou practiced in the communial *yeshiva* is the basis for "being *with* one another," yet retaining one's individuality (Buber, 1967).

Three constructs explain the dynamics of "reciprocal individualism": (1) the I or the "Single One" and his or her responsibility; (2) the Thou in the community of others; and

[9] Although Mead's (1934) individuality is also defined in terms of a self which is shaped by one's interaction with significant and generalized others, Mead's "generalized other" is normative, not concrete like Buber's conception of otherness in the living community, as Pfeutze points out in his excellent comparison between Mead and Buber: "More than one critic has confessed to a suspicion of 'white magic' in the process by which, starting with an animal organism, assuming roles, you end up with a well-rounded, integrated 'generalized other'" (Pfeutze, 1961:245).

Alienating Individualism; Reciprocal Individualism   159

(3) the "contrasting-binding" yet spontaneous sphere between the I and the others in the community.

PERSONAL RESPONSIBILITY OF THE "I"

The essential component of the "I" or the "Single One" is
"responsibility." Selfhood thus consists of our responsiveness
and of our responsibility both to ourselves and to others. The
individual's responsibility and uniqueness are grounded in
the belief that every human being is a unique creation of God
and hence it is his responsibility to unfold the unique goodness that was given to him (Friedman, 1972). Individualism
means, in this Kantian sense, that man cannot hide behind
any set of predicated rules (or "escape the freedom" of his
personal choice, to use the terms of Fromm's description of
the Protestant): "With my choice and decision and action—
committing or omitting . . . I answer for my hour. My
group cannot relieve me of this responsibility . . . and no
program, no tactical resolution, no command can tell me
how I, as I decide, have to do justice" (Buber, 1967:68).

The emphasis on the individual's responsibility to actualize
himself is illuminated in many Hassidic stories interpreted by
Buber. Thus Buber (1958a) cites Rabbi Shneur Zalman, who,
imprisoned in a Russian jail, was asked by the chief of gen-
darmes to explain the apparent paradox of the presumably
omniscient God asking Adam: "Where art thou?" The rabbi's
answer—that in this question God asks every person, "Where
are you in your world? How far along are you?"—is used by
Buber as a classic dictum of Hassidic self-realization. Similarly, Buber quotes the famous Rabbi Susya as having said
shortly before his death: "When I get to heaven, they will not
ask me, 'Why were you not Moses?' but 'Why were you not
Susya? Why did you not become what only you could become?'" (Buber, 1967:XIX).

In the concept of "distance and relation," Buber (1965)

further develops the meaning of individuation and self-differentiation. Thus, only by setting a distance from the other, by being independent and differentiated, can one appreciate the other as a whole person and enter into a meaningful relationship with him. Nevertheless, Buber's self-realizing concept of uniqueness is not synonymous with being preoccupied with oneself. It is merely a starting point for becoming oneself through responding to others. Thus, Buber's reciprocal "I" of being-in-community is continuous with the Jewish teaching of ethics (according to the "Mussar" Movement), which prohibits one's withdrawal from the world (see Tishby, 1970:118). Kierkegaard, according to his solitary conception of the "Single One," turns away from the world; Buber "stays with it."

THE RECIPROCAL "THOU" IN THE COMMUNITY OF OTHERS

Buber's "Thou," in terms of a community or a center, refers to an ever extending circle of others. In contrast to collectivistic groupism, it is not a domain where one surrenders one's will for the group but the very testing ground for one's commitment and responsibilities. Buber's concept of "center," the pulsing heart of the interacting community to which "its members have a common relation" (Buber, 1958b:135), can be understood in terms of the meaning that the traditional Jewish synagogue carried. In Hebrew, the word "synagogue" literally means a "house of gathering" (*beit knesset*), not only to pray, but also for people to meet, differentiate themselves from one another, and work out their situational problems. Compared to other "massed, mingled collectivities," the only commune that can be considered a "nonfailure" in Buber's eyes, owing to its dynamic, interactive nature, is the *kibbutz*. The *kibbutz*, according to Buber, emerged as a response to the problems Jews faced when they came together to Palestine, not on the basis of any abstract principle. In a genuine community people struggle *with* one another to solve their ever changing problems. To understand the dynamic nature of a genuine community, Buber insists that "a community need not be 'founded' . . . a community should not be made into a principle; it, too, should always satisfy a situation rather than an abstraction . . . a living togetherness, constantly renewing itself" (1958b:134, 135).

Buber's "Thou," however, should not be understood only in terms of a concrete congregation or a community center. The interrelatedness of the responsible "I" and the responsive "Thous" delineates the difference between the conception of salvation in Protestantism and in Judaism. While preoccupation with one's own salvation is the highest aim in Protestantism, in Judaism one is redeemed *only through the others* to whom he is responsible and who are responsible for him (*ibid.*). Thus, such Talmudic imperatives as "One who solicits mercy for his fellow while he himself is in need of the same thing will be answered first" (Talmud, *Shevuot*, p. 39a) or "all Israel are sureties one for another" (Talmud, *Baba Kama*, p. 92a) have featured the Jewish communal welfare system for many generations.

Accordingly, one's self-fulfillment and redemption as a differentiated "I" is conditioned by one's concomitantly being an unconditional "thou" to others.

The "Contrasting-Binding" Sphere between "I" and "Thou"

The sphere "between" the I and the Thou, to which I alluded earlier, refers to the dynamic "contrasting-binding" force between people, and its relation to reciprocal individualism may be understood in its spontaneous, nondoctrinaire nature. If nothing is final or certain, if nothing is absolutely settled between people but always open to debate, then each member in the interaction retains his individuality and responsibility in relation to the matter under dispute, yet is also bound to the other in the continuous search for solutions. Final solutions connote separateness; conflict implies living relationship.

The other aspect of the "interhuman-between" sphere is spontaneity, which can be understood by referring to Buber's (1965) distinction between "being" and "seeming." Relationships characterized by *being* are rooted in the belief that people are essentially good. Hence they can give themselves fully and spontaneously to each other without having to pose and pretend. By contrast, in relationships dominated by *seeming*, people calculate their role-taking behavior to hide their apparent badness and present themselves in a false, fragmented manner, which destroys the authentic, spontaneous interpersonal sphere vital for human existence.

According to Buber (1958b), the early settlers who gathered in the *kibbutz* gave themselves to each other spontaneously and did not follow any dogmatic collectivist principle. They only came with ideas to be modified. Although this is not to suggest that contemporary *kibbutzim* conform to Buber's ideal pattern, it may reflect typical communication patterns that subsequently developed in Israel.[10] These "contrasting-binding" modes of interrelationship may be illuminated by the following anecdotes:

Anecdote 1 (absurd disagreement): A driver stopped at

[10] It is certainly plausible that many of the contemporary secular Jews, notably Israelis, feel lonely as is generally implied in Schweid's recent monograph on *Judaism and the Solitary Jew* (1974). It seems, however, that Schweid's loose usage of the terms "loneliness" or "solitude" refers mostly to the identity crisis and rootlessness that many contemporary secular Jews experience as individuals or as a group. This does not necessarily mean that the Israeli, for example, feels isolated as an individual or separated from others, as the word "loneliness" connotes in behavioral terms.

a red light and asked a pedestrian for directions. A second pedestrian joined in, disagreeing with the directions given by the first. The light changed, and the driver drove on without knowing his way. After fifteen minutes of unsuccessful navigation, he ended up back at the same red light, where he found the two pedestrians—still arguing about the directions he had asked for.

Anecdote 2 (desired belongingness): A man and his wife sat in an almost empty movie theater. A group of five, the only other people in the theater, sat together in another corner. One of them came over to the couple and asked in an astonished tone why they wouldn't sit with everybody else.

In conclusion, alienating individualism may be operationalized in terms of an egoistic need for achievement and self-realization (E-nAch) associated with high feelings of loneliness and low affiliation needs. Reciprocal individualism may be operationalized in terms of a collectivistic need for self-fulfillment and achievement (C-nAch) associated with high affiliation needs and low feelings of loneliness.

Thus, "alienating individualism" and "reciprocal individualism" are modal systems of relationship. The extent of their prevalence within Western organizations, Japanese firms, *kibbutzim*, or communes is obviously a matter open for empirical testing.[11] To provide illustrative research findings that demonstrate how various aspects of these systems can be assessed, I shall conclude this chapter by describing results, relevant to this discussion, of a more comprehensive cross-cultural study on achievement and ethnicity (to be published separately).

[11] Research relevant to this suggested approach was done by Fayerweather (1959), who found that non-Protestant managers, such as Mexicans, had a significantly higher need for affiliation than Americans, whereas American managers had a significantly higher need for achievement. In this study, as in others, however, need achievement was not conceptualized in differential terms, nor were other individualistic variables considered.

Assessing Protestantism, Egocentrism, and Loneliness

In this study only differential need-achievement patterns were tested in relation to alienating and reciprocal individualism. Need achievement (nAch), one of the more frequently studied variables in modern psychology, seemed a most intriguing and challenging area in which to begin the study of differential individualism, since achievement motivation was hitherto defined primarily in what I termed the egoistic-need-achievement pattern (E-nAch) (see McClelland, 1961).

It was generally hypothesized that subjects who have high egoistic need achievement—a referent of "alienating individualism"—will express increased feelings of loneliness as compared to subjects who are high in collectivist need achievement (C-nAch)—a referent of "reciprocal individualism." It was also hypothesized that subjects who are low on the Protestant Ethic scale and/or were socialized in collective-oriented labor systems, such as collective farms, will have a high C-nAch and will feel less lonely than subjects with an urban-individualistic working background and/or a high score on the Protestant Ethic scale (who will have a high E-nAch and who will express increased feelings of loneliness).

METHOD

THE EGOISTIC/COLLECTIVE ACHIEVEMENT (E/C–NACH) QUESTIONNAIRE

To be consistent with previous cross-cultural studies of need achievement, a new instrument, designed according to Mehrabian's (1968) achievement questionnaire, was constructed to differentiate between the C-nAch and E-nAch achievement patterns (validity and reliability of Mehrabian's questionnaire was found to be high according to a retest done after ten weeks). The E/C-nAch questionnaire [12] comprised thirty preference questions. Part of the questions assess the subject's preference for actualizing himself and achieving for himself, even if it requires egoistic competition with others—i.e., "stepping on them"—causing others to lose or antagonizing others. The rest of the preference questions evaluated subjects' need to achieve and to realize themselves through others in the collectivity—i.e., to strive for accomplishments of the collectivity or to achieve in harmony with others.

The E-nAch preference questions were generally formulated according to McClelland's (1961) and Atkinson's (1960) definition of nAch, and the C-nAch questions were generally formulated according to DeVos's (1973) and Doi's (1973) definition of the non-Western collectivist achievement motive.

Subjects gave their answers on a seven-point scale ranging from "strongly agree" (the midpoint 4, "undecided," was eliminated to avoid evasive answers) to "strongly disagree."

Examples of E-nAch preference questions were "I prefer to hurt my fellow workers rather than give them a chance to excel at my expense," or "I prefer more money rather than more friends." If a subject strongly agreed with these statements, he received a high E-nAch score for them, and if he disagreed strongly he received a high C-nAch score. Examples of C-nAch questions were: "I prefer to help my family first of all, rather than advance myself economically," or "I prefer social success over economic success" (see Appendix for the full E/C-nAch questionnaire).

[12] The E/C-nAch questionnaire was constructed and standardized by Gera Shechter, who collaborated with me on the large-scale cross-ethnic study and who used part of the data as his master's thesis in psychology, which I supervised. I am most grateful for his devotion and ruthless criticism.

The E/C-nAch questionnaire at first included fifty-three preference questions. According to a pretest study administered to thirty subjects from various ethnic backgrounds, twenty-three items which had ambiguous connotations and/or were proved to have poor variance were eliminated. A split-half reliability test with the Spearman Brown correction (see Guilford, 1954) indicated that reliability of the thirty remaining items was .88 ($p < .005$).

BELCHER'S LONELINESS QUESTIONNAIRE

To test subjects' expressed feelings of loneliness, Belcher's (1973) loneliness questionnaire was used. This questionnaire was chosen not only because it included various aspects of alienation, anomie, and estrangement (which could be analyzed separately) but mostly because it also appeared to be the best available instrument for assessing subjective feelings of loneliness, which were of primary interest to the present study.

This instrument, which was found to have a reliability score of .83 ($p < .001$) in a test-retest procedure, included sixty items that were translated into Hebrew, and here, too, subjects expressed their feelings of loneliness on a six-point scale of agreement with statements such as "Most friendships end in disappointment," and "I feel I don't have a friend in the world."

THE SHORTENED PROTESTANT ETHIC SCALE

To assess subjects' endorsement of the Protestant Ethic orientation, Mirels and Garrett's (1971) shortened PE questionnaire was used (see Chapter 5).

RESULTS

As mentioned earlier, the research design described above was taken from a broader cross-cultural study that investi-

gated various aspects of achievement behavior among several
ethnic groups, which are not central to the main theme of
this book. Thus, only the results that seemed most relevant
for our discussion will be reported here briefly.

INTERVARIABLE CORRELATION

To establish the interrelationship between the variables
(scales) studied, a Pearson correlation test was performed on
a sample of 285 subjects. It was found that the three questionnaires correlated as expected beyond the .001 level of
confidence (see Table 7–1).

Table 7–1 shows that there is a significant correlation between the Protestant Ethic questionnaire (PE) and the loneliness questionnaire, which means that the more one endorses the Protestant value orientation, the more lonely he
feels. It also shows that there is a significant negative correlation between the PE questionnaire and the E/C-nAch questionnaire, which means that the more one endorses the
Protestant value system, the more egoistic is his need achievement, and, conversely, the less one accepts the Protestant
Ethic, the more collectivistic is his need achievement. Finally,
Table 7–1 indicates that there is a significant negative correlation between the loneliness and the E/C-nAch questionnaires, which means that the higher egoistic achievers feel
significantly more lonely than the collectivist achievers. Performing an analysis of variance between groups and within
each group on each scale, it was found that intergroup and

TABLE 7.1. **Intercorrelations Between PE, E/C-nAch, and Loneliness**

QUESTIONNAIRES	LONELINESS	PE	E/C-NACH
Loneliness	1.000	.051*	−.445*
PE	.051*	1.000	−.120*
E/C-nAch	.445*	−.20*	1.000

* p < .001

TABLE 7.2. Analysis of Variance of the Scales Between and Within Groups

SCALES		SOURCE OF VARIANCE		
		Between groups*	Within groups†	F
Loneliness	Sum squares	26182.98	179447.94	4.849‡
	Mean squares	3272.75	647.83	
E/C-nAch	Sum squares	49034.96	193953.25	8.75‡
	Mean squares	6129.37	700.19	
PE	Sum squares	3270.00	18866.58	7.26‡
	Mean squares	408.75	56.30	

* df = 8, † df = 277, ‡ p < .001

intragroup variance of each scale ($N = 285$) was significant at the .001 level of confidence (see Table 7–2).

COMPARING SUBJECTS FROM COLLECTIVE AND INDIVIDUALISTIC LABOR SYSTEMS

One of the more interesting and relevant findings of the large-scale study was when subjects living and working in a *kibbutz* were compared to subjects living and working in a city. It was assumed that in the *kibbutz,* where people do not receive personal salaries but are socialized to work for the collectivity and to be rewarded by its collective accomplishments, "reciprocal individualism" in terms of the C-nAch and its presumed correlates will be significantly higher, as Buber (1958b) suggested, compared to city workers who receive personal salaries and rewards and whose socialization might have been more influenced by the Western generalized "alienatory individualistic" orientation characterized by the E-nAch pattern. Thus, seventy city workers were compared to twenty-five *kibbutz* members. To minimize the possible intervening effects of cultural and other background variables, all subjects of the two groups were males of Euro-

TABLE 7.3.   **Mean of PE, E/C–nAch, and Loneliness among Kibbutz and City Workers**

	MEAN LONELINESS	MEAN E/C-NACH	MEAN PE
City subjects	138.79	127.86	33.23
Kibbutz subjects	137.04	133.88	31.76

pean, nonreligious background in the 18–52 age range who were engaged in manual work during the time of the study.

Comparing the means of the two groups with the *t* test, it was found that all comparisons were in the expected direction, but they did not reach the level of significance (see Table 7–3).

Although differences were not significant, the Pearson correlation test performed on each group separately showed that correlation between PE and E/C-nAch for city subjects was significant at the .05 level and correlation between E/C–nAch and loneliness was significant at the .005 level for the same group, while for the *kibbutz* subjects only the correlation between PE and E/C–nAch was significant at the .005 level.[13]

In order to obtain a broader picture of how collective versus individualistic background reflects differences in relation to the variables under consideration, a planned comparison analysis of variance (see Hays, 1973) was performed on a larger sample. Thus, 150 city dwellers were compared with 53 members of a *moshav,* a collective farm where members own some private property. These subjects had the same characteristics in terms of age, employment, and background as the subjects described above. Here results were as expected and highly significant. The contrasting analysis of variance showed that *moshav* members indeed feel signifi-

---

[13] Similar intervariable correlations and *t* test results were obtained when another sample of thirty-two "Kurdish" subjects, who also have a familistic-collective but non-Western working background, was compared to the seventy European subjects.

cantly less lonely than city dwellers ($F = 3.50$, $p < .001$). The analysis of variance showed too that the members had a significantly higher C-nAch score than city dwellers ($F = 7.43$, $p < .001$). However, contrasting the two groups on the PE scale showed that, while city subjects are more accepting of the values of the Protestant Ethic than the *moshav* people, as expected, this difference is not significant ($F = .166$, n.s.).

Conclusion

This study has generally indicated that the Protestant Ethic is indeed associated with an egoistic pattern of need achievement and with increased feelings of loneliness and alienation. It thus demonstrates that the price of the Protestant type of striving egoistically to purchase one's own salvation is indeed increased loneliness. It also demonstrates, for the first time, that failure to score high on a McClelland (1961) type of need-achievement test does not necessarily mean complete lack of achievement motivation, but that there is more than one pattern of need achievement and that the non-Protestant collectivist need-achievement pattern (which might be as strong as the egoistic nAch) produces less egoism and feelings of alienation and loneliness.

The group comparisons selected for presentation here suggest that, compared to the urban working background, socialization in a collective labor system, such as the *kibbutz* or the *moshav* (or in Japan?), indeed produces less loneliness and the collective type of need of achievement (C-nAch). Here it should be stressed again that although the PE scale correlated with the E-nAch and the loneliness scales, as expected, the correlation was not sufficiently powerful to produce significant differences between groups; hence the limited usefulness of this scale from our perspective (concentrating mainly on the Protestant work ethos) has once again become apparent, and there is reason to hope that its future reconstruction along the broader Calvinist lines mentioned in Chapter 5 will strengthen its predictive power. On the other hand, since results were generally as expected even though no "real" Protestants were tested, this study demonstrated that the egoistic vs. the collectivistic achievement aspect related to the Protestant-Western "alienating individualism" or to the non-Western "reciprocal individualism" can successfully be differentiated and tested on various groups. To obtain a more comprehensive assessment of "alienating" versus "reciprocal" individualistic patterns, it would obviously also be necessary to explore degrees of independence and self-determination vs. group dependence and lack of personal determination (as well as general low achievement motivation) among various ethnic groups characterized by degrees of individualistic or collectivistic orientations. In other words, it would be important to determine, for example, to what extent socialization toward a collective-achievement motivation facilitates or frustrates the development of one's individualistic identity. From the present limited perspective, we may nonetheless summarize that the "Protestant bias" was again shown to influence theory and research strongly, in this case on alienation and achievement motivation.

In the final chapter, the heart of the "Protestant bias" in terms of the theory of man and human change will be analyzed by a comparative study of the socio-historical roots of the pessimistic Protestant salvation ethic (therapy). To conclude this book by presenting what I would like to term a more optimistic paradigm of man, the Hassidic salvation ethic will be presented as a counter-paradigm to the Protestant deterministic conception of man's changeability.

Chapter Eight

Retrospective vs. Prospective Therapy: An Encounter Between the Protestant and Hassidic Salvation Ethics

The Protestant American is future-oriented but seeks salvation in his past; the Jew draws strength from the past but seeks salvation in his future.

(M. R.)

"Here and now" therapists (e.g. Rogers, 1942) and other critics of the so-called traditional psychodynamic or Freudian psychotherapeutic systems have often asked why these classical methods (not only psychoanalysis *per se*) insist on reconstructing personal history in order to cure current suffering (Goffman, 1961; Lofland, 1969; Rosenhan, 1973). Thus, the effective impact of such past-oriented, pain-reviving insight practices on a cure or on future behavior changes are seriously questioned (Nagel, 1959; Mowrer, 1961; Eysenck, 1966). Indeed, one may wonder how much energy can be left for future change if one spends a great deal of energy—sometimes for many years—to *relive*, albeit allegedly to *relieve*, past sufferings and buried memories.

Psychodynamic therapy is based on the assumption that neurotic symptoms of a suffering individual represent subconscious or repressed forbidden thoughts and impulses (e.g. classic Oedipal wishes), and the goal of analysis is accordingly structured to reduce current pains by reviving —bringing to consciousness—old painful thoughts (see Ford and Urban, 1964). Awareness of the causal relationship between old and new pains (insight) is therefore presumed to relieve neurotic suffering and enhance peace of mind. A description taken from a typical psychoanalytical textbook will suffice to illuminate this point: "As the process of psychoanalysis uncovered this patient's buried memories, with their associated emotions, he was made to *relive* emotionally all his early fears, frustrations, wishes, and rebellious reactions" (Polatin and Philitine, 1950:8–9. Italics added).

In essence, the traditional approaches to psychotherapy provoke two questions: (1) What are the historical models upon which contemporary psychodynamic therapy procedures are patterned? And (2) is the presumed phenomenon of repressing evil thoughts during childhood universal or culturally idiosyncratic?

In this final chapter I shall argue that (1) the conceptions and procedures of psychodynamic therapies are patterned after the Protestant methods of introspection and conversion and (2) the relative ineffectiveness as well as the self-torturing nature of the past-oriented processes of traditional therapy ("retrospective therapy") can best be understood when viewed in their historiosophical context. It will be also demonstrated that in Hassidic culture, which stands in contrast to the Protestant Ethic, (3) retrospective self-torture and repression of evil thoughts are forbidden, as a result of which neurotic guilt symptoms should be relatively absent; thus (4) it should be possible to conceptualize a future-oriented psychotherapeutic system ("prospective therapy") that utilizes mechanisms producing joyful experiences to bring about effective change.

"Retrospective Therapy"

It has often been acknowledged that the Reformation and the abolishment of the Church's function as an arbitrator between man and his God actually paved the way for the mass institutionalization of secular forms of psychotherapy (e.g. Mowrer, 1961). However, aside from citing the general resemblance between the priest's role as a confessor and the modern therapist's role as a listener, few attempts have been made to study systematically the traces of religious conceptions of man and the prescriptions for his salvation in modern psychotherapy.

The Protestant Conception of Conscience

Bercovitch cites several early Protestant writers who defined conscience as a "man's judgment of himself, according to the judgment of God of him" (1975:21). A succinct statement by Ryle points to the Protestant origin of such popular concepts among therapists as self-searching introspection, insight, and conscience: "The Protestants had to hold that a man could know the moral state of his soul and the wishes of God without the aid of confessors and scholars: they spoke therefore of the God-given 'light' of private conscience" (1949:159).

McNeill, in his extensive historical study of the cure of souls, indicates that Calvin himself associated the word "conversion" with "recovery," and, quoting from a Protestant prayerbook of 1552, he shows that the term "conscience" was used in relation to both pastoral counseling and self-examination: "If there be any of you who by the means aforesaid [self-examination] cannot quiet his own conscience . . . then let him come to me, or some other discreet and learned minister . . . and open his grief that he may receive such ghostly counsel, advice, and comfort" (McNeill, 1951:220). Furthermore, in 1602 the Cambridge Puritan William Perkins (cited by McNeill) used the term "conscience" to refer not only to the techniques of introspection and counseling but also to the endless process of self-torture that was a prominent feature of the Protestant experience: "Let a man commit any trespass or offense, though it be done in secret . . . yet conscience that knoweth it, will accuse him and terrify him and cite him before God and give him no rest" (*ibid.*, p. 264).

We can therefore see that the term "conscience" was used by early Protestants to refer to ruthless introspection, counseling, mental sufferings, and subsequent insight related to past transgressions. The operational meaning of these terms may have filtered down to contemporary therapy. However, to provide a full picture of how the self-torturing process of conversion was related to psychological cure and personal salvation, it would be useful to examine briefly the dynamics of conversion on the basis of examples taken from actual case histories.

Self-torturing Phases in Conversion

In his classic study of religious experiences, William James defines conversion in the broadest sense as the typical Christian process of experiencing religion:

> To be converted, to be regenerated, to receive grace, to experience religion, to gain assurance, are so many phrases which denote the process, gradual or sudden, by which a self hitherto divided, and consciously wrong, inferior and unhappy, becomes unified and consciously right [1901:194].

Starbuck maintains that "throughout Christianity, the spiritual event commonly called conversion has been characterized by 'more or less sudden' insight" (1901: p. 21). The seventeenth-century English Puritan Perkins identified ten stages in conversion. The first four preparatory stages were used to "breake and subdue the stubborness of our nature" (cited in Morgan, 1963:68). Pliability, then, presumably led to the general differentiation of good and evil and to the fourth stage of "legal fear." "In this crucial stage the individual perceived his helpless and hopeless condition and despaired of salvation" (*ibid.*). The next stages, which were presumably followed by eventual feelings of assurance and mercy, were nonetheless accompanied by a never ceasing combat against doubt and despair and by constant pleas for pardon.

It seems reasonable to compare the early stages of "breaking stubborness," which was intended to lead to awareness of sins and guilt, with the process in traditional therapy of breaking down defenses and façades, which should likewise lead to eventual insight. Similarly, Starbuck's (1901) "sudden insight" can be easily identified in modern therapy (e.g. Angyal, 1965:268). It is the *never-ceasing combat* against doubt accompanying these stages, however, that is of primary interest to us here. Morgan indicates that any assurance that came about without a prior experience of doubt, despair, and fear was considered "false assurance," and "even after he reached the stage of assurance, his doubts would continue" (1963:69).

Thus, whether conversion included ten stages or more, what seems important is that what can be termed "the three phases of evil" leading to relief and doubt-accompanied salvation are characterized by a continuous process of self-examination featured by self-torture. Paradoxically, although the first two phases are taken together as necessary conditions for the third, salvation itself is never assured: hence the "never-ceasing" doubt remains even during the third phase. The three phases consist of (1) past-oriented feelings of hopelessness and desperation (the realization that suffering is actually not reduced by awareness of what caused it); (2) self-contempt and constant doubt in regard to present identity (Am I saved or damned, loved or rejected, a success or a failure?); and (3) the awakening and insight phase leading to salvation.

PAST-ORIENTED SUFFERING

James (1901) noted that, upon looking back into their own past, two of the most insightful and successful Protestant celebrities felt that their efforts and success were futile and unrelated to their eventual feelings of hopelessness and despair. Goethe stated in 1842: "I will say nothing against the course of my existence. But at bottom it has been nothing but pain and burden, and I can affirm that during the whole of my 75 years, I have not had four weeks of genuine well-being." Similarly, Luther declared: "I am utterly weary of life. I pray the Lord will come forthwith and carry me hence" (James, 1901:146).

Paranoiac feelings caused by introspection and the revival of old guilt feelings are most clearly demonstrated in Alline's memories in 1806:

> My sins seemed to be laid open; so that I thought that every one I saw knew them . . . yea sometimes it seemed to me as if everyone was pointing me out as the most guilty wretch upon earth. I had now so great a sense of vanity and emptiness . . . the whole world could not possibly make me happy [*ibid.*, p. 165].

Similarly, Bercovitch notes, for example, that "Edward Taylor's self-scrutiny takes the form of a descent into 'A varnished pot of putrid excrements,' a labyrinth of illusion haunted by 'Fears, Heart-Aches, Grief' " (1975:16).

Actual physical fear accompanying introspection is reported in the following case: "Whilst in this state of philosophic pessimism . . . about my prospects . . . suddenly, there fell upon me . . . a horrible fear of my own existence.

. . . I awoke morning after morning with a horrible dread at the pit of my stomach" (James, 1901:166–67).

Finally, sadness, which increased markedly following an introspective-"insightful" journey into his subconscious personal past, is described by the French philosopher Jouffroy:

> Anxiously I followed my thoughts, as from layer to layer they descended toward the foundations of my consciousness. . . . I turned with them toward my childhood, my family, my country . . . memory, belief, it forced me to let go of everything. . . . The investigation went on more obstinate and more severe as it drew near its term. . . . I seemed to feel my earlier life. . . . The days which followed this discovery were the saddest of my life [*ibid.*, pp. 181–82].

Thus, Goethe's and Luther's success and Jouffroy's painful attempts to psychoanalyze himself by truly reliving his past ("I seemed to feel my earlier life") did not result in relief.

The dynamics of doubt pains

This phase, which Starbuck has termed the "storm and stress" experience, is characterized by restless, tormenting, vacillating waves of doubt (as to whether one is saved and loved or damned and rejected) accompanying efforts to relate past sins to present behavior. Again, Alline's experience provides a good example:

> I was now very moral in my life, but found no rest of conscience. . . . I soon began to be fond of carnal mirth. . . . I thought God would indulge young people with some recreation . . . and so got along very well in time of health and prosperity . . . but when I returned from my carnal mirth I felt as guilty as ever, and could sometimes not close my eyes for some hours [*ibid.*, pp. 178–79].

As in many cases, Alline's fluctuations and doubts tended to increase his own guilt feelings. In other cases the identity crisis associated with attempts to relate awareness of past sins to present efforts seem to be characterized by strong expressions of uncertainty and desperation. A woman who described herself as having been a naughty, nervous, irritable, jealous, and protesting child suffered later from "a morbid conscience . . . and misgivings about being one of the non-elect" (Starbuck, 1901:177). The famous John Bunyan declared at one point, "Nay, thought I, now I grow worse and worse; now I am farther from conversion than ever I was before" (James, 1901:164). Similarly, a student named Gratry wrote in 1880: "I suffered an incurable and intolerable desolation, verging on despair. I thought myself, in fact, rejected by God, lost, damned" (*ibid.*, p. 154). And finally, most desperate of all was the cry of one John Nelson: "Lord Thy will be done; damn or save!" (*ibid.*, p. 212).

James, Starbuck, and others provide ample cases describing the self-torturing phase of doubts and despair preceding conversion. The main point here is that, although salvation and relief did not necessarily result from past-oriented sufferings, revived pains and doubts were perceived as an absolute prerequisite of conversion, to the absurd point that a man would be alarmed if he did *not* suffer. The American nineteenth-century revivalist Finney stated: "Why! thought I, I never was so far from being concerned about my own salvation. . . . I tried to recall my convictions, to get back again the load of sins under which I had been laboring. I tried in vain to make myself anxious" (*ibid.*, p. 218). Moreover, while self-torture and inner struggles were apparently mandatory prerequisites for conversion, they admittedly led nowhere. Most instructive in this context is a passage from George Goodwin's popular early seventeenth-century poem:

> I sing my self; my civil Warrs within;
> The victories I howrely lose and win;
> The daily Duel, the continuall strife,
> The warr that ends not, till I end my life.
>
> (Quoted in Bercovitch, 1975:19.)

Similar to the traditional conversion process, in contemporary psychodynamic therapy the endless preoccupation with past failures and attempts to resolve old repressed conflicts seemed to have turned into a need and end in itself, although there are no measurable criteria to indicate how this procedure effects concrete changes in the patient (see Nagel, 1959).

AWAKENING AND CATHARTIC INSIGHT

Starbuck suggested that the experience of personal salvation can be defined as a gradual or sudden "awakening of power and insight" (1901:137) following an extended period of brooding, depression, morbid introspection, and guilt feelings. He terms the gradual process a volitional one and the sudden experience a self-surrender type of salvation. Two questions arise, however: (1) What is the precise relationship between the preceding suffering stages and the subsequent redeeming-insight? (2) What is the operational therapeutic meaning of insight-salvation? James contends that temporary exhaustion (probably preceding self-surrender) often forms part of the conversion crisis. He further suggests that in Protestant theology, as in psychology, redemption is a "free gift" caused by external forces (1901:214, 244).

As indicated earlier, the self-torturing conversion process did not always culminate in the yearned-for state of personal redemption and peacefulness. Bercovitch suggests, for example, that "self-examination serves not to liberate but to constrict" (1975:13). Thus, it is in light of the painful process preceding awakening that the relationship between those phases can be examined.

Consider first the following statements: "Lord, I have done all I can; I leave the whole matter with thee, and immediately there came to me a great peace," and "I finally ceased to resist and gave myself up" (James, 1901:211).

Similarly, the nineteenth century convert Nettleton surrendered and reached peacefulness after a violent struggle. Nettleton "ate nothing all day, locked himself in his room . . . crying aloud, How long, O Lord how long? After repeating this . . . several times, he says, I seemed to sink away into a state of insensibility. When I came to myself again . . . I felt submissive to the will of God" (*ibid.*, p. 217).

In these statements and in Nettleton's case, it appears that feelings of relief resulted from exhaustion, apathy, or surrender, as James suggested. However, while interpretation of redemption as a passive state of surrender seems consistent with Protestant psychology, there seem to be more in the "awakening-salvation" stage than simple receptive surrender.

In the eighteenth century David Brainerd described his experience as follows:

> One morning, while I was walking in a solitary place as usual, I at once saw that all my contrivances and projects to effect or procure deliverance and salvation for myself were utterly in vain. . . . I saw that there was no necessary connection between my prayers and the bestowment of divine mercy. . . . I had been heaping up my devotions before God, fasting, praying, etc. . . . I continued, as I remember, in this state from Friday morning till Sabbath evening . . . having been thus endeavoring to pray . . . for near half an hour: then . . . unspeakable glory seemed to open to the apprehension of my soul. I do not mean any external brightness, nor imagination of a body of light, but it was a new inward apprehension [*ibid.*, pp. 215–16].

It is possible that, in retrospect, Nettleton, Brainerd, and the others attributed their feelings of redemption and relief to their previous religious efforts. But from a more objective point of view it would be logical to assume that in the case of Brainerd, for example, after two intensive, exhausting, marathon days of desperate struggle to determine whether years of suffering and religious efforts had been fruitful or not, something drastic would happen. It could be expected that at such a stage one would either feel hopeless and leave the battlefield altogether (become insensible-psychopathic) or feel relieved and peaceful.

The experience of awakening that often follows conversion efforts appears to resemble conventional processes of therapy in at least two ways: (1) Since in psychotherapy, as in conversion, the goal of insight is consciousness and not cure (see Mowrer, 1961:107; Rieff, 1966:87), insight serves the cathartic purpose of releasing built-up tension and enhancing peace of mind rather than changing behavior. (2) In both conversion and therapy, insight does not reflect growth (although after years of analysis the patient obviously grows older) or self-surrender but often results from a process of *cognitive dissonance;* i.e., if a person has invested so much time and energy (and money?) to benefit from the therapeutic or conversion process, he *must* convince himself that his efforts were fruitful. Accordingly, he must bring himself to the point of an exhausting critical experience (e.g. a two-day marathon of introspection) so that he is able to hold on to some "unusual sign" and thus convince himself that by fulfilling the requirements (self-torture and insight) he has "earned" his "salvation." Thus, the very reduction of anxiety about achieving salvation may result in some inner peace.

The "Psychologization" of Conversion

It was noted earlier that "throughout Christianity, from the preaching of John the Baptist down to modern 'revival meeting,' a marked event in the spiritual life, commonly called 'conversion,' has been recognized" among Christians (see Starbuck, 1901:21). I shall attempt to show that the intrapsychic experience characterizing the conversion process for hundreds of years was not reserved exclusively for the devout Christian but has been secularized and integrated into modern developmental and therapeutic psychology. Moreover, the conversion experience seems to have been popularized and disseminated in the West through the advent of Puritanism. Paradoxically, however, it is this very Puritan-Calvinist version of conversion, hemmed in by the overbearing principle of predestination, that has limited the impact of the experience on behavior change (see Chapters 1 and 2).

In order to understand this paradox, one must remember that, until the Reformation, receiving grace was a rather simple matter. It was Calvin who introduced the stern, uncompromising dogma of preordained election, which could not be changed by man's efforts. While Calvinism was widely adopted by the sixteenth-century colonists because of its functional work ethos, the rational man of the seventeenth and eighteenth centuries could no longer accept the dysfunctional and irrational feelings of uncertainty and predicament produced by the belief in predestination. Thus, the historian Perry Miller states:

> The divines were acutely conscious that this [new rationalism] was demanding what their theory had made impossible, and they were struggling to find some possible grounds for proving the necessity of works without curtailing the absolute freedom of God to choose and reject regardless of man's achievements [1956:54].

The new doctrine, which made it possible to soften traditional Calvinism without curtailing its deterministic element, was the "covenant theology." This stipulated that God had made a binding contract with man to enable him to feel grace and assurance through the "new-old" conversion experience. Theoretically there were now two retrospective methods available to Protestants for "getting around" strict orthodox Calvinism: (1) to succeed materially, which assures man that he was *a priori* elected (see Chapter 1), and (2) to somehow experience grace through belief and religious conversion, which was man's part in the covenant.

Thus, paradoxically, "soft Calvinism" actually enhanced man's uncertainty and desperate striving for assurance, since now the way to God's grace seemed deceptively open, although "only God knows whether we have it or not" (Miller, 1950:73). In any event, although the ways to God were obscured, the new forms of Calvinism were nonetheless incorporated into American culture at large. As Miller put it: "Calvinism in the seventeenth century covered almost as many shades of opinion as did 'socialism' in the twenties" (*ibid.*, p. 50). But while the covenant theology disseminated conversion as the new psychological-rational inner-change process among Protestants, Protestantism preserved its pessimistic-painful flavor even vis-à-vis conversion by stipulating the predestinarian element that shadowed man's struggle for salvation.

Indeed, one may notice that, on the one hand, conversion, as a common Western intrapsychic experience leading to presumed change, was used by Starbuck as a basis for his developmental personality theory in psychology. Accordingly, Starbuck used the term "conversion" "in a very general way to stand for the whole series of manifestations just preceding, accompanying, and immediately following the apparently sudden changes of character involved" (1901:21). As might be expected, however, the conversion process was simultaneously used to describe psychopathological conditions. William James used the conversion model to explain the pathology of the sick soul and the divided self, thus implying that the stress of uncertainty over one's identity and election might shift one's self-perception from a sense of being elected to one of being damned, and vice versa. Similarly, Prince (1930) explained the phenomenon of a split personality by using terminology associated with conversion.

We can thus see that psychologists made generous use of the intrapsychic experience of conversion to explain both normal and abnormal development. It is therefore natural to expect that the pessimistic, self-torturing conceptualization of personality change would infiltrate the field of psychotherapy—albeit with disguised terminology.

Most striking is the "familiar" language used by Angyal to explain neurosis and the pains of despair during the "demolition" stage, which "must" accompany treatment:

> In the neurotic anxiety there is always a sense of approaching doom, of threatening death . . . the patient feels, without qualification, that no one loves him, that he harms the world. . . . Doubt is an essential element of phenomenal anxiety. . . . The work of demolition culminates in bankruptcy. . . . A sweeping experience of bankruptcy must come if the person is to break out of his neurotic enclosure. . . . It is essential for the success of therapy that the therapist recognize this despair [as] the crucial step forward, a fruit of his work [1965:79, 225].

Thus, the painful components of doubt, guilt, despair, and general self-torture which constitute neurosis are also necessary and integral components of therapy.

Our argument may therefore be concluded as follows: When traditional psychodynamic therapy is examined from the historical perspective presented above, the roots of the past-oriented and self-torturing nature of "retrospective therapy" can easily be identified, since in Protestant conversion the "fight against doubt and despair never ceased" (Morgan, 1963:69). Moreover, the retrospective orientation and the claims that Freudian therapy is ineffective in producing a concrete cure or measurable behavior changes (Nagel, 1959; Mowrer, 1961; Eysenck, 1966) can also be better understood. If the goal of therapy is to determine whether a man was born a successful-elect, whether he has sinned in the past, and whether God loves him now as a result of his self-torturing efforts to be pardoned, then the painful process of reliving repressed guilt is the only proper therapeutic method. Insight and salvation, achieved via the cathartic reliving effect, may bring him to accept himself as he is—i.e., as he was predestined to be.[1]

The theory's cultural bias, however, suggests that neither the phenomenon of repressed guilt feelings nor the need for a past-oriented, painful road to personal salvation is universally applicable. To give the reader a glimpse of a different culture, according to which past-oriented self-torture is forbidden and salvation is presumably purchased through the joyful process of "prospective therapy," I shall present selected salvation principles of the Hassidic ethic.

"Prospective Therapy"

To point out the similarity and continuity between Christian conversion systems and retrospective, pain-oriented therapy methods, I have used the historisophical case-study approach, or "spiritual autobiographies," which were popular soul-searching methods among Protestants (see Bercovitch, 1975). To contrast "retrospective therapy" with the Hassidic ethic that underlies "prospective therapy," I shall have to rely, however, mostly on the theosophical approach (analysis of ideological principles), since there are practically no autobiographical case studies in Hassidic literature (probably because of the explicit Hassidic prohibition against digging into one's past). I realize that this is a somewhat unorthodox comparison, but it is primarily the counter-positive paradigm of man in which we are interested here, not the comparative case study *per se*.

[1] In schizophrenic cases of "split personality," a person actually attempts to be somebody he was not before—i.e., someone he was not destined to be. It is indeed remarkable that schizophrenia is most prevalent in the West, although it is considered *the* most extreme expression of deviance there.

In the Hassidic movement, which originated in Eastern Europe during the eighteenth century, socialization and the inculcation of an optimistic doctrine of personal salvation are accomplished by reciting and transmitting from generation to generation the legends, parables, and biblical commentary advanced by the movement's leaders, the *Rebbes* (this may also explain why the few illustrative cases I shall cite below are, unfortunately, not very reliable from the historical standpoint). Since many schools of thought have emerged during the course of Hassidism's proliferation (e.g. the famous "Chabad" movement), I shall limit my analysis here mainly to the parables and commentary preserved in the name of the movement's founder, the Baal Shem Tov ("Master of the Good Name," 1700–1760),[2] who is known by the acronym "Besht" and whose basic philosophy generally guides all branches of the movement to this very day. To understand the inherent differences between the Protestant and Hassidic ethics in their underlying approaches to socialization and salvation, we must first apprehend the basically different conceptions and interpretations of good and evil that guide these two doctrines.

Holistic vs. Dualistic Conceptions of Evil

The theologian Porter, who compared the Jewish and Christian doctrines of sin, stated: "Man was to the Hebrew a unity. Body and soul were but the outer and inner sides of one being, [whereas to Christians] body and soul were regarded as two essentially contrasted and really unrelated

---

[2] Whether *all* or only part of the "Besht's literature" is truly the Besht's own sayings or part of the literature was "forged" and related by his students in his name (see Scholem, 1976) is unimportant from our point of view, since this literature has nonetheless been used for socialization among the Hassidim for at least the past two hundred years.

things" (1902:93). Thus, Porter maintained, "the resulting [Christian] ethics, the idea that virtue is to be attained by the conquest and subjugation of the body, in which evil has its seat and its power, were radically opposed to Hebrew thought" (*ibid.*, p. 94). Here, essentially, are the theosophical roots of the contrasting conceptions of good and evil and the methods for changing from evil to good that emanated from these doctrines.

According to the Jewish holistic approach, what appears to be evil can be utilized to serve good purposes. The evil impulse (*yetzer hara*), for example, is conceived as a dynamic force necessary for life (somewhat similar to Freud's notion of the sublimated sex drive). To the question of whether the evil impulse is good, there is a classic and much-cited answer in Jewish commentary: "Certainly, for without it man would not build a house, nor marry, nor beget children, nor engage in trade" (*Breshit Rabba* 89:7). Therefore, man need not torture himself over his past passions, for salvation is reached by reinterpreting his evil desires in the light of the positive energy they instilled in him. According to Christian "psychosomatic dualism" (the dichotomy between body and mind), however, "social dualism" (the dichotomy between people born good-elects or wicked-damned) is unchangeable, and one can cope with "cognitive dualism" (the dichotomy between good and evil thoughts, forbidden wishes, or passions) in only two ways: (1) torture of body [3] (the seat of evil) and of mind in regard to past sins, or (2) repression of forbidden thoughts, such as Oedipal passions. Although this is not to suggest that ascetic trends were unknown among various Jewish sects throughout its history, I shall now examine these problems in the light of the Hassidic philosophy,

---

[3] The burning of "witches" during the Middle Ages and thereafter was usually rationalized in dualistic terms, to justify the torturing of the sinful body in order to save the soul (see Huizinga, 1927). Kai Erikson told me, however, that Christian sinners were often burned "as an introduction to hell."

which came to be known as the most optimistic Jewish way of life.

The Hassidic Doctrine of Sparks

According to Jewish mystics known as the Kabbalists (especially the later Kabbalists), evil, or what appears to be evil, came into the world as a result of a cosmological-divine breaking (*"shevirah"*), which is called the "Breaking of the Vessels." The cathartic breaking of the vessels, which has many explanations in the literature of mysticism, caused a diffusion or a shattering of the divine light, which flew either back to its divine source or downward into the depths of the earth. In this way, it is said, the good elements—i.e., the divine sparks—came to be mixed with the so-called vicious elements—i.e., the shells (*"kelipot"*). Salvation (*"tikkun"*), then, means restoration of the divine order by raising or uplifting to its divine source the holy sparks that are scattered in the world (Scholem, 1941).

According to Hassidism, which brought heaven down to earth by reinterpreting Kabbalism in an optimistic-operational language accessible to the masses yearning for salvation, there is actually no evil in the world. What appears to be evil is only disguised by the shells. Hence in every earthly matter (*"gashmiyut"*) that might appear to be forbidden (e.g. eating, working, copulating, rejoicing) there are holy sparks that can be redeemed by peeling off the shells, so to speak, and raising them up to their divine source. Thus, it is reported, for example, that "once, when the Besht was observed eating excessively, he said, 'My intention in eating is to achieve what Moses achieved in the . . . two tablets of the ten commandments' " (Horodetzky, 1951, Vol. 1:28). Moreover, salvation entails man's obligation and responsibility (and free will) to redeem himself by unfolding the unique goodness given to him (see Chapter 7) and sanctifying his earthly activities—i.e., by uplifting the specific holy sparks allocated to him. It is in this spirit that one should understand the Besht's sayings.

The Transformation of Seeming "Evil"

As indicated above, the guiding principle of the Hassidic ethic is that goodness is to be uncovered in whatever appears to be evil. Paradoxically, then, seeming "evil" exists to serve goodness. Buber quotes the Besht as having said: "Indeed, even in the sins that a man does, dwell holy sparks. . . . And what is it that the sparks await? . . . It is the turning" (1958a:189). "Evil is the chair of goodness" is the Besht's favorite metaphor to stress that evil actually serves goodness. "The real uniqueness is the divine, and how can it include two opposites in one subject, good and evil? . . . But in actuality it is non-contradicting, since evil is the chair of good (Besht, 1975a:8). The verse "Turn from evil and do good" is repeatedly interpreted by the Besht as: "Use evil to do good" (ibid., p. 15).

A parable explaining how the "evil impulse" can be put to good use is the following:

> The evil impulse was given to try us in the way one tests a child, by making it difficult and confusing the simple to divert us . . . and if we are wise and we don't let Him defeat us, then God derives great pleasure, as in the case of the good, diligent son whose father has great pleasure when the guest tests him . . . but the son is not defeated [ibid., p. 37].

Thus, what appears as an "evil" impulse is only a strengthening and challenging device to teach man how to anticipate and overcome the obstacles life entails. Moreover, even the actual commitment of transgressions is interpreted by the Besht as serving good. The verse "there is no righteous man on earth who will do good without sinning [means] when a person does only good . . . the evil impulse seduces him, whereas when the evil impulse realizes that he has in him a part of the evil inclination, he will leave him alone" (*ibid.*, p. 30). A classic, much-cited example of how every event can be viewed positively might be: "Rav Levy Yitzchak of Barditchev (who came to be known as 'the great defender') once saw a Jew tarring the wheels of his wagon while praying with his phylacteries ('*Tefilin*') on his head and arm. Rav Yitzchak cried out joyfully: 'God in Heaven! See how great is the love of this Jew for you. Even when he tars his wheels, his thoughts are with you'" (see Horodetzky, 1951, Vol. 5:91). In general, however, this unitary approach to good and evil is not meant to suggest that sin should be idealized,[4] but that in retrospect one should not develop guilt feelings in relation to past transgressions but should, rather, transform and reinterpret them cognitively into positive energizing terms.

Redemption by Descending to the Other

In contrast to the lonely Protestant method of self-centered introspective conversion, in Hassidism one redeems oneself not through insight but through "exsight," not by being preoccupied with one's own problems but by being involved with the others to whom one is responsible. Thus, as mentioned in Chapter 7, the Talmudic saying, "One who solicits mercy for his fellow while he himself is in need of the same thing will be answered first" (*Shevuot*, p. 39a) has been featured in Jewish salvation ethics for generations. Here the

---

[4] This was the crucial difference between the Hassidic and the Frankist movement, which misinterpreted the holistic approach to good and evil by advocating and idealizing sin as the means for salvation (see Scholem, 1941).

holistic principle of good and evil receives full expression through the Hassidic notion of unification ("*achdut*") or generalization ("*hitkalelut*"), which is the exact opposite of Calvinist "social dualism." Since there are no really wicked people, anormative behavior can either be redeemed by the conforming person through the rule of unification (my virtues redeem the other) or be reinterpreted as serving the observant others. The Besht states: "If a person had the opportunity to see a transgression or hear about someone in whom he identifies a tiny component of this transgression and he feels [the need] to improve himself . . . then he will bring back the wicked after he includes him through unification, since all are one people" (1975a:21). Alternatively, anormative behavior may be interpreted so that "the one who does not attend [the house of Torah] becomes a chair for the one who does . . . when he provides for him" (*ibid.*, p. 41).

A corollary of the principle of generalization and mutual responsibility is the notion of the righteous ("*zaddik*") descent to uplift nonconforming others (see Dresner, 1960). Most instructive in this context is the method of cure by descent entailed in a parable by Rabbi Nachman of Bratzlav, which tells about a prince who believed himself to be a turkey and thus undressed and sat under the table, where he ate only sunflower seeds. While all the doctors hired by his father, the king, could not cure the prince, there was one wise man who got also undressed, sat with the prince under the table, introduced himself as a turkey, and ate sunflower seeds until the prince found it strange that a wise man should behave in such a fashion. Thus they both decided that turkeys could dress, eat other food, etc., and finally both came out from under the table and behaved like humans again (see Steinman, 1951:157).

What is of interest to us now is the question of how one deals with the inner experience of guilt and forbidden thoughts in the Hassidic culture.

Alien Thoughts and Repression

In essence, the operational roots of neurosis and repressed guilt feelings, with which Christian conversion and modern therapy deal, are thoughts. According to the presumably universal Oedipus complex, for example, the child represses his forbidden wish, not real attempts, to copulate with his mother and kill his father. Similarly, it may be assumed that most of the material with which Christian converts or patients in analysis deal comprises thoughts, passions, and desires that were repressed by the Protestant process of "cognitive dualism," according to which there is no legitimate outlet for forbidden thoughts. Fromm *et al.*, for example, contend that "every society excludes certain thoughts and feelings from being thought, felt and expressed [and, hence, even in a tribe of warriors] an individual who feels revulsion against killing. . . would probably develop a psychosomatic symptom" (1974:102). The assumption that people in all societies repress forbidden thoughts and develop neurotic guilt symptoms [5] is challenged, however, by the Beshtian-Hassidic methods for handling "alien thoughts."

In the Hassidic culture, alien thoughts are "garments and covers behind which the Holy One . . . conceals Himself" (see Buber, 1958a:204). Moreover, "sometimes an alien thought is sent to him" (see Besht, 1975a:62) "in order that he may redeem it" (Buber, 1958a:205). It is thus repeatedly stressed by the Besht that alien thoughts and impulses are not to be repressed or chased away but are to be utilized as positive energizers:

[5] While Freud's "guilt-releasing therapy" may often result in hedonistic-psychopathic interpretations of evil (see Mowrer, 1961), which may evoke feelings of retrospective election, Jung's Calvinistic psychology preaches acceptance of the damned-dark (i.e., the "shadow") elements as unchangeable, integral components of man (see Neumann, 1963).

> Who is the hero who conquers his impulse? . . . As in
> worldly matters . . . upon hearing an infiltrating thief,
> there is one who screams and thereupon the thief escapes,
> and there is one who prepares chains, and when the thief
> enters the room, he ties him up with iron chains. So it is
> with the righteous. There is one who will not let any alien
> thought come near him . . . and there is one who utilizes
> the passion or love and evil fear to worship God [1975a:37].

The classic parable often used by the Besht to explain
how cognitively to transform an alien thought is the following:

> External love, which comes to awaken him to love God, re-
> sembles the case in which the king's messenger sometimes
> comes with a gesture of love, and the one who is foolish
> takes pleasure and entertains himself with the messenger.
> But the wise man says, Why should I rejoice with the mes-
> senger? I shall go to the source of love, the king. . . . If an
> alien thought comes to a man during studies or prayers [6]
> . . . it is the spark that lies in the depth of the shells seeking
> to ascend to its source [*ibid.*, p. 45].

Accordingly, the Besht states:

> He should watch the thought . . . like adultery, he should
> bring it to its root . . . he should think, it is part of the
> world of love. . . . If he suddenly sees a beautiful woman
> . . . he shall think from whence does she have this beauty?
> If she would have been dead, she wouldn't have this face
> any more . . . therefore it comes from God's power that
> spreads within her [1975b:28–31].

Indeed, there are examples of how this technique of neutral-
izing forbidden passions was applied in real life (see, for
example, Horodetzky, 1951, Vol. 1: 77–78).

A most instructive example of how Hassidic leaders presented practical methods for working through alien thoughts

---

[6] Indeed, many thoughts developed in this book came up during
prayers.

by using preventative-ventilating procedures can be found in a letter written by Rabbi Elimelech from Liszank to his disciples:

> . . . and he should accustom himself . . . to tell the teacher . . . and even a loyal friend all his alien thoughts . . . which the evil impulse brings to his mind and head . . . and he should not hide anything out of shame and . . . he will find out that by telling these things . . . he breaks the power of the evil impulse so they will not be able to overcome him next time, besides the good advice which he can receive from his friend, which is an excellent device [Horodetzky, 1951, Vol. 2:166–67].

In summary, if "alien thoughts" and impulses are not repressed but are transformed cognitively, then hypothetically one should expect to find a relatively lower rate of neurotic guilt feelings among the Hassidic groups that adhere strictly to the Besht's instructions (according to Chabad's rational philosophy, alien thoughts should be expelled; see Shneurson, 1956). Indeed, Haring (1956) suggests that, in contrast to Western repression-guilt cultures, in shame cultures, such as Japan, one never feels guilt or sin, only loss of face (see Chapter 7).

In any event, although it remains an empirical problem to determine the degree of guilt feelings to be found among followers of Hassidism, one would expect that the ethical principle of transforming evil and "alien thoughts" would also be reflected in a more active and directive approach to socialization that forbids retrospective self-torture and prescribes prospective means for joyful salvation.

The Prohibition of Retrospective Self-torture

In complete contrast to the past-oriented despair and self-torture accompanying the processes of Protestant conversion and Freudian therapy, retrospective self-torture of any form is strictly prohibited in the Hassidic culture.[7] Schatz-Uffenheimer (1968) points out that the three major categoric imperatives prerequisite for the Hassidic life-style are the prohibitions against despair, dejection, and regret. Retrospective introspection involves the egocentric weighing of sins against merits, which prevents one from the prospective-active worship of God. Paradoxically, sadness, doubt, and despair, or "transgression worries," are considered to be the worst transgressions, since such self-torturing activities deal with a man's egoistic attempts to save his own soul instead of redeeming the holy sparks scattered in the world, and they cast doubt on man's spiritual ability to change himself. Accordingly, "turning" or repentance ("teshuva") requires nothing more than a future-oriented cognitive decision to change (see Schatz-Uffenheimer, 1968).

Buber cites the Rabbi of Ger, who warned against past-oriented self-torture:

> He who has done ill and talks about it and thinks about it all the time does not cast the base thing out of his thoughts . . . and so he dwells in baseness. He will certainly not be able to turn . . . and in addition to this he may be overcome by gloom. . . . Rake the muck this way, rake the muck that way—it will always be muck. Have I sinned, or have I not sinned? . . . In the time I am brooding over it, I could be stringing pearls for the delight of Heaven [1958a:164–65].

Turning, according to Buber, means much more than Christian repentance. While turning means future-oriented renewal and reversal of one's whole being, retrospective self-torture in repentance withholds the "best energies from the work of reversal" (ibid., p. 164).

It is of interest to note here that in view of the "anti-suffering" ethic, the question of inevitable physical self-

---

[7] Asceticism was in essence always condemned by the Jewish sages (see Urbach, 1971).

torture, such as fasting, was quite problematic in Hassidism. Thus ritual fasting was not viewed as an act of repentance in regard to an individual's past sins but was rationalized as man's participation in the sorrows of Heaven (see Schatz-Uffenheimer, 1968:43). It is reported for example:

> To the *maggid* [preacher or public commentator] of Koznitz came a man who, in order to mortify himself, wore nothing but a sack on his bare body and fasted from one Sabbath to the next. The *maggid* said to him, Do you think the Evil Urge is keeping away from you? It is tricking you into that sack. He who pretends to fast from Sabbath to Sabbath but secretly eats a little something every day is spiritually better off than you, for he is only deceiving others, while you are deceiving yourself [Buber, 1947:291].

The Besht further stressed that not only "weeping is very bad" but "even if he stumbled into sin, he should not be overly sad" (Besht, 1975b:15). Moreover, the Besht condemned sadness and regret for past sins as temptations of the evil impulse,[8] and he thus encouraged man to overcome his depression in spite of *actual* failure.

> Sometimes the evil inclination will mislead a man by telling him that he committed a great sin. . . . In this case the evil impulse simply wishes to sadden him. . . . One must be careful to detect this deceit and say . . . if in truth it was a sin, then God will have more joy on my account if I pay it no heed and refuse to be saddened by my transgression [*ibid.*, p. 14].

Indeed, it is known that the Besht never tortured himself but ate and drank like all people. When he heard that his faithful disciple tended to torture himself, he wrote to him angrily:

> My stomach is angry; don't put yourself in such a danger because this is the deed of melancholy and sadness and God

---

[8] Molinos, the founder of Quietism, similarly interpreted the tendency to repent as the temptation of Satan, but he went so far as to abolish the meaning of sin altogether (see Schatz-Uffenheimer, 1968).

does not prevail in sadness but is acquired through the commandment of being joyful [Horodetzky, 1951; Vol. 1:37].

Thus, although the natural inclination to repent via self-torture was never entirely eliminated, evidence indicates that the strict Beshtian Hassidic ethic severely condemns retrospective-egocentric self-torture.

If life, however, is to be conceived of as man's endless struggle against depression and desperation, mental exercises such as cognitive transformations of "alien thoughts" and even the proscriptive norms against sadness would seem insufficient. This is especially true for the ordinary man, yearning for salvation, unless active prescriptive norms are available to counteract melancholy. Thus, the most important and organismically involving principle in "prospective therapy" is the dynamic for producing energizing joy activities.

The "Feather Blanket" Principle for Producing Energizing Joy

The reflective impact of ecstatic singing and dancing capable of counteracting sadness can be compared to the effect of a feather blanket on the human body. When a person feels very cold and covers himself with a feather blanket, his body must first warm up the blanket slightly; only afterward does the blanket in return produce increasing warmth. To feel real joy, a group of people must first sing and dance in order to warm up the melody and the dance, and only thereafter can the ascending song and dance reproduce energizing joy. Yet, states the Besht, the bellows can inflame the fire only "if there is one spark left with which to reinflame the big fire" (1975a:48), so the coals of the melody should never be entirely extinguished.

According to Shochat (1951), the Besht's major contribution to the notion of joy in Hassidism was his insistence that the prerequisite for the soul's joy is earthly physical joy—

i.e., the "feather blanket" principle of social rejoicing to warm the soul. The ideal of eating, drinking, and rejoicing on the Sabbath is illustrated by the Hassidic parable about the prince who succeeded in overcoming his sadness only after he provided drinks for the masses, who eventually infected him with their happiness (*ibid.*, p. 14). Indeed, the periodic social gatherings among contemporary Hassidic groups, during which the Hassidim sing and dance together, or the "Hora" dances in *kibbutzim* seem to function as an antimelancholic bellows.

Unlike man's basic inability to change his fate in the predestinal conversion system, in the Hassidic culture man can, and is obliged to, influence Heaven and change himself by uplifting as many holy sparks as he can through the joyous sanctification of his earthly activities. Accordingly, states the Besht, "all his movements, business, and talks leave their impression on Heaven" (*ibid.*, p. 31). Adhesion (*devekut*) and ecstasy (*hitlahavut*) during prayer, eating, working, rejoicing, and even copulation, if accompanied by religious contemplation (which diverts attention from personal troubles), are, then, the behavioral means for the ordinary man to ascend to the highest level of the ideal Jew. Hence, dancing and drinking are perceived not as hedonistic ends but as acts of the "bellows" necessary to nourish the soul. Man's ups and downs, from spiritual prayer exercises down to any earthly activity, are conceived of as integral parts of the cosmological rhythm (*ratzo vashov*) necessary for the world's renewal and reproduction of positive energy in order to ascend higher and higher in the spiritual world.

Every act-producing motivation can accordingly be transformed into positive energy, and the notion of descending and ascending takes on a motivating-energizing meaning; i.e., the more one descends to accumulate strength and energy, the higher one will be able to ascend. As the Besht puts it: "By eating and drinking and engaging in trade, man ceases to study the Torah and worship God. Then the soul rests from its ecstasy and becomes stronger to return to higher adhesion" (*ibid.*, p. 10). Similarly, energizing adhesion can be achieved by all joy-producing actions, such as singing, "since the song causes adhesion" (see Shochat, 1951:33). Even the joy of joking before engaging in study is considered a legitimate energizing method by the Besht: "And through joy and a word of humor he ascends from smallness to greatness" (1975a:10). Moreover, it seems that the "feather-blanket" energizing principle was used by early Hassidim even to defend drunkards, since "even if they drink in the manner of drunkedness, it is desirable . . . since when the physical powers are strengthened, the mental powers will be strengthened" (see Shochat, 1951:37, 38).

Compelling descriptions of how the "feather-blanket," joy-producing energizing principle was activated as an antimelancholic device are ample. Thus one would expect that, at least during the High Holidays, which are days of repentance for past sins, people would fall into gloomy retrospective thoughts about their chances of being forgiven, Horodetzky reports, however, that

> . . . even during the High Holidays they [the Hassidim] would periodically dance in a circle, which included everybody, and they would sing and play special melodies and the *zaddik* [holy, righteous man, serving as charismatic leader of a Hassidic group] would also take part in the dance . . . this moment they would rise above reality, forget everything, dancing and singing for long hours and not feeling fatigue. During intermissions they would drink a little alcohol and tell holy stories and then return to dance [1951, Vol. 4:83].

Finally, whereas in the conversion process "assurance" is considered "false" if it is not preceded by inner struggles of despair and doubt, and in psychodynamic therapy achieving "insight" before reliving subconscious pains is regarded as external or even "psychopathic" verbalization, in Hassidism the very experience and expression of joy and happiness are a sign of assurance and basic trust. Rabbi Eliyahu Hacohen of Izmir maintained, for example, that a man's "face should be always smiling and joking, because this reflects his trust in God, [and conversely] if you see a man who is always sad, know that it is his lack of assurance that causes him sadness" (see Shochat, 1951:39). Thus Shochat concludes that it is in fact the "joy of assurance" which constitutes the essence of Hassidic joy (*ibid.*, p. 40).

Conclusion and Summary

In this final chapter I have discussed the inherent differences between the Protestant retrospective, self-torture approach to therapy and salvation and the Hassidic joy-oriented prospective system for redemption. I have suggested that, if traditional therapeutic procedures are examined in their historiosophical context, the relative ineffectiveness of these methods can be better understood.

A prospective approach to therapy does not advocate the denial of one's past or a "here and now" hedonism but the transfer of one's energies from egocentric preoccupation with past failures to sociocentric future-oriented efforts energized by joy-producing mechanisms.

Although the Hassidic perspective may constitute the general basis for the conceptualization of a new prospective "joy-therapy" to replace retrospective "*oy*-therapy," obviously this chapter has not offered concrete operational methods and therapeutic principles. Following the efforts developed throughout this volume, the point of departure here was that traditional therapy is rooted in a specific ethic; my purpose was to outline the principles of a different ethic as a potential source of a positivistic paradigm of man and a new therapeutic system. Naturally, careful experimentations and detailed documentation will be necessary to formulate the methodology of "prospective therapy." Although the principles of the Hassidic ethic may sound somewhat naive to modern secularized man, it should be remembered that the Hassidic life-system has crystallized during a period of nearly 250 years of actual socialization, which can be identified today among the many Hassidic groups (e.g. the "Chabad" movement), as well as in some communes.

In conclusion, if Western theories of deviance and especially modern psychotherapy methods are rooted in and affected by a pessimistic ethical-religious conception of man, as this book has attempted to show, change must begin by adopting a more optimistic philosophy of man. Then, although the world does not change with the change of paradigms, as Thomas Kuhn noted, perhaps the change in the social scientist's view of the world may undermine the rigid division of people into big bad wolves and innocent lambs.

Appendix

The Egoistic/Collectivistic (E/C-nAch) Questionnaire

Instructions

The following questionnaire deals with personal attitudes. The statements are presented in the following form: "I prefer (A) to (B)." For example: "I prefer going to the movies to reading a book." You are requested to register your agreement with each statement according to the given scale. Please pay attention. If you agree *very much* with the statement "I prefer doing (A) to doing (B)," this would mean that you prefer (A) much more than (B). If you strongly disagree with the statement "I prefer doing (A) to doing (B)," this means you prefer (B) much more to (A).

Read the following statements carefully and put an X in the column that expresses your degree of agreement with the statement most accurately.

Example: If you very much agree with the statement "I prefer working at any job to not working at all" put an X in column 7, which is to the extreme right in the first row, as follows:

1	2	3	5	6	7
disagree strongly	disagree much	disagree somewhat	agree somewhat	agree much	agree strongly
					X

[Note: Midpoint number 4, "undecided," was eliminated to avoid evasive answers. See p. 165.]

If you completely disagree with this statement, put an X under column 1, which is to the extreme left, as follows:

1	2	3	5	6	7
disagree strongly	disagree much	disagree somewhat	agree somewhat	agree much	agree strongly
X					

In the same way, you may put an X under the intermediate degrees, according to your agreement or disagreement with the statement.

	disagree strongly 1	disagree much 2	disagree somewhat 3	agree somewhat 5	agree much 6	agree strongly 7
1. I prefer to honor obligations to a friend rather than to an employer.						
2. I prefer working for a goal in which I'm the only recipient of approval to working for a goal where many people participate and win approval together.						
3. I think more about my future than about the present lives of others.						

	disagree strongly 1	disagree much 2	disagree somewhat 3	agree somewhat 5	agree much 6	agree strongly 7
4. I prefer competitive conditions in which I have an advantage to conditions where all the people involved have approximately the same ability.						
5. I find it important to do my work as well as possible, even if this harms my relationship with fellow workers.						
6. In my spare time I prefer to spend time on topics related to my job rather than with my friends.						
7. I prefer to give up a personal career rather than argue with my family about the profession I will work in.						
8. As a business administrator, I would rather fire a veteran worker for inefficiency than keep him at work because of his great social contribution to fellow workers.						
9. I prefer working overtime at my job to busying myself with public activity in my spare time.						

	disagree strongly 1	disagree much 2	disagree somewhat 3	agree somewhat 5	agree much 6	agree strongly 7
10. I prefer working on a piece-work-bonus system, which is slightly more risky but enables me to earn more, to working according to a permanent salary like all my fellow workers.						
11. I prefer firing old veterans and conscientious workers in my business, in order to profit more, to letting them continue to work according to their ability in spite of the fact that I will profit less.						
12. I'd rather change my job because of advancement difficulties than argue with fellow workers.						
13. I prefer being successful in financial ventures to being successful socially.						
14. I'd rather hurt my fellow workers slightly in order to advance personally than sustain good relations but remain a longer time in the same position.						

	disagree strongly 1	disagree much 2	disagree somewhat 3	agree somewhat 5	agree much 6	agree strongly 7
15. I prefer to keep my personal property for myself rather than contribute part to some social goals.						
16. I prefer to do all I can for my fellow workers rather than lose their friendship.						
17. I prefer to hurt my fellow workers rather than give them a chance to excel at my expense.						
18. I prefer to finish important business at work rather than spend vacations with my family and friends.						
19. I'd rather be considered unsociable than leave a job in which I am successful.						
20. I prefer more money rather than more friends.						
21. I prefer to harm my fellow worker rather than give him a job that I want for myself.						
22. I prefer social success rather than economic success.						
23. I prefer more friends and less money rather than more money and fewer friends.						

	disagree strongly 1	disagree much 2	disagree somewhat 3	agree somewhat 5	agree much 6	agree strongly 7
24. I prefer to work alone with greater earnings rather than with a group of friends and less earnings, even though with friends the atmosphere is more pleasant.						
25. I prefer a social engagement to a business dinner in an expensive restaurant.						
26. I prefer to help my family first of all rather than advance myself economically.						
27. I prefer one fat bank account to one hundred good friends.						
28. I think I hate to lose friends more than I love to earn money.						
29. I'd rather get to the top without regard for the price involved than be held back because of sentiments.						
30. I prefer being successful for my own sake to dedicating myself to others.						

Bibliography

ABBIE, A. A. *The Original Australians.* London: F. Muller, 1969.

ADAMS, C. F. *Massachusetts, Its Historians and Its History.* Boston: Houghton Mifflin, 1893.

ADAMS, C. F. *Some Phases of Sexual Morality and Church Discipline in the Colonial New England.* Proceedings of the Massachusetts Historical Society, Boston, Second Series, Vol. VI, 1890.

ADORNO, T. A., *et al. The Authoritarian Personality.* New York: Harper & Row, 1950.

ALBERT, R. S., *et al.,* "The Psychopathic Personality: A Content Analysis of the Concept." *Journal of General Psychology,* Vol. 60, 1959.

ALEXANDER, F. "The Neurotic Character." *International Journal of Psychoanalysis,* Vol. 2, 1930.

ALEXANDER, F., and SELESNICK, S. T., *The History of Psychiatry.* New York: Harper & Row, 1966.

ALLPORT, G. W. "Mental Health: A Generic Attitude." *Journal of Religion and Health,* Vol. 4, 1964.

American Psychiatric Association. *Diagnostic and Statistical Manual.* Washington, D.C.: APA, 1952, 1958.

ANDERSON, N. H. "Likeableness Ratings of 555 Personality-Trait Words." *Journal of Personality and Social Psychology,* Vol. 9, 1968, No. 3.

ANGYAL, A. *Neurosis and Treatment: A Holistic Approach.* New York: Wiley, 1965.

ARONFREED, J. *Conduct and Conscience.* New York: Academic Press, 1968.

ATKINSON, J. W. "The Achievement Motive." *Journal of Abnormal and Social Psychology,* Vol. 60, 1960.

BARNES, H. E., and N. K. TEETERS. *New Horizons in Criminology.* Englewood Cliffs, N.J.: Prentice-Hall, 1965.

BECKER, H. S. " 'Whose Side Are We On?' " *Social Problems,* Vol. 4, Winter 1967.

BECKER, H. S. *Outsiders.* New York: Free Press, 1963.

BECKER, H. S., *et al. Boys in White.* Chicago: University of Chicago Press, 1961.

BELCHER, N. J. *The Measurement of Loneliness: A Validation Study of the Belcher Extended Loneliness Scale (Bels).* Chicago: Illinois Institute of Technology, 1973.

BELL, D. *The End of Ideology.* New York: Free Press, 1972.

BEN MAIMON, M. *Mishne Torah* (Hebrew), Vol. I. Tel Aviv: Pardes, 1955.

BENEDICT, R. *The Chrysanthemum and the Sword: Patterns of Culture.* Glencoe, Ill.: Free Press, 1954.

BERCOVITCH, S. *The Puritan Origins of the American Self.* New Haven: Yale University Press, 1975.

BERGER, P. L., and T. LUCKMANN. *The Social Construction of Reality.* Harmondsworth, England: Penguin, 1966.

BESHT, I. *Keter Shem Tov.* (Hebrew). Jerusalem: Rosen, 1975a.

BESHT, I. *Zavaat Harivash* (Hebrew). New York: Kehot Publication Society, 1975b.

BLAUNER, R. *Alienation and Freedom.* Chicago: University of Chicago Press, 1964.

BRAGINSKY, B. M., *et al. Methods of Madness.* New York: Holt, Rinehart & Winston, 1969.

BRENDT, R. H., and C. BRENDT. *The World of the First Australians.* Chicago: University of Chicago Press, 1964.

BUBER, M. *Tales of the Hassidism—The Early Masters.* New York: Schocken, 1947.

BUBER, M. *Hassidism and Modern Man.* New York: Harper & Row, 1958a.

BUBER, M. *Paths in Utopia.* Boston: Beacon Press, 1958b.

BUBER, M. *The Knowledge of Man.* New York: Harper Torchbooks, 1965.

BUBER, M. *Between Man and Man.* New York: Macmillan, 1967.

BURGESS, R. L., and R. L. AKERS, "A Differential Association-Reinforcement Theory of Criminal Behavior." In D. R. Cressey and D. A.

Ward (eds.), *Delinquency, Crime and Social Processes.* New York: Harper & Row, 1969.

BURROWS, E. G., and M. E. SPIRO. *An Atoll Culture.* New Haven: Human Relations Files, 1957.

BUSS, A. H. *Psychopathology.* New York: Wiley, 1966.

CALVIN, J., *A Compend of the Institutes of the Christian Religion.* Edited by H. T. Kerr. Philadelphia: Westminster (United Presbyterian Church in the U.S.A.), 1939.

CAMERON, N. *Personality Development and Psychopathology.* Boston: Houghton Mifflin, 1963.

CAMPBELL, D. *The Puritans in Holland, England and America.* Vol. II. New York: Harper & Brothers, 1892.

CAMPBELL, D. *Arabian Medicine and its Influence on the Middle Ages.* New York: Dutton, 1926.

CAMUS, A. *The Stranger.* Harmondsworth, England: Penguin Books, 1968.

CAPLAN, R. B. *Psychiatry and the Community in Nineteenth Century America.* New York: Basic Books, 1969.

CAUDILL, W. "Around the Clock Patient Care in Japanese Psychiatric Hospitals: The Role of the 'Tsukitoi'." *American Sociological Review,* Vol. 26, 1961.

CHAUNCY, C. *Seasonable Thoughts on the State of Religion in New England.* Boston: Rogers & Fowle, 1743.

CLECKLEY, H. *The Mask of Sanity.* St. Louis: Mosby, 1964.

CLEMMER, D. *The Prison Community.* New York: Holt, Reinhart & Winston, 1958.

CLOWARD, R., and L. OHLIN. *Delinquency and Opportunity.* Glencoe, Ill.: Free Press, 1960.

COHEN, A. K. *Delinquent Boys: The Culture of a Gang.* Glencoe, Ill.: Free Press, 1955.

COHEN, A. K. *Deviance and Control.* Englewood Cliffs, N.J.: Prentice-Hall, 1966.

COHEN, H. L. "Educational Therapy: The Design of Learning Environment." In J. M. Shlien (ed.), *Research in Psychotherapy.* Washington, D.C.: American Psychological Association, 1968.

COLEMAN, J. C., *Abnormal Psychology and Modern Life.* Chicago: Scott, Foresman, 1964.

COOKRIDGE, E. H. *The Third Man.* New York: Putnam, 1968.

CRESSEY, D. R., and D. A. WARD. *Delinquency, Crime and Social Processes*. New York: Harper & Row, 1969.

DAVIS, K. "Mental Hygiene and the Class Structure." *Psychiatry*, Vol. 1, 1938.

DAHLSTROM, W. G., and G. S. WELCH. *An MMPI Handbook*. Minneapolis: University of Minnesota Press, 1960.

DE VOS, G. A. *Socialization for Achievement*. Berkeley: University of California Press, 1973.

DEUTSCH, A. *The Mentally Ill in America*. New York: Columbia University Press, 1949.

DINITZ, S. *et al.* "Psychopathy and Autonomic Responsivity: A Note on the Importance of Diagnosis." *Journal of Abnormal Psychology*, Vol. 82, 1973.

DOI, T. *The Anatomy of Dependence*. Tokyo: Kodansha International, 1973.

DORE, R. *Education in Tokugava Japan*. Berkeley: University of California Press, 1965.

DRAGUNS, J. G. "Values Reflected in Psychopathology: The Case of the Protestant Ethic." *Ethos*, Vol. 2, 1974, No. 2.

DRESNER, S. H. *The Zaddik*. New York: Schocken Books, 1960.

DURKHEIM, E. *Sociology and Philosophy*. New York: Free Press, 1974.

DURKHEIM, E. *The Division of Labor in Society*. New York: Free Press, 1964.

EASTWOOD, M. R., and M. H. TREVELYAN. "Psychosomatic Disorders in the Community." *Journal of Psychosomatic Research*, Vol. 16, 1972.

Encyclopaedia Britannica, Vol. 4. Chicago: Encyclopaedia Britannica Inc., 1970.

EDGERTON, R. B. "On the 'Recognition' of Mental Illness." In S. C. Plog and R. B. Edgerton (eds.), *Changing Perspectives in Mental Illness*. New York: Holt, Rinehart & Winston, 1969.

EISENSTADT, S. N. (ed.). *The Protestant Ethic and Modernization*. New York: Basic Books, 1968.

EPSTEIN, S. M. "Toward a Unified Theory of Anxiety." In Maher, B. (ed.), *Progress in Experimental Personality Research*. New York: Academic Press, 1967.

ERIKSON, K. T. "The Functions of Deviance in Groups." *Social Problems*, Vol. 7, Fall 1959.

ERIKSON, K. T. "Notes on the Sociology of Deviance." *Social Problems*, Vol. 9, Spring 1962.

ERIKSON, K. T. *Wayward Puritans.* New York: Wiley, 1966.

EYSENCK, H. J. *The Dynamics of Anxiety and Hysteria.* New York: Praeger, 1957.

EYSENCK, H. J. *The Effects of Psychotherapy.* New York: International Science Press, 1966.

FARNHAM, W. (ed.). *Twentieth Century Interpretations of Doctor Faustus.* Englewood Cliffs, N.J.: Prentice-Hall, 1969.

FAYERWEATHER, J. *The Executive Overseas.* Syracuse, N.Y.: Syracuse University Press, 1959.

FENICHEL, D. *The Psychoanalytic Theory of Neurosis.* London: Routledge & Kegan Paul, 1963.

FISCHOFF, B. "Aspects of Historical Judgement: The Effects of Temporal Perspective and Outcome Knowledge on Judgments under Uncertainty," Ph.D. dissertation. Hebrew University of Jerusalem, May 1974.

FISCHOFF, B. "Hindsight: Thinking Backward?", *ORI Research Monograph* No. 14, 1974; also in *Psychology Today,* Vol. 3, 1975.

FLUSSER, D. "The Dead Sea Sect and Pre-Pauline Christianity." In *Aspects of the Dead Sea Scrolls* Scripta Hierosolymitana, Vol. 4. Publications of the Hebrew University of Jerusalem, 1958.

FORD, D. H., and H. B. URBAN. *Systems of Psychotherapy.* New York: Wiley, 1964.

FORTUNE, R. F. "Sorcerers of Dobu." In *Archipelago of East New Guinea.* London: Routledge & Sons, 1932.

FOUCAULT, M. *Madness and Civilization.* New York: Random House, 1965.

FRANKENSTEIN, C. *Psychopathy.* New York: Grune & Stratton, 1959.

FREIDSON, E. "Disability as Social Deviance." In M. B. Sussman (ed.), *Sociology and Rehabilitation.* Washington, D.C.: American Sociological Association, 1965.

FREUD, S. *Complete Psychological Works.* London: Hogarth Press, 1966.

FRIEDMAN, M. "Dialogue and the Unique in Humanistic Psychology." *Journal of Humanistic Psychology,* Vol. 12, 1972, No. 2.

FROMM, E. *The Fear of Freedom.* London: Routledge & Kegan Paul, 1960.

FROMM, E., *et al. Zen Buddhism and Psychoanalysis.* London: Souvenir Press, 1974.

GARDNER, H. *Milton's Satan and the Theme of Damnation in Elizabethan Tragedy.* Vol. 1. London: English Studies, 1948.

GARFINKEL, H. "Conditions of Successful Degradation Ceremonies." *American Journal of Sociology,* Vol. 61, 1956.

GIBBS, J. P. "Issues in Defining Deviant Behavior." In R. A. Scott and J. D. Douglas (eds.) *Theoretical Perspectives on Deviance.* New York: Basic Books, 1972.

GLASER, D. *The Effectiveness of a Prison and Parole System.* Indiannapolis: Bobbs Merrill, 1964.

GOFFMAN, E. *The Presentation of Self in Everyday Life.* New York: Doubleday, 1959.

GOFFMAN, E. *Asylums.* Chicago: Aldine, 1961.

GOFFMAN, E. *Stigma.* Englewood Cliffs, N.J.: Prentice-Hall, 1965.

GOLDMAN, R. K. and G. A. MENDELSOHN. "Psychotherapeutic Change and Social Adjustment: A Report of a National Survey of Psychotherapists." *Journal of Abnormal Psychology,* Vol. 74, 1969.

GOLDSTEIN, JOSEPH, BURKE MARSHALL, and JACK SCHWARTZ. *The My Lai Massacre and Its Cover-up: Beyond the Reach of Law?* New York: Free Press, 1976.

GOUGH, H. G. "A Sociological Theory of Psychopathy." *American Journal of Sociology,* Vol. 53, 1948.

GOUGH, H. G., and D. R. PETERSEN. "The Identification and Measurement of Predispositional Factors in Crime and Delinquency." *Journal of Consulting Psychology,* Vol. 16, 1952.

GRAY-LITTLE, B. "The Salience of Negative Information in Impression Formation among Two Danish Samples." *Journal of Cross-Cultural Psychology,* Vol. 4, 1973, No. 2.

GREENING, T. C. "Encounter Groups from the Perspective of Existential Humanism." In T. C. Greening (ed.), *Existential Humanistic Psychology.* Belmont, Calif.: Brooks/Cole, 1971.

GROB, G. *The State and the Mentally Ill.* Chapel Hill: University of North Carolina Press, 1966.

GUILFORD, J. P. *Psychometric Methods.* New York: McGraw-Hill, 1954.

HALEY, J. "The Famility of the Schizophrenic: A Model System." In G. Handel (ed.), *The Psychosocial Interior of the Family.* Chicago: Aldine, 1967.

HALLORAN, R. *Japan: Image and Realities.* Tokyo: C. E. Tuttle, 1969.

HARE, R. D. *Psychopathy: Theory and Research.* New York: Wiley, 1970.

HARE, R. D. "Psychopathy." In P. Venables and M. Christie (eds.), *Research in Psychophysiology.* New York: Wiley, 1975.

HARE, R. D. "The Origins of Confusion." *Journal of Abnormal Psychology,* Vol. 82, 1973, No. 3.

HARE, R. D., and D. CRAIGEN. "Psychopathy and Physiological Activity in a Mixed Motive Game Situation." *Psychophysiology,* Vol. 11, 1974.

HARING, D. *Personal Character and Cultural Milieu.* Syracuse, N.Y.: Syracuse University Press, 1956.

HARRINGTON, A. *Psychopaths.* New York: Simon & Schuster, 1972.

HARTER, M. R. "Excitability Cycles and Cortical Scanning: A Review of Two Hypotheses of Central Intermittency in Perception." *Psychological Bulletin,* Vol. 68, 1967.

HAVENS, J., *et al. Psychology and Religion.* New York: Van Nostrand, 1968.

HAYS, W. L. *Statistics for the Social Sciences.* New York: Holt, 1973.

HECKHAUSEN, H. *The Anatomy of Achievement Motivation.* New York: Academic Press, 1967.

HERCHMAN, D. *New England Memorial.* Boston: 1771. *The History of New England from 1630–1649.* Boston: Little, Brown, 1853.

HOBBES, T. *Leviathan.* London: Oxford University Press, 1958.

HOFSTADTER, R. *Social Darwinism in American Thought.* Boston: Beacon Press, 1968.

HOLLINGSHEAD, A. B., and F. C. REDLICH. *Social Class and Mental Illness.* New York: Wiley, 1958.

HONIGMAN, J. J. *Culture and Personality.* New York: Harper & Rutlers, 1954.

HORODETZKY, S. A. *Hassidism and the Hassidim* (Hebrew). Tel Aviv: Devir, 1951.

HOSPERS, J. "What Means This Freedom?" in B. Berofsky (ed.), *Free Will and Determinism.* New York: Harper & Row, 1966.

HUGHES, P. *Witchcraft.* Harmondsworth, England: Penguin Books, 1965.

HUIZINGA, J. *The Waning of the Middle Ages.* New York: Doubleday, 1927.

HUTTON, B. *School for Spies.* London: Neville Spearmen, 1961.

IRWIN, J. *The Felon.* Englewood Cliffs, N.J.: Prentice-Hall, 1970.

INGRAM, G. L., et al. "An Experimental Program for the Psychopathic Delinquent: Looking in the 'Correctional Wastebasket'." Journal of Research in Crime and Delinquency, Vol. 7, 1970.

ISRAEL, J. Alienation from Marx to Modern Sociology. Boston: Allyn & Bacon, 1971.

JACOBS, J. "Jack and the Beanstalk," in M. Williams and M. Dalphin (eds.), The New Junior Classics. Vol. I. New York: P. F. Collier & Sons, 1949.

JAHODA, M. Current Concepts of Positive Mental Health. New York: Basic Books, 1958.

JAMES, W. (1901). The Varieties of Religious Experience. London: Fontana Library, 1960.

JOHNSON, F., ed. Alienation. New York: Seminar Press, 1973.

JUNG, C. P. The Development of Personality. New York: Pantheon Books, 1954.

KATCHER, A., and J. KATCHER. "The Restructuring of Behavior in a Messianic Cult." In R. Endleman (ed.), Personality and Social Life. New York: Random House, 1967.

KITANO, H. H. L. "Japanese-American Mental Illness." In Plog and Edgerton, Changing Perspectives in Mental Health, 1969 (see Edgerton).

KITSUSE, J. I. "Societal Reactions to Deviant Behavior: Problems of Theory and Method." Social Problems, Vol. 9, Winter 1962.

KUHN, T. S., The Structure of Scientific Revolutions. Chicago: University of Chicago Press, 1969.

LAING, R. D. The Politics of Experience. New York: Ballantine, 1967.

LEMERT, E. G. Human Deviance, Social Problems and Social Control. Englewood Cliffs, N.J.: Prentice-Hall, 1967.

LIFTON, R. J. Thought Reform and the Psychology of Totalism. New York: W. W. Norton, 1961.

LINTON, R. The Cultural Background of Personality. New York: Appleton-Century, 1945.

LOFLAND, J. Deviance and Identity. Englewood Cliffs, N.J.: Prentice-Hall, 1969.

LOMBROSO, C. (1876). Crime: Its Causes and Remedies. Montclair, N.J.: Montclair, 1912.

LOUBSER, J. J. "Calvinism, Equality, and Inclusion: The Case of Afrikaner Calvinism." In S. N. Eisenstadt (ed.), The Protestant Ethic and Modernization. New York: Basic Books, 1968.

LUKES, S. Individualism. New York: Harper Torchbooks, 1973.

LYKKEN, D. T. "A Study of Anxiety in the Sociopathic Personality." *Journal of Abnormal Psychology*, Vol. 55, 1957, No. 1.

LYMAN, S. M., and M. D. SCOTT. *A Sociology of the Absurd*. New York: Appleton-Century-Crofts, 1970.

MANN, J. H. "Experimental Evaluation of Role-Playing." *Psychological Bulletin*, Vol. 53, 1956.

Massachusetts Historical Society, Vols, 4, 14, 44.

MATHIS, H. I. *Emotional Responsivity in the Antisocial Personality*. Doctoral dissertation, George Washington University. Ann Arbor, Mich.: University Microfilms, 1970, 71–12.

MATZA, D. *Delinquency and Drift*. New York: Wiley, 1964.

MATZA, D. *Becoming Deviant*. Englewood Cliffs, N.J.: Prentice-Hall, 1969.

MAY, R. *The Meaning of Anxiety*. New York: Ronald Press, 1950.

McCLELLAND, D. C. *The Achieving Society*. New York: Van Nostrand, 1961.

McCLELLAND, D. C. "The Effects of the Protestant Reformation on Need for Achievement." In L. Hudson (ed.), *The Ecology of Human Intelligence*. London: Penguin, 1970.

McCORD, W., and J. McCORD. *The Psychopath*. Princeton, N.J.: Van Nostrand, 1964.

McCORKLE, L. W. and R. KORN. "Resocialization within Walls." In N. Johnson *et al.* (eds.), *The Sociology of Punishment and Correction*. New York: Wiley, 1962.

MACDONALD, A. P. "More on the Protestant Ethic." *Journal of Consulting and Clinical Psychology*, Vol. 39, 1972, No. 1.

McNAMARA, J. H. "Uncertainties in Police Work." In D. J. Bordua (ed.), *The Police: Six Sociological Essays*. New York: Wiley, 1967.

McNEILL, J. T. *A History of the Cure of Souls*. New York: Harper & Brothers, 1951.

MEAD, G. H. *Mind, Self and Society*. Chicago: University of Chicago Press, 1934.

MEAD, G. H. "The Problems of Society—How We Become Selves." In M. H. Moore (ed.), *Movements of Thought in the Nineteenth Century*. Chicago: University of Chicago Press, 1936.

MEHRABIAN, A. "Male and Female Scales of Tendency to Achieve." *Educational and Psychological Measurement*, Vol. 28, 1968.

MERTON, R. K. "Puritanism, Pietism, and Science." *Sociological Review*, Vol. 28, 1936.

MERTON, R. K. *Social Theory and Social Structure.* New York: Free Press, 1957.

MIDDLEKAUFF, R. *The Mathers.* New York: Oxford University Press, 1971.

MILGRAM, S. "A Behavioral Study of Obedience." *Journal of Abnormal and Social Psychology,* Vol. 67, 1963.

MILLER, J. C. (ed.). *The Colonial Image.* New York: George Braziller, 1962.

MILLER, P. *Errand into the Wilderness.* New York: Harper Torchbooks, 1956.

MILLER, P., and T. H. JOHNSON (eds.). *The Puritans.* Vol. I. New York: Harper Torchbooks, 1963.

MILLON, T. *Modern Psychopathology.* Philadelphia: Saunders, 1969.

MILTON, O., and R. G. WAHLER (eds.) *Behavior Disorders.* Philadelphia: Lippincott, 1969.

MINTURN, L. *et al. Mothers of Six Cultures: Antecedents of Child Rearing.* New York: Wiley, 1964.

MIRELS, H. L., and J. B. GARRETT. "The Protestant Ethic as a Personality Variable." *Journal of Consulting and Clinical Psychology,* Vol. 36, 1971.

MITCHELL, J. "Cons, Square-Johns, and Rehabilitation." In B. J. Biddle and E. J. Thomas (eds.), *Role Theory: Concepts and Researchs.* New York: Wiley, 1966.

MORGAN, E. S. *The Puritan Dilemma.* Boston: Little, Brown, 1958.

MORGAN, E. S. *Visible Saints: The History of a Puritan Idea.* Ithaca, N.Y.: Cornell University Press, 1963.

MOWRER, O. H. *The Crisis in Psychiatry and Religion.* New York: Van Nostrand, 1961.

MOWRER, O. H. *The New Group Therapy.* New York: Van Nostrand, 1964.

MURASE, T., and F. JOHNSON. "Naikan, Morita, and Western Psychotherapy." *Archives of General Psychiatry,* Vol. 31, 1974.

NACHSHON, I., and M. ROTENBERG. "Perception of Violence by Institutionalized Offenders." *Journal of Criminal Law and Criminology,* Vol. 68 (1977): 454–457.

NAGEL, E. L. "Methodological Issues in Psychoanalytic Theory." In S. Hook (ed.), *Psychoanalysis, Scientific Methods and Philosophy.* New York: New York University Press, 1959.

NEUMANN, E. *Depth Psychology and New Morality.* Tel Aviv: Schocken, 1963.

NUNNALY, J. C. *Popular Conceptions of Mental Illness.* New York: Holt, Reinhart & Winston, 1961.

OLESON, V. L., and E. W. WHITTAKER. *The Silent Dialogue.* San Francisco: Jossey-Bass, 1968.

PAGE, J. D. *Psychopathology.* New York: Aldine Atherton, 1971.

PASTORE, N. "A note on Changing Toward Liked and Disliked Persons." *Journal of Social Psychology,* Vol. 52, 1960.

PETRIE, A. *Individuality in Pain and Suffering.* Chicago: University of Chicago Press, 1967.

PFEUTZE, P. E. *Self, Society, and Existence.* New York: Harper Torchbooks, 1961.

PHILLIPS, L., and J. G. DRAGUNS. "Classification of the Behavior Disorders." In P. H. Mussen (ed.), *Annual Review of Psychology,* Vol. 22, 1971.

PLATT, A. M. *The Child Savers.* Chicago: University of Chicago Press, 1969.

PLATT, A. M., and B. L. DIAMOND. "The Origins and Development of the 'Wild Beast' Concept of Mental Illness and Its Relation to Theories of Criminal Responsibility." *Journal of the History of the Behavioral Sciences,* Vol. 1, 1965.

POLATIN, P. and E. C. PHILITINE. "Psychoanalytic Treatment." In H. Herma and G. M. Kurth (eds.), *Elements of Psychoanalysis.* New York: World, 1950.

PORTER, F. C. "The Yecer Hara," *Yale Bicentennial Publications, Biblical and Semitic Studies.* New York: Charles Scribner's Sons, 1902.

PRICE, R. H. *Abnormal Behavior.* New York: Holt, Reinhart & Winston, 1972.

PRINCE, M. *The Dissociation of a Personality.* London: Longmans, Green, 1930.

PRITCHARD, J. B. (ed.). *Ancient Near Eastern Texts.* Princeton, N.J.: Princeton University Press, 1955.

QUAY, H. C. "Dimensions of Personality in Delinquent Boys as Inferred from the Factor Analysis of Case History Data." *Child Development,* Vol. 35, 1964.

RACHMAN, S. *The Meaning of Fear.* Harmondsworth, England: Penguin, 1974.

RACHMAN, S. J., and J. TEASDALE. "Aversion Therapy: An Appraisal." In C. M. Frank (ed.), *Behavior Therapy Appraisal and Status.* New York: McGraw-Hill, 1969.

RADZINOWICZ, L. *Ideology and Crime*. New York: Columbia University Press, 1966.

Records of the Colony of Massachusetts, Vol. 4, 1652, 1676.

REIMER, H. "Socialization in the Prison Community." In *Proceedings of the American Prison Association*, 1937.

RIEFF, P. *The Triumph of the Therapeutic*. New York: Harper & Row, 1966.

RIESMAN, D. *Individualism Reconsidered*. London: Free Press of Glencoe, 1954.

ROBBINS, P. R., R. H. TANCK, and H. S. MEYERSBURY. "A Study of Three Psychosomatic Hypotheses." *Journal of Psychosomathic Research*, Vol. 16, 1972.

ROBBINS, R. H. *The Encyclopedia of Witchcraft and Demonology*. New York: Crown Publishers, 1959.

ROGERS, C. R. *Counseling and Psychotherapy*. Cambridge, Mass.: Riverside Press, 1942.

ROSEN, B. C. "Socialization and the Achievement Motivation in Brazil." *American Sociological Review*, Vol. 27, 1962.

ROSENHAN, D. L. "On Being Sane in Insane Places," *Science*, Vol. 79, January, 1973.

ROTENBERG, M. "Conceptual and Methodological Notes on Affective and Cognitive Role-Taking (Sympathy and Empathy): An Illustrative Experiment with Delinquent and Non-Delinquent Boys." *Journal of Genetic Psychology*, Vol. 125, 1974.

ROTENBERG, M. *Mental Patients' Involvement in "Normal" and "Abnormal" Primary Roles in Front of Staff and Patients*. Jerusalem: Hebrew University, 1975.

ROTENBERG, M., and B. L. DIAMOND. "The Biblical Conceptions of Psychopathy: The Law of the Stubborn and Rebellious Son." *Journal of the History of the Behavioral Sciences*, Vol. 7, 1971, No. 1.

ROTENBERG, M., and I. NACHSHON. "Impulsiveness and Aggression among Israeli Delinquents." *British Journal of Social and Clinical Psychology*, 1978.

ROTENBERG, M. and T. R. SARBIN. "Impact of Differentially Significant Others on Role Involvement: An Experiment with Prison Social Types." *Journal of Abnormal Psychology*, Vol. 77, 1971.

ROTENBERG, M., et al. 1976 (unpublished research data on altruism).

RUEL, M. (ed.). *Social Anthropology and Language*. Tavistock: ASA monographs, 1971.

RUTMAN, B. *Winthrop's Boston.* Chapel Hill: University of North Carolina Press, 1965.

RYLE, G. *The Concept of Mind.* New York: Barnes & Noble, 1949.

SARBIN, T. R. "On the Futility of the Proposition that Some People Be Labeled 'Mentally Ill.'" *Journal of Consulting Psychology,* Vol. 31, 1967.

SARBIN, T. R. "The Scientific Status of the Mental Illness Metaphor." In Plog and Edgerton, *Changing Perspectives in Mental Illness,* 1969 (see Edgerton).

SARBIN, T. R. "Schizophrenia: From Metaphor to Myth." Unpublished paper, 1971.

SARBIN, T. R., and N. ADLER. "Self-Reconstitution Processes: A Preliminary Report." *The Psychoanalytic Review,* Vol. 57, 1970–71.

SARBIN, T. R., and V. L. ALLEN. "Role Theory." In G. Lindsay and E. Aronson (eds.), *Handbook of Social Psychology.* Reading, Mass.: Addison-Wesley, 1968.

SARNA, N. M. *Understanding Genesis.* New York: McGraw-Hill, 1966.

SCHACHT, R. *Alienation.* New York: Doubleday, 1970.

SCHACHTER, S., and B. LATANE. "Crime, Cognition and the Autonomic Nervous System." In M. R. Jones (ed.), *Nebraska Symposium on Motivation.* Lincoln: University of Nebraska Pres, 1964.

SCHALLING, D., and A. ROSEN. "Porteus Maze Differences between Psychopathic and Non-Psychopathic Criminals." *British Journal of Social and Clinical Psychology,* Vol. 7, 1968.

SCHALLING, D., et al. "Spontaneous Autonomic Activity as Related to Psychopathy." *Biological Psychology,* Vol. 1, 1973.

SCHATZ-UFFENHEIMER, R., *Quietistic Elements in 18th Century Hassidic Thought* (Hebrew). Jerusalem: The Magnes Press, 1968.

SCHEFF, T. J. *Being Mentally Ill.* Chicago: Aldine, 1966.

SCHEIN, E. H. "The Chinese Indoctrination Program for Prisoners of War: A Study of Attempted Brainwashing." In E. E. Maccoby et al. (eds.), *Readings in Social Psychology.* New York: Holt, Rinehart & Winston, 1958.

SCHMIDT, H. O., and C. P. FONDA. "The Reliability of Psychiatric Diagnosis: A New Look." In H. Quay (ed.), *Research in Psychopathology.* Princeton, N.J.: Van Nostrand, 1963.

SCHOLEM, G. G. *Major Trends in Jewish Mysticism.* New York: Shocken Books, 1941.

SCHOLEM, G. G. *Devarim Bego* (Hebrew). Tel Aviv: Am-Oved, 1976.

SCHUR, E. M. *Labeling Deviant Behavior.* New York: Harper & Row, 1971.

SCHWEID, E. *Judaism and the Solitary Jew* (Hebrew). Tel Aviv: Am-Oved, 1974.

SCHWITZGEBEL, R. "Short-Term Operant Conditioning of Adolescent Offenders on Socially Relevant Variables." *Journal of Abnormal Psychology,* Vol. 72, 1967.

SCOTT, R. A. *The Making of Blind Men.* New York: Russell Sage Foundation, 1969.

SCOTT, R. A. "A Proposed Framework for Analyzing Deviance as a Property of Social Order." In R. A. Scott and J. D. Douglas (eds.), *Theoretical Perspectives on Deviance.* New York: Basic Books, 1972.

SECORD, P. F., and C. W. BACKMAN. "An Interpersonal Approach to Personality." In B. H. Maher (ed.), *Progress in Eperimental Personality Research.* New York: Academic Press, 1965.

SERENY, G. *The Case of Mary Bell.* London: Mathuen, 1972.

SHAFFER, J. B. P., and M. D. GALINSKY. *Models of Group Therapy and Sensitivity Training.* Englewood Cliffs, N.J.: Prentice-Hall, 1974.

SHAVER, P. R., and K. E. SCHEIBE. "Transformation of Social Identity: A Study of Chronic Mental Patients and College Volunteers in a Summer Camp Setting." *Journal of Psychology,* Vol. 66, 1967.

SHEPARD, T. *The Sincere Convert.* London, 1646.

SHEPARD, T. *The Works of Thomas Shepard.* Boston: Doctrinal Tract and Book Society, 1853.

SHERIF, M., and HOVELAND, C. I. *Social Judgment: Assimilation and Contrast, Effects in Communication and Attitude Change.* New Haven: Yale University Press, 1961.

SHNEURSON, S. Z. *Tanya* (Hebrew). New York: Kehat, 1956.

SHOCHAT, A. "On Joy in Hassidism." *Zion* (Hebrew), 1951, 16:1–2.

SKRZYNEK, G. J. "The Effects of Perceptual Isolation and Arousal on Anxiety: Complexity Preference and Novelty Preference in Psychopathic and Neurotic Delinquents." *Journal of Abnormal Psychology,* Vol. 74, 1969.

SLATER, P. E. *The Pursuit of Loneliness.* Boston: Beacon Press, 1970.

SOLOMON, R. L., and J. D. CORBIT. "An Opponent-Process Theory of

Motivation: I Cigarette Addiction." *Journal of Abnormal Psychology,* Vol. 81, 1973.

SROLE, L., and T. S. LANGER. "Protestant, Catholic, and Jew: Comparative Psychopathology." In S. C. Plog and R. B. Edgerton (eds.), *Changing Perspectives in Mental Health.* New York: Holt, 1969.

STARBUCK, E. D. *The Psychology of Religion.* London: Walter Scott Paternoster Square, 1901.

STEINMAN, E., *Kitvey Rabi Nachman Mibratzlav* (Hebrew). Tel Aviv: Keneset, 1951.

STENNING, D. "Pastoral Fuluani of Northern Nigeria." In J. L. Gibbs, *Peoples of Africa.* New York: Holt, 1965.

STEPHEN, L. *The English Utilitarians.* Vol. 1. London: Duckworth, 1950.

STRONG, S. M. "Social Types in a Minority Group: Formulation of a Method." *American Journal of Sociology,* Vol. 48, 1943.

SUDNOW, D. *Passing On.* Englewood Cliffs, N.J.: Prentice-Hall, 1967.

SUTHERLAND, E. H., and D. R. CRESSEY. *Principles of Criminology.* Philadelphia: Lippincott, 1955.

SYKES, G. M. "The Corruption of Authority." *Social Forces,* Vol. 34, 1956.

SYKES, G. M., and D. MATZA. "Techniques of Neutralization: A Theory of Delinquency." *American Sociological Review,* Vol. 22, 1967.

SYKES, G. M., and S. L. MESSINGER. "The Inmate Social System." In R. A. Cloward *et al.* (eds.), *Theoretical Studies in Social Organization of the Prison.* New York: Social Science Research Council, 1960.

SZASZ, T. S. *The Myth of Mental Illness.* New York: Haeber, 1961.

SZASZ, T. S. *The Manufacture of Madness.* New York: Delta, 1970.

TALMON, Y. *Family and Community in the Kibbutz.* Cambridge, Mass.: Harvard University Press, 1972.

The Babylonian Talmud. London: translated by M. S. Soncino Press, 1938.

TISHBY, I. *Hebrew Ethical Literature* (Hebrew). Jerusalem: M. Newman, 1971.

TOCH, H. H. "Psychological Consequences of the Police Role." In A. E. Niederhoffer and A. S. Blumberg (eds.), *The Ambivalent Force: Perspectives on the Police.* Waltham, Mass.: Gina, 1970.

TRACHTENBERG, J. *Jewish Magic and Superstition.* New York: Atheneum, 1974.

TREVOR-ROPER, H. R. "Witches and Witchcraft." *Encounter,* Vol. 28, 1967.

TRICE, H. M., and P. M. ROMAN. "Delabeling, Relabeling and Alcoholics Anonymous." *Social Problems,* Vol. 17, Spring 1970.

TURNER, R. H. "Role-Taking, Role-Standpoint and Reference Group Behavior." *American Journal of Sociology,* Vol. 61, 1956.

ULLMAN, L. P., and L. KRASNER. *A Psychological Approach to Abnormal Behavior.* New York: Prentice-Hall, 1969.

URBACH, E. E. *The Sages: Their Concepts and Beliefs* (Hebrew). Jerusalem: The Magnes Press, 1971.

VOGEL, E. F., and S. H. VOGEL. "Permissive Dependency in Japan." In H. K. Geiger (ed.), *Comparative Perspectives on Marriage and the Family.* Boston: Little, Brown, 1958.

VOLD, B. *Theoretical Criminology.* New York: Oxford University Press, 1958.

WARREN, A. B., and J. M. JOHNSON. "A Critique of Labeling Theory from the Phenomenological Perspective." In Scott and Douglas (eds.), *Theoretical Perspectives on Deviance.*

WEBER, M. *The Protestant Ethic and the Spirit of Capitalism.* London: Unwin University Books, 1930.

WILLIAMS, T. R., and M. WILLIAMS. "Socialization of the Student Nurse." *Nursing Research,* Vol. 8, 1959.

Winthrop's Journal, Vol. II, 1630, 1642, 1645.

WHITING, B. B. (ed.). *Six Cultures: Studies in Child Rearing.* New York: Wiley, 1963.

WHYTE, W. H., JR. *The Organization Man.* New York: Doubleday Anchor Books, 1956.

YABLONSKY, L. *The Tunnel Back: Synanon.* New York: MacMillan, 1965.

ZAX, M. and E. L. COWEN. *Abnormal Psychology.* New York: Holt, Reinhart & Winston, 1972.

ZILBOORG, G. *A History of Medical Psychology.* New York: Norton, 1941.

ZUBIN, J. "Classification of the Behavior Disorders." In P. R. Farnsworth (ed.), *Annual Review of Psychology.* Palo Alto, Calif.: Annual Reviews, 1967.

Index

Achievement, 1, 2, 23, 36, 100, 129, 146–48, 150, 154, 171, 183; *see also* Need achievement
"Adhesion," 199, 200
Adler, N., 88, 139
Adrenalin, 71
Africa, 66, 91, 115; East, 19; North, 113
Aggression, xvii, 104, 152
Alchemic practices, 92, 112–14, 117–20
Alcoholism, 85
Alien thoughts, 193–95, 198
Alienation, xxi, 142–45, 149–51, 153, 155, 166, 170, 171
Amae (desired dependence), 152, 154, 155
America, 10, 11, 13, 31n, 39, 60, 103–11, 149, 150, 163n, 179, 184
Anomie, 123, 124, 144
Anthropology, 86, 120n
Antilabeling, 22, 82, 96, 137
Antisocial behavior, 42, 45
Anxiety, 29, 46–48, 53, 54, 69–71, 151, 158, 179, 185
Apathy, 44, 60, 63, 181
Arabs, 4n, 92, 120n; Christian, 106
Asia, 66, 115
Asthma, 54, 55
Authoritarianism, 141
Autonomic functions, 47, 60, 63, 64, 70
Autonomy, 36, 146, 148, 155, 166
Autosuggestion, 86, 88
Avoidance learning, 70

Badness, xviii, 30, 49, 85, 93, 127
Becker, H. S., 57, 89
Behaviorism, xvii, xix, 11, 12, 37, 51, 53, 61, 63, 100

Being, 125; contingent, 124–28, 130, 131, 135, 137, 139, 142; primary, 125, 131–36, 138–40, 142; secondary, 125, 131–33, 135, 136, 139, 142
Bercovitch, S., 29, 39, 40, 174, 177, 180
Besht (Baal Shem Tov), 187, 189–95, 197–201
Blacks, 82
Blood pressure, 58
Boredom, 47, 62, 70–75
Brainwashing, 88, 89
Buber, Martin, 157–62, 168, 190, 196
Bunyan, John, 29, 179

Cadavers, 56–58
Calling, 11, 33, 147
Calvin, John, 2, 8–12, 16, 23, 49, 76, 96, 183
Calvinism, xviii, xxi, 1, 3, 8–10, 13, 16, 21, 23, 26n, 29, 33, 35–38, 97, 100–103, 106, 109–11, 145–47, 149, 151, 171, 174, 183, 184, 192, 193n; secular, 147; "soft," 34, 36, 184
Camus, Albert, 44, 56
Capitalism, 1, 10, 11, 144
Catharsis, 182, 186, 189
Catholicism, 11, 103, 157n
Chabad movement, 187, 195, 202
Changeability, human, xviii, xxi, 2, 8, 16, 21, 43, 45, 48, 98, 171, 182, 183, 193n
Chauncy, C., 26, 27
Children, 141, 152, 173
Christianity, 4n, 8, 20, 139, 175, 182, 183, 186–88, 193, 196

225